THE VOICE OF
MY SERVANTS

THE VOICE OF MY SERVANTS

APOSTOLIC MESSAGES ON TEACHING, LEARNING, AND SCRIPTURE

EDITED BY SCOTT C. ESPLIN AND RICHARD NEITZEL HOLZAPFEL

RELIGIOUS STUDIES CENTER
BRIGHAM YOUNG UNIVERSITY

Published by the Religious Studies Center, Brigham Young University, Provo, Utah
http://rsc.byu.edu/

Printed in the United States of America by Sheridan Books Inc.

ISBN: 978-0-8425-2773-6
$23.99

Cover photo © Intellectual Reserve Inc.

Library of Congress Cataloging-in-Publication Data

The voice of my servants : apostolic messages on teaching, learning, and scripture / edited by Scott C. Esplin and Richard Neitzel Holzapfel.
    p. cm.
  Includes index.
  ISBN 978-0-8425-2773-6 (hardcover : alk. paper) 1. Teaching--Religious aspects--Church of Jesus Christ of Latter-day Saints. 2. Learning and scholarship--Religious aspects--Church of Jesus Christ of Latter-day Saints. 3. Church of Jesus Christ of Latter-day Saints--Sacred books. 4. Mormon Church--Sacred books. I. Esplin, Scott Clair. II. Holzapfel, Richard Neitzel.

  BV1471.3.V65 2010
  268'.89332--dc22

2010031225

Contents

Contents

Acknowledgments

We appreciate the generous assistance provided by the Religious Studies Center faculty and staff in bringing this publication to light. Special acknowledgment is given to Joany O. Pinegar for coordination, R. Devan Jensen for content gathering and editing, Brent R. Nordgren for production, Jeffrey M. Wade for cover design, and Jonathon R. Owen for layout. We also thank Brent R. Esplin and Nathan D. Grover, who helped review the initial selections.

INTRODUCTION

IN A REMARKABLE REVELATION GIVEN to the Prophet Joseph Smith in November 1831, the Lord said, "What I the Lord have spoken, I have spoken, and I excuse not myself; and though the heavens and the earth pass away, my word shall not pass away, but shall all be fulfilled, *whether by mine own voice or by the voice of my servants, it is the same*" (D&C 1:38; emphasis added). Later, the Lord added, "For he that receiveth my servants receiveth me" (D&C 84:36). Since the earliest days of the Restoration, the Latter-day Saints have come to appreciate how the Lord communicates to his people through those sustained as prophets, seers, and revelators.

One of the chief missions of a prophet is to teach truth. "A prophet is a teacher," observed Elder John A. Widtsoe. "That is the essential meaning of the word. He teaches the body of truth, the gospel, revealed by the Lord to man; and under inspiration explains it to the understanding of the people. He is an expounder of truth."[1]

While Moses rightly wished, "Would God that all the Lord's people were prophets, and that the Lord would put his spirit upon them!" (Numbers 11:29), the mantle to authoritatively expound the gospel message nevertheless rests on fifteen chosen men—the prophets, seers, and revelators of The Church of Jesus Christ of Latter-day Saints. Appointed by revelation, they fulfill a unique charge on the earth. President J. Reuben Clark Jr. described their responsibility. "It should be in mind," President Clark declared, that some of the General Authorities have had assigned to them a special calling; they possess a special gift; they are sustained as prophets, seers, and revelators, which gives them a special spiritual endowment in connection with their teaching of the people. They have the right, the power, and authority to declare the mind and will of God to his people, subject to the over-all power and authority of the President of the Church. Others of the General Authorities are not given this special spiritual endowment and authority covering their teaching; they have a resulting limitation, and the resulting limitation upon their power and authority in teaching applies to every other officer and member of the Church, for none of them is spiritually endowed as a prophet, seer, and revelator.[2]

Seasoned by time and coupled with an endowment of spiritual light, the prophets, seers, and revelators of our time offer messages with special meaning for all who seek gospel insight. "Perhaps young men do speak of the future because they have no past, and old men of the past because they have no future," quipped President Boyd K. Packer. "However," he continued, "there are 15 old men whose very lives are focused on the future. They are called, sustained, and ordained as prophets, seers, and revelators. It is their right to see as seers see; it is their obligation to counsel and to warn."[3] Fulfilling their divine mandate, the prophets in this dispensation have authored a large collection of essays, articles, and addresses expounding God's truths to his children. In particular, they have addressed issues related to gospel teaching, learning, and scripture.

Established in 1975, the Religious Studies Center at Brigham Young University has regularly published landmark scholarship on Latter-day Saint scripture, doctrine, history, and culture. Among this collection are more than seventy significant essays by General Authorities addressing a wide range of topics. This book contains selections from that collection authored by prophets, seers, and revelators and published by the Religious Studies Center over the past thirty-five years. The articles come from the center's journal, the *Religious Educator*, from addresses to religious educators, and from conference proceedings and publications at Brigham Young University.

TEACHING

Among these pieces are insightful ways to improve gospel teaching. President Thomas S. Monson begins the collection, offering counsel for effective communication. Modeling how "we let the Lord be our guide in developing communication skills," President Monson stresses that improved "communication . . . accompanied by spirituality" allows the Lord to "work through His servants to accomplish His purposes."[4] President Henry B. Eyring further challenges teachers to raise their sights about gospel teaching and find ways that the pure gospel of Jesus Christ can "go down into the hearts of students by the power of the Holy Ghost."[5] Looking outward, President Dieter F. Uchtdorf discusses a doctrinal basis for global interaction, offering ways the Church can teach and lead in a cross-cultural world. Offering practical advice on how to more effectively teach, Elder Richard G. Scott stresses teaching by the Spirit, emphasizing the reality of personal communication with God, kindling a love of the scriptures, and encouraging students to "come unto Christ" as four fundamentals for gospel teaching. President Gordon B. Hinckley likewise offers four imperatives for success in religious education, charging teachers to continue learning, maintain balance, lead with love, and find joy in their journeys. Finally, Elder Bruce R. McConkie emphasizes the significance of gospel teaching in the Lord's plan, offering a divine commission for how it is to be done.

LEARNING

Prophetic commentaries on gospel scholarship regularly highlight the dual responsibility of both the teacher and the learner in inspired learning. In this volume, President Boyd K. Packer reminds readers that the home should be the main source for gospel learning. "This shield of faith is handmade in a cottage industry. What is most worth doing ideally is done at home," he writes. "It can be polished in the classroom, but it is fabricated and fitted in the home, handcrafted to each individual."[6] Elder Dallin H. Oaks expands the understanding of personal revelation in the process of learning, outlining purposes of divine communication and principles governing its use. Elder Robert D. Hales continues the theme, describing how, through committed study and faith, gospel learning can become a lifelong endeavor. Takng an example from the Book of Mormon, Elder Jeffrey R. Holland offers an astute analysis of the brother of Jared's rending the veil of unbelief and how it models our own process of learning by faith. Elder David A. Bednar further develops the student's role in gospel learning. Elder Bednar observes, "I suspect we emphasize and know more about a teacher teaching by the Spirit than we do about a learner learning by faith."[7]

SCRIPTURE

While numerous prophetic talks emphasize teaching and learning, others provide insightful analysis of scripture itself. Assisting students of the Old Testament, Elder Russell M. Nelson scans the breadth of the ancient witness of Christ, establishing "strong and significant links between ancient and modern Israel."[8] Turning to modern revelation, Elder D. Todd Christofferson elaborates on the sacramental covenant, highlighting the responsibility to "always remember [Christ]" in all we do. President James E. Faust focuses his attention on the New Testament, emphasizing ways this biblical witness of the life and ministry of the Master informs our understanding of the gospel of Jesus Christ. Finally, Elder Neal A. Maxwell further explores the depths of the great latter-day witness for Christ, analyzing how the Book of Mormon answers "the great question . . . , is there really a redeeming Christ?"[9]

These messages highlight ways modern prophets have disseminated the gospel. The Lord and his servants emphasize that obedience to their messages opens the gates to heaven's choicest blessings as one treats the voice of his servants as if from the Lord himself (see D&C 1:38; 21:6). "Where else can you go for guidance?" asked President Harold B. Lee. "Where is there safety in the world today? Safety can't be won by tanks and guns and the airplanes and atomic bombs. There is only one place of safety and that is within the realm of the power of Almighty God that he gives to those who keep his commandments and listen to his voice, as he speaks through the channels that he has ordained for that purpose."[10] Following the teaching and message of prophets provides a spiritual anchor for Saints today. "The authorities which the Lord has placed in his Church constitute for the people of the Church a harbor, a place of refuge, a hitching post, as it were," promised President Spencer W. Kimball. "No one in this Church will ever go far astray who ties himself securely to the Church authorities whom the Lord has placed in his Church. This Church will never go astray; the Quorum of the Twelve will never lead you into bypaths; it never has and never will. . . . The Lord has chosen them; he has given them specific responsibilities. And those people who stand close to them will be safe."[11]

While some of these addresses were originally delivered to specific audiences, like scripture, the voice of the Lord's servants applies to all mankind. It is hoped that this volume will help facilitate greater access to their timely and timeless messages. We invite our readers to "come, listen to a prophet's voice, and hear the word of God."[12]

Scott C. Esplin

Richard Neitzel Holzapfel

NOTES

1. John A. Widtsoe, *Evidences and Reconciliations* (Salt Lake City: Bookcraft, 1960), 257.

2. J. Reuben Clark Jr., "When are the Writings or Sermons of Church Leaders Entitled to the Claim of Scripture?" address to seminary and institute personnel (Provo, UT: Brigham Young University, July 7, 1954).

3. Boyd K. Packer, "The Snow-White Birds," *BYU Speeches*, August 29, 1995.

4. Thomas S. Monson, "How to Communicate Effectively," *Religious Educator* 11, no. 3 (2010): 5–6.

5. Henry B. Eyring, "We Must Raise Our Sights," *Religious Educator* 2, no. 2 (2001), 3.

6. Boyd K. Packer, "The One Pure Defense," *Religious Educator* 5, no. 2 (2004), 8.

7. David A. Bednar, "Seek Learning by Faith," *Religious Educator* 7, no. 3 (2006), 1.

8. Russell M. Nelson, "Remnants Gathered, Covenants Fulfilled," in *Voices of Old Testament Prophets* (Salt Lake City: Deseret Book, 1997), 3.

9. Neal A. Maxwell, "The Book of Mormon: A Great Answer to 'The Great Question,'" in *First Nephi, The Doctrinal Foundation*, ed. Monte S. Nyman

and Charles D. Tate Jr. (Provo, UT: Religious Studies Center, Brigham Young University, 1988), 1.

10. Harold B. Lee, "Closing Remarks," *Ensign*, January 1974, 125.

11. Spencer W. Kimball, in Conference Report, April 1951, 104.

12. Joseph S. Murdock, "Come, Listen to a Prophet's Voice," *Hymns* (Salt Lake City: The Church of Jesus Christ of Latter-day Saints, 1985), no. 21.

Part 1

TEACHING

President Thomas S. Monson is President of The Church of Jesus Christ of Latter-day Saints. Address published in *Religious Educator* 11, no. 3 (2010): 1–8.

1

HOW TO
COMMUNICATE
EFFECTIVELY

COMMUNICATION BETWEEN PEOPLE HAS BEEN a principal problem throughout recorded history. It is complicated further when translation is involved.

Many years ago this country had some diplomatic problems which resulted in riots and general civil disturbances. Just when it appeared that agreement had been reached between Panama, the Canal Zone, and the United States, diplomatic relations came apart because the parties differed as to the meaning of a single word. In the English language text, the two parties agreed to "discuss" differences.

The Spanish language text used the word *negociar*—"to negotiate." Americans assumed that negotiation meant (according to *Funk and Wagnalls Standard College Dictionary*) "a conference or discussion designed to produce an agreement." They felt this was synonymous with "discussion." Panamanians thought that "to negotiate" implied a willingness to *renegotiate* existing treaties. It took months, patience, and the services of communications experts to bring about the ultimate understanding.

In another instance, the realization that the question of war or peace could depend upon effective communication brought about the establishment of the hotline between the world's nuclear capitals at the time, Washington and Moscow, to avoid an inadvertent pushing of the panic button.

We have a communication problem as we wage war against the

powers of the adversary and strive to help members of the Church to live by gospel principles. I suppose we can take some courage from the fact that the Master had His problems with communication, even though He possessed great understanding of people.

On one occasion Jesus was speaking from a ship to a great multitude gathered on the shore. In the course of His remarks, He related the parable of the sower.[1] When He finished, the disciples asked Him, "Why speakest thou unto them in parables? He answered and said unto them, Because it is given unto you to know the mysteries of the kingdom of heaven, but to them it is not given."[2]

And then He said the ears of these particular people were dull of hearing and their eyes were closed. "But blessed are your eyes," the Savior told His disciples, "for they see: and your ears, for they hear."[3] He then continued His sermon, relating several other parables.

Perhaps the disciples were too embarrassed to interrupt again because Jesus had told them it was given to them to understand the

Vincent Van Gogh, *The Sower*. Kröller-Müller Museum, Otterlo, Netherlands.

mysteries of heaven. But when the multitude had gone, "his disciples came unto him, saying, Declare unto us the parable."[4]

If the Master found it necessary to repeat and explain in order to have effective communication, I suppose we should not feel discouraged when we fail to communicate effectively at the first recitation.

Effective communication is essential to effective motivation. The leader must first educate himself, develop enthusiasm, and perfect himself in the skill he desires to teach (communicate). He must then project his feeling on the subject until it is shared by the follower. This is the process of most effective motivation.

Effective communication always includes these three Cs: *clear, concise*, and *confirm*.

CLEAR

One must make his presentation *clear*. The first rule of clarity is to have a well-defined goal or objective—to know what you wish to accomplish through your communication. Unless you can define this goal clearly to yourself, it is not likely your audience will understand it and be motivated.

Another way in which clarity can be improved is by use of illustrations. Since words have different meanings to various people, the additional definition through supporting illustrations is usually helpful. There are many types of illustrations.

First, words and motions. Jesus made *parables* a part of nearly every teaching situation. So often did He use this teaching device that Evangelists recorded at one point that "without a parable spake he not unto them."[5] Jesus said He used parables in teaching because they conveyed to the hearer religious truth exactly in proportion to the hearer's faith and intelligence. To the unlearned, the parable had story interest and some teaching value. To the spiritual, it conveyed much more, including the mysteries or secrets of the kingdom of heaven. Thus the parable is suited alike to simple and learned. It teaches all people to find divine truth in common things.

For the purpose of teaching in our day, the Savior's parables have the added advantage of taking on more and more meaning as we understand more about the objects and symbols He used in his parables. These stories also can be suited to a variety of applications.

Closely related to parables are the *brief comparisons* the Master often used to illustrate ideas, such as: "It is better that one man should perish than that a nation should dwindle and perish in unbelief."[6] "Follow me, and I will make you fishers of men."[7] "Let your light so shine before men that they may see your good works, and glorify your Father which is in heaven."[8] "By their fruits ye shall know them."[9]

Illustrative stories provide another excellent means of teaching to aid clarity. It is easy for people to project themselves into stories of living people and their experiences. The Lord frequently used this technique. In the case of the widow's mite, He illustrated a lesson in charity: "This poor widow hath cast in more than they all: for these have of their abundance cast in unto the offerings of God: but she of her penury hath cast in all the living that she had."[10] Real stories involving real people provide an excellent vehicle to promote clarity.

A third type of illustration involving words and motions is the *demonstration*. This is particularly helpful when attempting to teach skills that have some mechanical aspects. Examples of situations in which demonstrations could profitably be used include teaching techniques in public speaking, methods of conducting oral evaluations and interviews, effective use of visual aids, and athletic skills. Pictures can be used. The old adage that "a picture is worth a thousand words" can be supported by many examples.

Objects provide another means of clarifying a message. These might be objects from surroundings or from apparel—objects prepared by the speaker for the occasion. Some examples of utilizing objects from surroundings might be (1) using organ pipes to illustrate how priesthood power works *through* the individual when he is in tune or (2) using a light switch to demonstrate the need to take a voluntary action (turn on the switch) yourself in order to get light (as from the Lord).

CONCISE

Next is *concise*. Make your presentation concise. To be concise means to express much in few words. The amount of time spent in communicating an idea may vary depending on the complexity of the subject matter and the previous knowledge of members of the audience. But communication is improved when each word, each sentence, each paragraph is meaningful and pertinent to the objective.

Guidelines for making a concise presentation could include (1) study and research until you know you have information that is worthy of presentation; (2) write your thoughts on paper as they come, without concern for style or polish; (3) arrange ideas in logical order.

Some prefer a formula for organizing material into a logical sequence, such as PREP—*point, reason, example, point.* The name of a well-known opera has been used as a letter key to a motivation formula. AIDA in this instance stands for gain *attention,* sustain *interest,* incite *desire,* get *action.*

Eliminate irrelevant ideas, illustrations, and humor which reaches too far for an application. Because of the difficulty of getting full attention, there is a temptation with some to include interesting material even though it is not entirely relevant. When the organizing stage has been completed, reduce every sentence to the fewest necessary words. Last, learn the material well enough to present it as it has been prepared.

Confirm

Finally comes *confirm.* To see what has been learned, confirm what you have taught. Fragmentary listening, misinterpretation of ideas, and mistaken meanings of words may cause misunderstandings. It is important, therefore, to have a method of checkup, feedback, and correction of mistaken impressions whenever possible. One labor negotiator found a very effective way to cool down heated arguments and improve communication in labor and management disputes. The referee made a rule that the representative of labor could not present his viewpoint until he could explain management's viewpoint to the satisfaction of the management representative, and vice versa.

Here are two of the methods that have been used successfully to improve communication skills: (1) *Improve your vocabulary* by keeping a dictionary available when reading or writing. Check words about which you have a question to see if your understanding of their meaning is the same as the dictionary definition. The listening vocabulary should be greater than the one you use to speak or write so you can learn on a higher level than that on which you speak or write. (2) *Read aloud* as a drill when the opportunity to do so presents itself. This strengthens the voice and makes it more clear. It helps the reader to enunciate words more clearly, carefully, and naturally. It helps to prevent speech mannerisms and monotonous patterns because the reader has an opportunity to use other people's word combinations. The reader should also practice voice inflection and develop a wider range of tones to make the voice more interesting.

The Lord, through His prophets, has given counsel concerning the importance of communication skills. He has also emphasized the need of spirituality as a part of effective communication. When Moses was called to lead the children of Israel out of bondage, he recognized his weakness as a speaker—a communicator. Nevertheless, he had the Spirit of the Lord with him. The Lord, after some reassuring, gave him Aaron as a mouthpiece. He didn't give Aaron the job of leading but assigned that to Moses, who had the other leadership skills that were necessary to perform the task.[11]

Paul counsels that we should seek spiritual gifts so that we might speak unto men "to edification, and exhortation, and comfort." He then counsels that clarity is even more important than the gift of tongues. "For if the trumpet give an uncertain sound, who shall prepare himself to the battle?" Who shall be motivated? "So likewise ye, except ye utter by the tongue words easy to be understood, how shall it be known what is spoken? for ye shall speak into the air."[12]

When we let the Lord be our guide in developing communication skills, He can help us to be humble, to present ourselves to the right people at the proper time and in an atmosphere where we will be trusted and worthy of a listening ear. When communication skills are accompanied by spirituality, the Lord can work through His servants to accomplish His purposes. Hundreds of thousands of newly baptized members of the Church and the many missionaries who taught them the gospel provide a living testimony of effective communication.

One spring day, a humble boy, motivated by a sincere desire to know the truth, sought an audience with his Heavenly Father. The glorious vision which followed, the words from the Father, "*This is My Beloved Son. Hear him!*"[13] the message from the Master, and the response of faithful service and supreme sacrifice by that boy, even Joseph Smith, were communication at its finest.

As we ourselves prepare to communicate effectively, may this beautiful example govern our thinking and prompt our actions.

Notes

1. See Matthew 13:1–43.
2. Matthew 13:10–11.
3. Matthew 13:16.
4. Matthew 13:36.
5. Mark 4:34.
6. 1 Nephi 4:13.
7. Matthew 4:19.
8. Matthew 5:16.
9. Matthew 7:20.
10. Luke 21:3–4.
11. See Exodus 4:10–16.
12. 1 Corinthians 14:3, 8–9.
13. Joseph Smith—History 1:17.

President Henry B. Eyring is a member of the First Presidency. Address at the Church Educational System Religious Educators Conference at Brigham Young University on August 14, 2001, published in *Religious Educator* 2, no. 2 (2001): 1–11.

2

We Must Raise
Our Sights

I AM GRATEFUL FOR THAT MUSIC, beautifully sung, and perfectly chosen for the message and for the purpose that I believe I have been given tonight. I'm grateful to Brother Stanley Peterson for his introduction. One of the things that is most pleasant in my being allowed to be the commissioner of education and still go on associating with you and with people like you and Brother Peterson is that from time to time I have the chance to sense the appreciation of the Savior for you and for him. I think you need to know that I have had clear and unmistakable evidence that the Lord knows Brother Peterson and has watched over him and is grateful and is pleased. I believe he was inspired to have the volunteers and missionaries stand so that I might for a second feel not *my* gratitude but the Master's gratitude.

I was also touched by the opening prayer, to have someone who has given such long full-time service be asked to pray. Because again, as he prayed, I had a sense that some of you who are full-time people have labored in obscurity. But you are not obscure, and your work is known.

I am grateful to be with you and for our opportunity to teach the gospel to the young people of the Church. They hold the future in their hands. The Church has always been one generation away from extinction. If a whole generation were lost, which will not happen, we would lose the Church. But even a single individual lost to the gospel of Jesus Christ closes doors for generations of descendants, unless the Lord reaches out to bring some of them back. Our trust from the Lord as teachers of youth is great. And so is our opportunity.

The world in which our students choose spiritual life or death is changing rapidly. When their older brothers and sisters return to visit the same schools and campuses they attended, they find a radically different moral climate. The language in the hallways and the locker rooms has coarsened. Clothing is less modest. Pornography has moved into the open. Tolerance for wickedness has not only increased, but much of what was called wrong is no longer condemned at all and may, even by our students, be admired. Parents and administrators have in many cases bent to the pressures coming from a shifting world to retreat from moral standards once widely accepted.

The spiritual strength sufficient for our youth to stand firm just a few years ago will soon not be enough. Many of them are remarkable in their spiritual maturity and in their faith. But even the best of them are sorely tested. And the testing will become more severe.

The youth are responsible for their own choices. And there are many others to help them. Faithful parents and priesthood and youth leaders shore up the faith of the students we teach. But ours is a unique opportunity. Students at our Church universities and colleges have been required to take our religion classes. The prophets of God have repeatedly endorsed seminary and institute classes and urged the youth to become our students. We are given a regular, often daily, opportunity to meet with them where the word of God from the scriptures is the text and we are their trusted guides.

You and those who have gone before you have done a wonderful work. The world has changed but so has our curriculum. Students in seminary and institute and in our campus religion classes are reading the scriptures and understanding them. If you were not teaching with us twenty-five years ago, you may not sense the great sweep of that change. Where once there was a wealth of material calculated to hold the wandering interest of young people and even entertain them, the words of the scriptures are now doing the holding. In your classes students know the scriptures beyond what their older brothers and sisters, or their parents, did. You have made the scriptures live for them.

But they need more. Too many graduates of seminary fail to qualify for the mission field. Too many of our faithful students never receive the blessings of the temple ordinances. The proportion of those tragedies among them will increase if we do not change.

The place to begin is with our aim, our vision of what we seek in the lives of our students. We have always sought to enroll and hold students in our classes. We have aimed to see them persist to graduation. We have always had a goal that they will qualify for the mission field and for temple marriage and then remain faithful. Those are lofty, difficult goals, but we must raise our sights.

Too many of our students want the blessings of a mission and the temple and yet fail to endure to claim them. For many of our students, next year is a long way away, and beyond a year looks like forever. To them, missions and the temple are far distant, in some time when the joys of youth have flown away. Those goals are distant enough that too many, far too many, say to themselves: "Well, I know I may have to repent some day, and I know that a mission and temple marriage will require big changes, but I can always take care of that when the time comes. I have a testimony. I know the scriptures. I know what it takes to repent. I'll see the bishop when it's time and I'll make the changes later. I'm only young once. For now, I'll go with the flow."

Well, the flow has become a flood and soon will be a torrent. It will become a torrent of sounds and sights and sensations that invite temptation and offend the Spirit of God. Swimming back upstream to purity against the tides of the world was never easy. It is getting harder and may soon be frighteningly difficult.

We must raise our sights. We must keep the goals we have always had: enrollment, regular attendance, graduation, knowledge of the scriptures, the experience of feeling the Holy Ghost confirm truth. In addition, we must aim for the mission field and the temple. But students need more during the time they are our students. That is when they make the daily choices that will bless or mar their lives. That is when the pressures of temptation and spiritual confusion are increasing.

The Pure Gospel Changes Hearts and Lives

The pure gospel of Jesus Christ must go down into the hearts of students by the power of the Holy Ghost. It will not be enough for them to have had a spiritual witness of the truth and to want good things later. It will not be enough for them to hope for some future cleansing and strengthening. Our aim must be for them to become truly converted to the restored gospel of Jesus Christ while they are with us.

Then they will have gained a strength from what they are, not only from what they know. They will become disciples of Christ. They will be His spiritual children who always remember Him with gratitude and in faith. They will then have the Holy Ghost as a constant companion. Their hearts will be turned outward, concerned for the temporal and spiritual welfare of others. They will walk humbly. They will feel cleansed, and they will look on evil with abhorrence.

The Book of Mormon describes such a change and testifies that it is possible. The accounts are found everywhere in the book. One evidence is the experience of the people of King Benjamin, the master teacher:

> And now, it came to pass that when king Benjamin had thus spoken to his people, he sent among them, desiring to know of his people if they believed the words which he had spoken unto them.
>
> And they all cried with one voice, saying: Yea, we believe all the words which thou hast spoken unto us; and also, we know of their surety and truth, because of the Spirit of the Lord Omnipotent, which has wrought a mighty change in us, or in our hearts, that we have no more disposition to do evil, but to do good continually.
>
> And we, ourselves, also, through the infinite goodness of God, and the manifestations of his Spirit, have great views of that which is to come; and were it expedient, we could prophesy of all things.
>
> And it is the faith which we have had on the things which our king has spoken unto us that has brought us to this great knowledge, whereby we do rejoice with such exceedingly great joy.
>
> And we are willing to enter into a covenant with our God to do his will, and to be obedient to his commandments in all things that he shall command us, all the remainder of our days,

that we may not bring upon ourselves a never-ending torment, as has been spoken by the angel, that we may not drink out of the cup of the wrath of God.

And now, these are the words which king Benjamin desired of them; and therefore he said unto them: Ye have spoken the words that I desired; and the covenant which ye have made is a righteous covenant.

And now, because of the covenant which ye have made ye shall be called the children of Christ, his sons, and his daughters; for behold, this day he hath spiritually begotten you; for ye say that your hearts are changed through faith on his name; therefore, ye are born of him and have become his sons and his daughters. (Mosiah 5:1–7)

That mighty change is reported time after time in the Book of Mormon. The way it is wrought and what the person becomes is always the same. The words of God in pure doctrine go down deep into the heart by the power of the Holy Ghost. The person pleads with God in faith. The repentant heart is broken and the spirit contrite. Sacred covenants have been made. Then God keeps His covenant to grant a new heart and a new life, in His time.

TEACH THE PURE GOSPEL IN A SIMPLE WAY

Whether the miracle comes in a moment or over years, as is far more common, it is the doctrine of Jesus Christ that drives the change. We sometimes underestimate the power that pure doctrine has to penetrate the hearts of people. Why did so many respond to the words of the missionaries when the Church was so young, so small, and seemingly so strange? What did Brigham Young and John Taylor and Heber C. Kimball preach in the streets and on the hills of England? They taught that the Lord had opened a new dispensation, that He had given us a Prophet of God, that the priesthood was restored, that the Book of Mormon was the word of God, and that we had a glorious new day. They taught that the pure gospel of Jesus Christ had been restored.

That pure doctrine went down into the hearts then, as it will now, because the people were starved and the doctrine was taught simply. The people of England, and our students, were seen long before by a prophet of God named Amos: "Behold, the days come, saith the Lord God, that I will send a famine in the land, not a famine of bread, nor a thirst for water, but of hearing the words of the Lord: and they shall wander from sea to sea, and from the north even to the east, they shall run to and fro to seek the word of the Lord, and shall not find it. In that day shall the fair virgins and young men faint for thirst" (Amos 8:11–13).

Most of those early converts in England had known they were hungry for the true word of God. Our students may not know that they are fainting from famine, but the words of God will slake a thirst they did not know they had, and the Holy Ghost will take it down into their hearts. If we make the doctrine simple and clear, and if we teach out of our own changed hearts, the change for them will come as surely as it did for Enos. Listen to his account, so similar to the others:

> Behold, it came to pass that I, Enos, knowing my father that he was a just man—for he taught me in his language, and also in the nurture and admonition of the Lord—and blessed be the name of my God for it—
>
> And I will tell you of the wrestle which I had before God, before I received a remission of my sins.
>
> Behold, I went to hunt beasts in the forests; and the words which I had often heard my father speak concerning eternal life, and the joy of the saints, sunk deep into my heart.
>
> And my soul hungered; and I kneeled down before my Maker, and I cried unto him in mighty prayer and supplication for mine own soul; and all the day long did I cry unto him; yea, and when the night came I did still raise my voice high that it reached the heavens. (Enos 1:1–4)

And then the miracle came:

> And there came a voice unto me, saying: Enos, thy sins are forgiven thee, and thou shalt be blessed.

And I, Enos, knew that God could not lie; wherefore, my guilt was swept away.

And I said: Lord, how is it done?

And he said unto me: Because of thy faith in Christ, whom thou hast never before heard nor seen. And many years pass away before he shall manifest himself in the flesh; wherefore, go to, thy faith hath made thee whole. (vv. 5–8)

Then Enos describes the first effects: "Now, it came to pass that when I had heard these words I began to feel a desire for the welfare of my brethren, the Nephites; wherefore, I did pour out my whole soul unto God for them" (v. 9). He ends with a description of the lasting effects:

And it came to pass that I began to be old, and an hundred and seventy and nine years had passed away from the time that our father Lehi left Jerusalem.

And I saw that I must soon go down to my grave, having been wrought upon by the power of God that I must preach and prophesy unto this people, and declare the word according to the truth which is in Christ. And I have declared it in all my days, and have rejoiced in it above that of the world.

And I soon go to the place of my rest, which is with my Redeemer; for I know that in him I shall rest. And I rejoice in the day when my mortal shall put on immortality, and shall stand before him; then shall I see his face with pleasure, and he will say unto me: Come unto me, ye blessed, there is a place prepared for you in the mansions of my Father. Amen. (vv. 25–27)

A Deep Change in Our Students

What we seek for our students is that change. We must be humble about our part in it. True conversion depends on a student seeking freely in faith, with great effort and some pain. Then it is the Lord who can grant, in His time, the miracle of cleansing and change. Each person starts from a different place, with a different set of experiences, and so a different need for cleansing and for change. The Lord knows that place, and so only He can set the course.

But for all of our students, we can play a vital part. Enos remembered the words of eternal life that he had been taught. So did Nephi, and so did the people of King Benjamin. The words had been placed in memory in such a way that the Holy Ghost could take them deep into the heart. We are teachers whose charge is to place those words so that when the student chooses and pleads, the Holy Ghost can confirm them in the heart and the miracle can begin.

THE PURE DOCTRINE TAUGHT IN PLAINNESS

Much of the power of the Book of Mormon is that it presents the pure doctrine so plainly. For instance, as if He were speaking to us, the Lord through prophets gave us these words in 2 Nephi: "And now, behold, my beloved brethren, this is the way; and there is none other way nor name given under heaven whereby man can be saved in the kingdom of God. And now, behold, this is the doctrine of Christ, and the only and true doctrine of the Father, and of the Son, and of the Holy Ghost, which is one God, without end. Amen" (2 Nephi 31:21). And the Lord repeats Himself, as if we might misunderstand:

> And this is my doctrine, and it is the doctrine which the Father hath given unto me; and I bear record of the Father, and the Father beareth record of me, and the Holy Ghost beareth record of the Father and me; and I bear record that the Father commandeth all men, everywhere, to repent and believe in me.
>
> And whoso believeth in me, and is baptized, the same shall be saved; and they are they who shall inherit the kingdom of God.
>
> And whoso believeth not in me, and is not baptized, shall be damned.
>
> Verily, verily, I say unto you, that this is my doctrine, and I bear record of it from the Father; and whoso believeth in me believeth in the Father also; and unto him will the Father bear record of me, for he will visit him with fire and with the Holy Ghost. (3 Nephi 11:32–35)

And He goes on to say it yet again:

> Verily, verily, I say unto you, that this is my doctrine, and whoso buildeth upon this buildeth upon my rock, and the gates of hell shall not prevail against them.
>
> And whoso shall declare more or less than this, and establish it for my doctrine, the same cometh of evil, and is not built upon my rock; but he buildeth upon a sandy foundation, and the gates of hell stand open to receive such when the floods come and the winds beat upon them.
>
> Therefore, go forth unto this people, and declare the words which I have spoken, unto the ends of the earth. (vv. 39–41)

You wonderful teachers already put great effort and sacrifice into your preparation to teach the word, into your teaching, and into caring for students. You more than study, you ponder the words of God. You declare them with faith and with testimony. You fast and plead in prayer for help, for your students and for yourselves. You teach the pure doctrine with testimony and in clarity.

A Higher Vision

But there is more. We can raise our sights by adding greater faith that the change promised by the Lord will come to our students. The teachers of the Church Educational System had faith that the students would take the scriptures into their lives, and they did. Of all the great contributions Stan Peterson can look back on with satisfaction, it is that he was a major force in allowing that miracle, that I think he will someday find, when the Lord shows him the sweep of things, was, if not his greatest contribution, one of the greatest. He drew from you the faith that a mighty change could come.

You can now add your faith that more of our students will make the choices that lead to true conversion. The Lord always keeps His promises. We can exercise our faith that He will keep His word, for our students and for ourselves.

You have already been prepared. You have felt the desire to repent and be cleansed when these words went down into your heart:

> And assuredly, as the Lord liveth, for the Lord God hath spoken it, and it is his eternal word, which cannot pass away, that they who are righteous shall be righteous still, and they who are filthy shall be filthy still; wherefore, they who are filthy are the devil and his angels; and they shall go away into everlasting fire, prepared for them; and their torment is as a lake of fire and brimstone, whose flame ascendeth up forever and ever and has no end.
>
> O the greatness and the justice of our God! For he executeth all his words, and they have gone forth out of his mouth, and his law must be fulfilled.
>
> But, behold, the righteous, the saints of the Holy One of Israel, they who have believed in the Holy One of Israel, they who have endured the crosses of the world, and despised the shame of it, they shall inherit the kingdom of God, which was prepared for them from the foundation of the world, and their joy shall be full forever. (2 Nephi 9:16–18)

You have also felt your heart swell with love just as it is described in the words from Moroni (think of your own experiences—remember): "And the remission of sins bringeth meekness, and lowliness of heart; and because of meekness and lowliness of heart cometh the visitation of the Holy Ghost, which Comforter filleth with hope and perfect love, which love endureth by diligence unto prayer, until the end shall come, when all the saints shall dwell with God" (Moroni 8:26).

Each of you have at some time in your life, because of the power of the Atonement, felt relief when a temptation no longer seemed appealing to you, exactly as in the words in Alma: "And it came to pass that when Ammon arose he also administered unto them, and also did all the servants of Lamoni; and they did all declare unto the people the selfsame thing—that their hearts had been changed; that they had no more desire to do evil" (Alma 19:33).

And you've felt spots on your soul fade just as it did for these servants of God, described in these words from Alma:

Therefore they were called after this holy order, and were sanctified, and their garments were washed white through the blood of the Lamb.

Now they, after being sanctified by the Holy Ghost, having their garments made white, being pure and spotless before God, could not look upon sin save it were with abhorrence; and there were many, exceedingly great many, who were made pure and entered into the rest of the Lord their God.

And now, my brethren, I would that ye should humble yourselves before God, and bring forth fruit meet for repentance, that ye may also enter into that rest. (Alma 13:11–13)

And you have also felt this: you have felt yourself look up, and feast on the words of the Master and His love, just as promised in the words of Jacob, and just as some of you may have experienced in this very hour we are together: "O all ye that are pure in heart, lift up your heads and receive the pleasing word of God, and feast upon his love; for ye may, if your minds are firm, forever" (Jacob 3:2).

You know what I know. As a witness of Jesus Christ, I testify that the promises are true. Our Heavenly Father lives. Jesus is the Christ. By faith in Him and keeping His commandments, we and our students can have eternal life. I know that the word of God can be carried into the hearts of men and women by the power of the Holy Ghost. And I know that the blessing the Lord has given so freely since the world began, of a new heart, unspotted and filled with His pure love, is still offered in His true Church. I testify that He has called you to teach and that He invites all who will to become His true disciples, His sons and His daughters.

A Concluding Blessing

Now as I close I need to share with you the desire of my heart. I have prayed that I might have the opportunity to bless you. You know about blessings. *All blessings are contingent.* I know what I want you to have, and I know what I want for your students and for your families. But it is not enough that I want it. I had to know, is it what God is now ready to give? Are you ready to do what you must do to receive the gift? Are your students ready? I have prayed to know that, and I have been given assurance, both as to the blessing He would give you, and that you and your students are prepared to receive the blessing.

The reason I take a moment to explain this to you is that I need to explain to you the way you exercise unwavering faith. Faith is not to hope. Faith is not simply to know God *could* do something. Faith is to know He will. And I testify to you that our Heavenly Father and Jesus Christ are prepared to bless our students. I now leave a blessing with you.

This is my blessing: I bless you that as you exercise unwavering faith in the Lord Jesus Christ and in His Atonement, you will see mighty change multiplied in the lives of your students. As I sought the power to give this blessing I was told that many of you have already seen, often, change in your students beyond what you know is even reasonable to hope for, and so you knew the power of the Atonement was working in their lives. I bless you that you will see that magnified, both in the extent of change and in the numbers who will be touched.

I bless you in that same way in your families.

Now as I leave you that blessing, I need of course to also caution you. Teach the doctrine simply. You don't need to give discourses on true conversion. I have tried tonight to be an example. I could have told stories of the mighty change. I chose not to do that on this occasion, although I have at other times. I tried to give to you the words that the Lord has given us, with faith that the Holy Ghost would take them into your hearts, and that the desire to exercise your faith would come from that.

My hope would be this: not that you would speak a great deal to your students about the mighty change nor the blessing from Brother Eyring. It would be better if you simply taught with unshakable faith the simple doctrine taught so well in the Book of Mormon. Then, alone, as you kneel in prayer, in great faith, express the confidence you have in them and the love you have for them.

I have been given assurance that many will respond to the pure doctrine when it is taught in humility and with testimony and by those who themselves are feeling the effects of the Atonement in their lives.

You have seen the effects of the Atonement in your life. You don't need to speak of that to the students. They will sense it in the way you teach. They will know.

I could have told you of my own wrestles. I could have told you of my own experiences. I felt a restraining hand which seemed to say: Don't do that. Do the simple thing. Teach the doctrine of Jesus Christ, simply, clearly, from the Book of Mormon.

Bear testimony without unduly focusing on examples from your own lives, but rather, having faith that students have been prepared, and each of them will see in their own lives the application of the scriptures that you will read with them.

I have been given that assurance, that the Holy Ghost will teach them and bear witness to them not only of what is true but of what they should do. Each will be given a different course. Each will be blessed in a different way. The Lord may not reveal to you where they are or what they must do, but He will to them. I so assure you.

I love you. The Savior loves you. There is great safety as the young people of the Church accept the gospel into their lives. There will be safety even in the times of great difficulty that are coming. There is a protection that they will have—because of the mighty change that has come in their hearts. They will choose righteousness and find that they have no more desire to do evil. That will come. It will not come in an instant, it will come over time. But you will, I promise you, in the year ahead, see miracles of strengthening among your students, and they will strengthen each other. And there will be a fortification created by the gospel of Jesus Christ through your faith and through your great efforts.

I say to you again, in the name of Jesus Christ, He loves you. He knows you. You will, in this service, feel His love. I so testify as His servant in the name of Jesus Christ, amen.

President Dieter F. Uchtdorf is a member of the First Presidency. Address at the LDS International Society's fourteenth annual conference at Brigham Young University in August 2003, published in *Global Mormonism in the 21st Century* (Provo, UT: Religious Studies Center, Brigham Young University, 2008), 294–306.

3 THE CHURCH IN A CROSS-CULTURAL WORLD

The theme of this year's conference, "The Gospel, Professional Ethics, and Cross-Cultural Experience," is certainly an area of special concern for The Church of Jesus Christ of Latter-day Saints and its worldwide membership. It has special significance for Latter-day Saint professionals who are more and more involved in international affairs due to the ongoing process of globalization and the integration of markets, transportation, and communication systems as we have never witnessed before. In a way, this development enables countries, corporations, institutions, and individuals to reach around the world faster, farther, and deeper than ever before.

Many of us are crossing these borders of different cultures frequently. Elder Neal A. Maxwell would suggest that Latter-day Saint international professionals should have their citizenship first in the kingdom of God, but then carry their passport with all its consequences into the professional world and not the other way around. This also reminds me of a comment made by Elder Dallin H. Oaks after his call to the Quorum of the Twelve Apostles that he wanted to be remembered as an Apostle who formerly was a judge and not as a judge serving as an Apostle.

The dictionary defines *culture* as the sum of ways of living, built up by a group of human beings and transmitted from generation to generation. *Cross-cultural* is defined as pertaining to or contrasting two or more such cultures, and the dictionary suggests that ethics is the body of moral principles or values held by or governing a culture, group, or individual.

I commend all of you who are participating in the International Society. I have read several of your newsletters, published presentations, and papers from prior conferences. In my thinking, you are not only building links and bridges between nations and countries but also between cultures and traditions and, most important, between revealed truths and the world of your professional lives.

Division versus Integration

As I grew up in Europe following the Second World War, the political system then was symbolized by a single word—*division*—and by a name and a location—*the Berlin Wall*. It was the Cold War system. The globalization we are experiencing now is a different system. The world has become an increasingly interwoven place. Today, whether you are a country, institution, or a company, your opportunities come increasingly from who you are connected to and how you are connected. This system of globalization is also impressively characterized by a single word—*integration*—and by a name and a location—*www*, or the *World Wide Web*.

So in a broad sense, we have come from a world of division and walls to a system built increasingly around integration. This type of globalization is bringing the world closer together. Borders are coming down, and the rewards will be measured in better standards of living, less poverty around the world, more respect and deference for diversity of culture, and peace for all mankind. I believe we all agree that we still have a long way to go.

Globalization is facilitated by openness and trust. Yet openness is today considered as much a liability as a virtue. The tragic and traumatic impact of 9/11 and the Iraq War have brought increased focus on insecurity and uncertainty, which translates into extreme caution for anyone considering travel and investments. The emphasis is not so much on opportunities but on avoiding risks of any kind. We have also discovered in the past that some of the links and connections that made globalization work so effectively across cultures can also transmit a crisis. The Asian currency crisis of the late 1990s was transmitted through a worldwide financial system that had become much more integrated than almost anyone understood. That made it possible for the crisis to spread quickly through Asia, triggering a huge economic collapse in Russia and coming close to bringing Wall Street to its knees.

In the recent past, a similar impact coming from Asia, this time not just financial, had huge worldwide ramifications for all walks of life. The SARS virus is easily transmitted through our open global travel network. The SARS virus can hitch an airplane ride and get anywhere in twenty-four hours.

We are also living in a cynical time. Trust in public institutions, corporations, and organized religion is declining. We read daily newspaper accounts and hear media reports that describe the decline of moral decency and the erosion of basic ethical conduct. They detail the corrupting influence of dishonesty, from small-time childish stealing or cheating to major embezzlement and fraud, child or spouse abuse, and misappropriation of money or goods.

A TIME OF GREAT OPPORTUNITIES

In this time of uncertainty, mistrust, fear, rumors of war, and political road rage, is there still hope for integration and openness across different cultures? Is there still room for virtues and divine principles?

Yes, there is, but we must understand that the axiomatic and eternal principle of agency demands that there be "an opposition in all things" (2 Nephi 2:11) to ensure that meaningful choices can be made, not only between good and evil but also from among an array of righteous alternatives.

Moral agency refers not only to the capacity "to act for [ourselves]" (2 Nephi 2:26) but also to the accountability for those actions. Exercising agency is a spiritual matter (see D&C 29:35); it consists of either receiving the enlightenment and commandments that come from God or resisting and rejecting them by yielding to the devil's temptations (see D&C 93:31). Without awareness of alternatives, an individual could not choose, and that is why being tempted by evil is as essential to agency as being enticed by the Spirit of God (see D&C 29:39).

We believe that every man and woman, irrespective of race, culture, nationality, or political or economic circumstance, has the power to determine what is right and what is wrong. In the Book of Mormon we read, "For behold, the Spirit of Christ is given to every man, that he may know good from evil; wherefore, I show unto you the way to judge; for every thing which inviteth to do good, and to persuade to believe in Christ, is sent forth by the power and gift of Christ; wherefore ye may know with a perfect knowledge it is of God" (Moroni 7:16).

Church leaders have counseled wisely about how to handle temporal matters to produce rich spiritual revenue. President N. Eldon Tanner taught, "Material blessings are a part of the gospel if they are achieved in the proper way and for the right purpose."[1] And President Spencer W. Kimball said that money is "compensation received for a full day's honest work. It is . . . reasonable pay for faithful service. It is . . . fair profit from the sale of goods, commodities, or service. It is . . . income received from transactions where all parties profit."[2]

One reason for today's decline in moral values is that the world has invented a new, constantly changing, undependable standard of moral conduct, often referred to as "situational ethics." Now individuals consider good and evil adjustable according to each situation. Some wrongly believe that there is no divine law, so there is no sin (see 2 Nephi 2:13). This is in direct contrast to the proclaimed, God-given, absolute standards which we find in the Ten Commandments and in other revealed sources that represent the commandments of God.

For Latter-day Saints, obedience to divine imperatives and the pursuit of ultimate happiness are correlated elements in the maturing of human beings. We believe that this ethical maturity derives from experience, including religious experience; from rational and practical deliberation; from the mandates, both general and specific, that recur in scriptures; and from the counsel given by living prophets.

Divine laws are instituted by God to govern His creations and kingdoms and to prescribe behavior for His offspring. The extent of the divine laws that He reveals to mankind may vary from dispensation to dispensation, according to the needs and conditions of mankind, as God decrees, and as they are given through and interpreted by His prophets. These laws are important to the individual and for the social aspects of the human family eternally. The scriptures teach, "That same sociality which exists among us here will exist among us there [in the eternal worlds], only it will be coupled with eternal glory, which glory we do not now enjoy" (D&C 130:2).

Modern revelation brings the human existence to a clear, divine, and eternal perspective. Latter-day Saints believe in an ethic of divine approbation; to discern the will of God and receive assurance that one is acting under God's approval are the ultimate quest of discipleship. This may be called Spirit-guided morality.

CHILDREN OF A LOVING HEAVENLY FATHER

Latter-day Saints believe that all human beings are God's children and that He loves all of us. He has inspired not only people of the Bible and the Book of Mormon but other people as well to carry out His purposes through all cultures and parts of the world. God inspires not only Latter-day Saints but also founders, teachers, philosophers, and reformers of other Christian and non-Christian religions. The restored gospel holds a positive relationship with other religions. Intolerance is always a sign of weakness. The Latter-day Saint perspective is that of the eleventh article of faith: "We claim the privilege of worshiping Almighty God according to the dictates of our own conscience, and allow all men the same privilege, let them worship how, where, or what they may" (Articles of Faith 1:11).

The Church teaches that members must not only be kind and loving toward others but also respect their right to believe and worship as they choose. George Albert Smith, the eighth President of the Church, publicly advocated the official Church policy of friendship and tolerance: "We have come not to take away from you the truth and virtue you possess. We have come not to find fault with you nor to criticize you. . . . We have come here as your brethren . . . to say to you: 'Keep all the good that you have, and let us bring to you more good, in order that you may be happier and in order that you may be prepared to enter into the presence of our Heavenly Father.'"[3]

On February 15, 1978, the First Presidency of the Church issued the following declaration:

The great religious leaders of the world such as Mohammed, Confucius, and the Reformers, as well as philosophers including Socrates, Plato, and others, received a portion of God's light. Moral truths were given to them by God to enlighten whole nations and to bring a higher level of understanding to individuals. . . . Our message therefore is one of special love and concern for the eternal welfare of all men and women, regardless of religious belief, race, or nationality, knowing that we are truly brothers and sisters because we are the sons and daughters of the same Eternal Father.[4]

In the words of Orson F. Whitney, an Apostle, the gospel "embraces all truth, whether known or unknown. It incorporates all intelligence, both past and prospective. No righteous principle will ever be revealed, no truth can possibly be discovered, either in time or in eternity, that does not in some manner, directly or indirectly, pertain to the Gospel of Jesus Christ."[5]

President Spencer W. Kimball set the tone in relationships with other religions and cultures. In a major address to Church leaders, he said, "The pattern . . . has not been to demand rights but to merit them, not to clamor for friendship and goodwill but to manifest them and to give energy and time beyond rhetoric." Citing a statement by the First Presidency, he said: "With our wide ranging mission, so far as mankind is concerned, Church members cannot ignore the many practical problems that require solutions. . . . Where solutions to these practical problems require cooperative action with those not of our faith, members should not be reticent in doing their part in joining and leading in those efforts where they can make an individual contribution to those causes which are consistent with the standards of the Church."[6]

"Go Ye Therefore, and Teach All Nations"

The Church has a history of reaching out to other nations and cultures beginning immediately after the Church was organized again in April 1830. Early missionaries fearlessly taught the gospel in Native American lands before the Church was fully organized. As early as

1837, the Twelve Apostles were in England; in 1844 they were in the Pacific Islands; by 1850 they had been to France, Germany, Italy, Switzerland, and the Middle East. This was during a time when the Church was facing severe persecution and extreme financial difficulties.

The Church has become a great cosmopolitan church. It rejoices in the tremendous growth of the work across the world. We are thankful for the deep faith and faithfulness of members of the Church. We all look upon one another as brothers and sisters, regardless of the land we call home. We belong to what may be regarded as the greatest community of friends on the face of the earth.

Church members now live in nearly every country of the world. Church congregations around the world will increasingly reflect the diversity of the nations in which they are located. There are members in at least 150 of the 230 countries of the world. Church members speak approximately 170 different languages as their first language. Therefore, the Church as a whole, worldwide, is becoming more diverse in terms of national, racial, cultural, and linguistic characteristics of its members.

Across all the different nations, we are guided and united by the ethical principles of the thirteenth article of faith: "We believe in being honest, true, chaste, benevolent, virtuous, and in doing good to all men; indeed, we may say that we follow the admonition of Paul—We believe all things, we hope all things, we have endured many things, and hope to be able to endure all things. If there is anything virtuous, lovely, or of good report or praiseworthy, we seek after these things" (Articles of Faith 1:13).

This article of our faith is one of the basic declarations of our theology. It is an all-encompassing statement of the ethics of our behavior. There would be less rationalizing over some elements of our personal conduct which we try to justify with one excuse or another if we would closely follow this declaration. The restored gospel offers the more excellent way; it suggests we seek answers to life's crucial questions from God, who is the source of all true wisdom. "Fear not to do good. . . . Look unto me in every thought" (D&C 6:33, 36).

Diversity by its very nature implies differences. Not all differences are of equal value; some differences can be very positive, and some can be destructive. For example, Latter-day Saints, though we are "required to forgive all men" (D&C 64:10), cannot accept and tolerate the gross evils that are so prevalent in societies today. We hear often of the need for people to be tolerant of differences they observe in others. We agree insofar as tolerance implies genuine respect for another, but we disagree if tolerance means acceptance of sin, which God Himself rejects. "For I the Lord cannot look upon sin with the least degree of allowance" (D&C 1:31).

Ethical decline is accelerated when individuals and eventually societies become indifferent to divine values once widely shared. Now is the time to stand up and be counted and not to step aside or duck. We actually have an obligation to lift people out of endangering routine and help them face the challenges of the future. Leaders and followers are both accountable to Him who gave us life. In a democratic society much is required of leaders and followers, and individual character matters so much in both.

The ultimate, key source for Christian behavioral ethics, and therefore for Latter-day Saints, is found in Jesus Christ's Sermon on the Mount, which sacred message He reemphasizes by providing us with a second witness in the Book of Mormon. Based on those principles, a world community could be established where we are "of one heart and one mind, and [dwell] in righteousness" (Moses 7:18).

There is no question about it; we cannot separate ourselves from others. Our common interests are too great. The English poet John Donne said, "No man is an Island, entire of itself; every man is a piece of the Continent, a part of the main."[7]

By crossing boundaries, continents, and countries, we are establishing contact with different cultures, religions, and traditions. Naturally some challenges arise. In many countries, The Church of Jesus Christ of Latter-day Saints is viewed as an American church. Church leaders strongly emphasize that it is a universal church for all people everywhere, with a responsibility to share the gospel with all of God's children. There is an increased awareness of cultural differences as well as a willingness to work within those differences. The Apostle Paul pronounced that all men and women are God's beloved children. To the

Athenians, Paul said, God "hath made of one blood all nations of men for to dwell on all the face of the earth" (Acts 17:26).

Nephi expressed the same vision: "[Christ] inviteth them all to come unto him and partake of his goodness; and he denieth none that come unto him, black and white, bond and free, male and female; . . . and all are alike unto God" (2 Nephi 26:33).

Sadly, however, deep divisions of race, ethnicity, politics, economic status, and cultures still separate people throughout the world. These divisions corrode, corrupt, and destroy relationships between neighbors and prevent the establishment of societies where there is "no contention in the land, because of the love of God which did dwell in the hearts of the people" (4 Nephi 1:15).

We can be a positive influence as we meet the people of the world. Often people of other cultures look up to us, and it is important that we are not looking down on them.

Roger Loveless, *Brotherhood.*

It takes great courage to put away old hatred, divisions, and tribal traditions that constrict and confine people into a blind succession of destructive behavior toward others. Jesus, who knew perfectly the corrosive effects of such behavior, gave us a higher law when He said: "Ye have heard that it hath been said, Thou shalt love thy neighbour, and hate thine enemy. But I say unto you, Love your enemies, bless them that curse you, do good to them that hate you, and pray for them which despitefully use you, and persecute you; that ye may be the children of your Father which is in heaven: for he maketh his sun to rise on the evil and on the good, and sendeth rain on the just and on the unjust" (Matthew 5:43–45).

Today the power of the restored gospel brings to pass the kind of miracle Paul described to the Saints at Ephesus: "Without Christ, [we are] aliens, . . . having no hope. . . . [But] through [Christ] we both have access by one Spirit unto the Father. Now therefore ye are no more strangers and foreigners, but fellow citizens with the saints, and of the household of God" (Ephesians 2:12, 18–19).

THE WORLD A GLOBAL VILLAGE

The world is becoming, to some degree, a global village with a diverse population. Even in the United States it is expected that by the year 2050 the so-called racial minorities will have taken over and will surpass in numbers the Anglo majority. The children and grandchildren of today's Americans will live in a society where everyone is a member of a minority group. Therefore, we must look beyond superficial stereotyping, which influences too much of our thinking about the worth of those who seem on the surface to be different than we are and sometimes leads us to judge them prematurely. We must learn to look at others through the eyes of love, not as strangers and foreigners but as individuals, fellow children of God, of one blood with us. The Apostle Paul taught, "By love serve one another" (Galatians 5:13).

Becoming a worldwide religion in spirit as well as in organizational matters is much more than building chapels and translating documents. As we embark to experience the universal brotherhood we seek, all of us must be prepared to make some alterations in our views of one another.

We will need to increase our empathy and cross-cultural sensitivity and progressively discard prejudices incompatible with brotherhood. The different cultural and ethnical backgrounds bring challenges into members' lives.

We also need to make a clear distinction between our cultural and other preferences and the gospel of Jesus Christ. The gospel has flourished and has been blessed and sanctioned by God under numerous kinds of governments and economic and cultural systems. There must be some accountability, of course, between these preferences and systems and the gospel. In political terms, one key is freedom: freedom unfettered by practices that limit the exercise of religious conscience or that relegate classes of citizens to servitude, bondage, oppression, or exploitation—freedom that is compatible with the gospel. Governments that actively foster freedom of conscience and opportunity and protect it for all of its citizens are our implicit friends. This is true whether they happen to agree with the political policy of the United States or not. This is not an American church. The Church is beyond the nation-state because no state is an official representative of God. So why is it to our advantage to make a distinction between the gospel we possess and our own political, economic, and cultural preferences?

A Global Church of Jesus Christ

To become a worldwide Church in various cultures and nations, the doctrinal truths of the restored gospel will be the guiding star, not our political background, not even some of the present Church programs. It is the Spirit that counts.

A diverse Latter-day Saint people cannot have brotherhood if one of its segments insists on being always right, all the time, on everything. The gospel is transcendent truth—man-made political and social institutions are not. In social, cultural, and political areas, we cannot expect that widely divergent people should adhere to the same specific perspectives. It is certain that some aspects of culture, ideology, and political practices are more compatible with gospel principles than others, and from that point they are temporally preferable, but only the principles of the restored gospel of Jesus Christ constitute eternal truth.

Jesus Christ is the central figure in the doctrine of The Church of Jesus Christ of Latter-day Saints. Complete salvation is possible only through the life, death, Resurrection, doctrines, and ordinances of Jesus Christ, and in no other way. "We talk of Christ, we rejoice in Christ, we preach of Christ, we prophesy of Christ, . . . that our children may know to what source they may look for a remission of their sins" (2 Nephi 25:26). Jesus is the model and exemplar of all who seek to acquire the divine nature. Thus, the Messiah's mission to "preach good tidings unto the meek," to "bind up the brokenhearted, to proclaim liberty to the captives, and the opening of the prison to them that are bound" (Isaiah 61:1; see also Luke 4:18–19) extends into our days and into the life beyond.[8]

Jesus Christ is the God of the whole earth and invites all nations and people to come unto Him. To worship Christ, the Son of God, and to acknowledge Him as the source of truth and redemption, as the light and life of the world, is the only way and the answer to all the challenges of our time (see John 14:6; 2 Nephi 25:29; 3 Nephi 11:11).

The charge and commandment given by the Savior Himself to His Apostles in the meridian of time applies equally to us today: "Go ye therefore, and teach *all nations*, baptizing them in the name of the Father, and of the Son, and of the Holy Ghost: . . . I am with you alway, even unto the end of the world" (Matthew 28:19–20; emphasis added).

Did the early Apostles, then, live up to this charge? Their real test came when God answered the prayers of a Roman centurion from Caesarea called Cornelius, a just man who feared God and was of good report, and instructed him to send for Peter to teach and to baptize him. After initial doubt and resistance, followed by fervent prayer and willingness to embrace divine revelation, "then Peter opened his mouth, and said, Of a truth I perceive that God is no respecter of persons: but in every nation he that feareth him, and worketh righteousness, is accepted with him" (Acts 10:34–35).

The people of the earth are all our Father's children. They are of great diversity and many varied religious persuasions. They are our brothers and sisters. May we cultivate tolerance, respect, and love for one another and stand up for the truth with sweet boldness to magnify the charge given to us by the Lord today is my humble prayer.

NOTES

1. N. Eldon Tanner, in Conference Report, October 1979, 117–18.
2. Spencer W. Kimball, in Conference Report, October 1953, 52.
3. George Albert Smith, *Sharing the Gospel with Others*, comp. Preston Nibley (Salt Lake City: Deseret Book, 1948), 12–13.
4. Spencer J. Palmer, *The Expanding Church* (Salt Lake City: Deseret Book, 1978), frontispiece.
5. Spencer J. Palmer, "World Religions (Non-Christion) and Mormonism," in *Encyclopedia of Mormonism*, ed. Daniel H. Ludlow (New York: Macmillan, 1992), 4:1589.
6. Spencer W. Kimball, "Living the Gospel in the Home," *Ensign*, May 1978, 100; see also Richard P. Lindsay, "Interfaith Relationships: Christian," *Encyclopedia of Mormonism*, 2:694.
7. Angela Partington, ed., *The Oxford Dictionary of Quotations*, 4th ed. rev. (Oxford: Oxford University Press, 1996), 253.
8. See Topical Guide, "Salvation for the Dead" and "Spirits in Prison."

Elder Richard G. Scott is a member of the Quorum of the Twelve Apostles. Address at the Church Educational System Religious Educators Symposium at Brigham Young University on August 14, 1987, published in *Religious Educator* 11, no. 1 (2010): 1–15.

4 FOUR FUNDAMENTALS FOR THOSE WHO TEACH AND INSPIRE YOUTH

THE TIME DEVOTED TO THE preparation of this message has been rewarded with the deepest feelings of love, thanksgiving, and gratitude to the Lord for His mercy and kindness in providing us with the holy scriptures, for the indescribable blessing of prayer, and, when we have given sufficiently of ourselves, for the blessing of answer to prayer.

I likewise have feelings of gratitude for the declarations of the prophets that demonstrate a love for the scriptures and lead us to study, ponder, and apply them in our lives.

I have a profound feeling of love for each of you who have participated in this symposium, who so willingly devote yourselves to teaching the gospel to Father in Heaven's children. I likewise sense deep feelings of love. That love gives encouragement to try to express the feelings of my heart this morning in a way that can be understood to bless the lives of the students you, with such tender care, so willingly serve.

Some of your students may ask, "Why are we studying the Old Testament when President Ezra Taft Benson has spoken so vigorously about the need to know the Book of Mormon?"

In the 1986 October conference, our beloved prophet, President Benson, said:

That sacred and holy book has been of inestimable worth to the children of men. In fact, it was a passage from the Bible that inspired the Prophet Joseph Smith to go to a grove of trees near his home and kneel in prayer. What followed was the glorious vision that commenced the restoration of the fulness of the gospel of Jesus Christ to the earth. That vision also began the process of bringing forth new scriptures to stand shoulder to shoulder with the Bible in bearing witness to a wicked world that Jesus is the Christ and that God lives and loves His children and is still intimately involved in their salvation and exaltation. . . .

Today we have three new books of scripture: the Book of Mormon, the Doctrine and Covenants, and the Pearl of Great Price. I love all of these sacred volumes. (In Conference Report, October 1986, 100–101; or *Ensign*, November 1986, 78–79)

These statements from the living prophet of God indicate the importance of all scripture. Each of your students needs to determine personally how he or she will follow the admonition of the prophet to know and to live the teachings of the Book of Mormon. However, this year's course in seminary and institute provides you with the opportunity to open the curtains of understanding to many who otherwise may never on their own find the treasures contained within the Old Testament.

I express gratitude to those who prepared the curriculum for this year and, particularly this morning, to all who have labored so diligently to prepare the workshops and messages of this symposium to further facilitate the understanding of the sacred contents of the Old Testament. They have provided you with suggestions, teaching aids, and methods to help your students find the diamonds of truth that sometimes must be carefully mined from the pages of the Old Testament. How wonderful it is that you have the opportunity to invite your students to drink of the waters of truth the Lord has placed in the Old Testament.

You have come to know that your students learn from you in three ways:

What they hear,

What they see, and

What they feel.

What they *hear* results from your painstaking preparation for each class encounter. Each skill you develop, each teaching capacity you exercise helps them benefit from what they hear.

What they *see* is more than the visual aids you use within the classroom. Paramount and predominant in what they observe is the example of your own life—how you work; how you react to challenges in and out of the classroom; for those of you with families, how you treat them. How you live is constantly under observation. It impacts the lives of your students even in moments when you are least aware that you are being an example.

But the greatest impact of all is what they *feel* in your presence in the classroom and elsewhere. Your commitment to teach the precious children of our Father in Heaven is not alone the long hours you spend in preparation for each class, nor the many hours of fasting and prayer that you may become a more effective teacher. It is the commitment to a life every hour of which is purposefully lived in compliance with the teachings and example of the Savior and of His servants. It is a commitment to constant striving to be evermore spiritual, evermore devoted, evermore deserving to be the conduit through which the Spirit of the Lord may touch the hearts of those you are trusted to bring to a greater understanding of His teachings.

I have observed the influence of some of you, the tremendous consequences of your devoted service as instruments of truth. Years ago, when the first missionaries were being called from South America, they were few in number, enthusiastic but lacking in formal preparation. I contrast that now with the repeated example observed in many areas in South America, Central America, and Mexico, areas with which I am most familiar. There are now young men and young women who have an understanding of the truths of the gospel, a commitment to live them and to teach them to others. Years ago, the peer leaders in the missions were invariably from North America. That is no longer the case. We find equally prepared, devoted, and capable priesthood bearers from the other countries. Much of that preparation has come from laborious, patient testifying and teaching of others like you. From such efforts, there has come a core of capable, devoted, scripturally oriented leaders. One example will illustrate:

Ten years ago, a stake president was called in an area of Mexico. For nine years, he did his devoted best with relatively slow growth resulting. The stake was reorganized. A twenty-seven-year-old returned missionary, who taught seminary and institute, was called as the stake president. He and his similarly trained counselors understand the doctrine, teach and serve as guided by the Spirit, and lead from the scriptures. The result is wondrous.

I think of one of your number whom I love very much who was given the opportunity to accept a position at considerably increased salary or to continue in the Church Educational System. It was not difficult for him or his wife to determine that they would accept fewer material blessings to continue the singular privilege of teaching truth to precious children of Father in Heaven. I am grateful for that determination and for the potent influence on the many youth that continues to result from it.

I know that each of you has been willing, and many have made great sacrifices to serve in the Church Educational System on a full-time, part-time, or Church-service basis. How can I tell you how we appreciate you, how we need you, how we love you? How can one measure the eternal consequences of your selfless service and willingness to give and to give more? How can we thank your children who likewise make sacrifices to support you in this sacred service?

Long ago, you realized that the willingness of your students to listen to your counsel, to open their hearts to you privately, to place you on a pedestal of respect and honor and appreciation is not entirely merited by your capacity or service. It is a gift of God to open hearts and minds of those willing to be taught. It is a great blessing from the Lord that you may teach each individual truth, encourage resolute determination to live righteously, and serve generously. In those sacred moments when we ponder the most important things in life, I am confident you recognize the singular privilege and enormous blessing of being a teacher of youth. I feel blessed to be in your presence today. There radiate from you a power and a genuine love that touches me to the depths of my soul. These feelings encourage me to speak of those thoughts that I have felt so strongly to communicate this morning.

As I am lifted to the heights by the teachings of our prophet, President Benson, and consider the depth of understanding, the clarity of communicating truth embodied in his sermons, I feel the influence of a spiritual giant. I ask myself, "Who led the child to love the Lord and His teachings?" Parents, of course, and inspired teachers. They helped kindle and encourage the flame of testimony in this inspiring prophet of God.

You have a similar opportunity. More than what you teach, more than what you show or say, the spirit that radiates from you will affect your students. A truly effective, inspiring teacher of youth cannot be marginal in conviction, intermittent in testimony, or wavering in obedience.

I stand before you in honest recognition of my own weakness, having prayed, pondered, and labored intently that I might find a way to communicate understandably four fundamentals that I know will help you teach youth. May they be considered in all you do. I pray for the ability to communicate through the Spirit and for you to receive the message by the Spirit.

Teach by the Spirit

The first fundamental I would emblazon in your mind and heart is teach by the Spirit. You never know the extent of your influence when you teach by the Spirit.

Some years ago, a young man listened to a radio broadcast in which Elder Joseph Fielding Smith said that Joseph Smith was instructed of the Lord by revelation. The word *revelation* captured the young man's interest and penetrated deeply into his consciousness. The experience left an imprint that had a pivotal influence on his life. He has devoted his life to the study, understanding, teaching, and illuminating of the scriptures.

Through prayer and quiet, persistent effort over years, he helped touch hearts, which led to the opportunity to study the original manuscript of Joseph Smith's translation of the Bible. That and other extensive work helped establish the authenticity of the published translation. He made significant contribution to the Latter-day Saint edition of the scriptures. That man is Robert J. Matthews, dean of Religious Education and professor of ancient scripture at Brigham Young University.

This next example will further illustrate the vital importance of teaching by the Spirit. I am sure that the essence of the experience that I now relate has been felt time and again in your own life. I mention it so that you may remember that the most lasting impressions, the greatest teaching, and the most enduring effects for good will result from your ability to invite the Spirit of the Lord to touch the hearts and minds of those you teach.

A few years ago, I had an experience I will not forget. It occurred during a priesthood meeting. A humble, unschooled priesthood leader in Mexico struggled to teach truths of the gospel contained in his lesson material. It was obvious how deeply they had touched his life. I noted the intense desire he had to communicate those principles. He recognized that they were of great worth to the brethren present. His manner evidenced a pure love of the Savior and love of those he taught.

His love, sincerity, and purity of intent permitted a spiritual influence to envelop the room. I was so touched that, in addition to receiving again a witness of the truths that he presented, I began to receive some personal impressions as an extension of those principles taught by the humble instructor. These impressions were intended for me personally and were related to my assignments in the area.

As each impression came, it was faithfully recorded. I recognized that because a teacher had taught by the Spirit, I had been given precious truths that were greatly needed for me to be more effective in the service of the Lord. In part, I recorded: "You are to continue to build the Church on the foundation of true principles but with increased expression of love you have been blessed to feel for the great Lamanite people." There followed specific directions, instructions, and conditioned promises that have altered the course of my life.

Subsequently, I visited the Sunday School class where a very well-educated individual presented his lesson. That experience was in striking contrast to the one enjoyed in the priesthood meeting. While technically correct, the lesson did not have the same spiritual effect. The subject was Joseph Smith. The content of the lesson, information the class would likely never otherwise hear. The instructor used his highly developed expertise, yet the message lacked spiritual power.

This second experience so contrasted with the first that strong impressions came again. I began to write down those impressions. One begins with the statement: "Teach and testify to instruct, edify and lead others to full obedience, not to demonstrate anything of self. All who are puffed up shall be cut off." Another entry reads, "You are nothing in and of yourself, Richard."

In this experience, there came such an outpouring of impressions that I felt it inappropriate to try and record them in the midst of a Sunday School class. I sought a more private location. There I continued to write as accurately and as faithfully as possible the feelings that flooded into my mind and heart.

After each powerful impression was recorded, I meditated upon it, pondered the feelings I had received to determine if I had accurately expressed them. Then I studied their meaning and application in my own life.

Subsequently, I prayed expressing what I thought I had been taught by the Spirit. When that feeling of peace and serenity confirmed what I had sought, I asked if there were yet more that I should be given to understand. There came further impressions, and the process was repeated until I received treasured specific direction that has immeasurably enriched my life.

This experience embodies principles I know to be true regarding communication from the Lord to His children here on earth. It illustrates how as you teach by the Spirit, an environment can be established that will permit the Lord to communicate personalized messages through the Holy Ghost to meet an individual's need. I feel, in part at least, that is what this scripture teaches:

"He that receiveth the word by the Spirit of truth receiveth it as it is preached by the Spirit of truth. . . . Wherefore, he that preacheth and he that receiveth, understand one another, and both are edified and rejoice together" (D&C 50:21–22).

I believe that we often leave the most precious personal direction of the Spirit unheard because we do not record and respond to the first promptings that come to us when we are in need or when impressions come in answer to urgent prayer.

Will you help your students understand these principles?

TEACH THE REALITY OF PERSONAL COMMUNICATION WITH GOD

The second fundamental I would strongly emphasize is teach the reality of personal communication from and to God. Help each individual understand how to pray worthily and how to receive and recognize answers from God.

Honestly, I only partially comprehend that process. Yet application of principles I only begin to understand have repeatedly changed the course of my life. It has brought further knowledge, truth and motivation that could not have been known in any other way. It has shown me undiscovered truths about myself, reduced unnecessary dependence upon others, and repeatedly filled my heart, mind, and soul with such overpowering joy and such all-pervading peace as to be beyond my power to express. It has directed my thoughts and acts in efforts to help others in need, and given me specific information and knowledge unattainable by other means critical to my efforts to act as an instrument to unravel tangled lives.

Personal communication from and to God through the Holy Spirit to me is as real as life itself and far more precious than all the treasures of the earth. Please help those you serve feel the vital importance of prayer in their life. Let them know of your witness of the reality of communication with God.

You have spent years studying the scriptures and the declarations of inspired servants of the Lord relating to spiritual communication. You have pondered those truths and faithfully endeavored to try to apply them in your life. Sacred personal experiences have resulted for your own guidance and direction. While you likely will not feel prompted to share specifics of that sacred counsel, testify that it occurs so that your students, trusting your example, will venture forth in faith.

Have you learned the lesson it took me so long to recognize? When I first received Church assignments that embodied counseling and training others, I was very anxious to share personal experiences considered to have some application in the lives of those individuals. This sharing was based upon an honest desire to help. As further experience was gained, I seemed to have more examples from my own life, or lessons learned from others, that I was eager to share to benefit others. Again, this sharing was done with great sincerity and a desire to help.

As the years have passed, I find that I am now much less moved to suggest to others the specific things I have learned. Rather, I am powerfully motivated to share with them *how* the most treasured lessons were learned from the Spirit.

There have been many people who have deeply touched and molded my life. Yet I have come to recognize that the guidance, understanding, enlightenment, and experience most treasured have come directly from the Lord through the Holy Spirit.

You know that the Lord has given us no magic wand to provide immediate answers to life's challenges. You know there is no secret formula for solutions. You have confirmed that God communicates with us on the basis of simple, understandable, verifiable principles. Please testify of that knowledge to those you teach. Let them feel the certainty of your witness that the Lord answers prayers when we live worthily and ask in faith.

Kindle a Love of the Scriptures

The third fundamental I would stress is please kindle a love of the scriptures in the mind and heart of each precious youth. Help ignite within them that flame of unquenchable fire that motivates those who have felt it with a desire to know evermore of the word of the Lord, to understand His teachings, to apply them, and to share them with others.

A love of the scriptures can be encouraged in two ways:

First, walk with them step-by-step through many passages of the sacred word of the Lord. Help them feel your enthusiasm, respect, and love for the scriptures.

Second, help them learn to read, ponder, and pray privately to discover the power and peace that flow from the scriptures.

To appreciate the value of reading scriptures together, consider this counsel of President Marion G. Romney:

> I urge you to get acquainted with this great book [the Book of Mormon]. Read it to your children, they are not too young to

understand it. I remember reading it with one of my lads when he was very young. On one occasion I lay in the lower bunk and he in the upper bunk. We were each reading aloud alternate paragraphs of those last three marvelous chapters of Second Nephi. I heard his voice breaking and thought he had a cold, but we went on to the end of the three chapters. As we finished he said to me, "Daddy, do you ever cry when you read the Book of Mormon?"

"Yes, Son," I answered. "Sometimes the Spirit of the Lord so witnesses to my soul that the Book of Mormon is true that I do cry."

"Well," he said, "that is what happened to me tonight."

I know not all of them will respond like that, but I know that some of them will, and I tell you this book was given to us of God to read and to live by, and it will hold us as close to the Spirit of the Lord as anything I know. Won't you please read it? (in Conference Report, April 1949, 41)

Your engendering in youth a love of the scriptures can prevent tragedy. I am overwhelmed with the thoughts of what will occur in the lives of those under your influence as they live to prevent the consequence of deep sin in their lives because they accept truth and live it. These words of President Spencer W. Kimball eloquently depict what I mean:

"An ounce of prevention is worth a pound of cure" says the old adage. My experience would lead me to believe that the odds are greater. When I see the simple scraping of the upper arm and the application of a little vaccine in the prevention process, I compare it with what I suffered in my twenties with the dreaded smallpox when I could have died, remembering a couple of minutes for a vaccination against many days for the disease to run its course. And when I see one wince so little at the poke of a needle against typhoid fever, I contrast that moment with the many weeks of dizziness and distress and intense fever which nearly burned me out, followed by weeks of starvation and pain and hunger and weakness, trying to gain back my strength. Then

I believe that our function is in prevention rather than, or in addition to, cure, with full assurance that as the one increases, the other decreases. The less prevention the more need of cure processes, and the more prevention the less cure is needed. The more needles, the fewer hospital beds, psychiatrists' couches, and bishops' offices. ("What I Hope You Will Teach My Grand-children," address to seminary and institute personnel, Brigham Young University, July 11, 1966, 8)

Help youth understand that personal scripture study is a joyous lifetime pursuit. President Kimball observed: "I ask us all to honestly evaluate our performance in scripture study. It is a common thing to have a few passages of scripture at our disposal, floating in our minds, as it were, and thus to have the illusion that we know a great deal about the gospel. In this sense, having a little knowledge can be a problem indeed. I am convinced that each of us, at some time in our lives, must discover the scriptures for ourselves—and not just discover them once, but rediscover them again and again" ("How Rare a Possession—the Scriptures!" *Ensign*, September 1976, 4).

Elder Howard W. Hunter noted: "Those who delve into the scriptural library . . . find that to understand requires more than casual reading or perusal—there must be concentrated study. It is certain that one who studies the scriptures every day accomplishes far more than one who devotes considerable time one day and then lets days go by before continuing" (in Conference Report, October 1979, 91; or *Ensign*, November 1979, 64).

The Prophet Joseph Smith said:

Search the scriptures . . . and ask your Heavenly Father, in the name of His Son Jesus Christ, to manifest the truth unto you, and if you do it with an eye single to His glory nothing doubting, He will answer you by the power of His Holy Spirit. You will then know for yourselves. . . . You will not then be dependent on man for the knowledge of God; nor will there be any room for specu-lation. No; for when men receive their instruction from Him that made them, they know how He will save them. Then again we say: Search the Scriptures, search the Prophets and learn what portion of them belongs to you and the people of [this] century. (*Teachings of the Prophet Joseph Smith*, comp. Joseph Fielding Smith [Salt Lake City: Deseret Book, 1938], 11–12)

President Benson teaches powerfully from the scriptures, both publicly and privately. I was blessed to be present recently when he set apart a new mission president. Then he drew his chair close to the president and his wife, opened the scriptures, and began to read and comment on verse after verse for almost an hour. Consider just one comment made that will be motivating inspiration throughout that president's mission. President Benson said, "Your mission will soar on the Book of Mormon."

With counsel applicable to each of us who teach of the scriptures, President Marion G. Romney states:

> You can't teach the gospel unless you know it. . . .
>
> So I would suggest that you do study the gospel and study it every day. You should never let a day go by that you don't read it.
>
> Now, I don't know much about the gospel other than what I've learned from the standard works. When I drink from a spring I like to get the water where it comes out of the ground, not down the stream after the cattle have waded in it. . . . I appreciate other people's interpretation, but when it comes to the gospel we ought to be acquainted with what the Lord says and we ought to read it. You ought to read the gospel; you ought to read the Book of Mormon and the Doctrine and Covenants; and you ought to read all of the scriptures with the idea of finding out what's in them and what the meaning is and not to prove some idea of your own. Just read them and plead with the Lord to let you understand what he had in mind when he wrote them. . . . Become converted to it. Become acquainted with the language of the scriptures and the teachings of the scriptures.
>
> After you have done that, you have to live it. You can't learn the gospel without living it. Jesus didn't learn it all at one time.

He went from grace to grace. . . . You can't understand [the gospel] just by reading it and knowing the words; you have to live it. (address at coordinators' convention, Seminaries and Institutes of Religion, April 13, 1973, 4)

Oh, how your students would be blessed if we were to teach as did Nephi: "I, Nephi, did exhort them to give heed unto the word of the Lord; yea, I did exhort them with all the energies of my soul, and with all the faculty which I possessed, that they would give heed to the word of God and remember to keep his commandments always in all things" (1 Nephi 15:25).

Help your students interlock scriptures throughout the standard works. Greater understanding of gospel principles will result. Consider the statement of the Master in the Sermon on the Mount before His sacrifice:

"Be ye therefore perfect, even as your Father which is in heaven is perfect" (Matthew 5:48).

Now ponder His statement to the Nephites: "Therefore I would that ye should be perfect even as I, or your Father who is in heaven is perfect" (3 Nephi 12:48).

Jesus' inclusion of Himself as an example in the second reference after His resurrection has great meaning.

One has to be impressed with the value of the Old Testament scriptures by considering the impact just a few of them had on the people of the Book of Mormon. Consider one example from Nephi: "And I did read many things unto them which were written in the books of Moses; but that I might more fully persuade them to believe in the Lord their Redeemer I did read unto them that which was written by the prophet Isaiah; for I did liken all scriptures unto us, that it might be for our profit and learning" (1 Nephi 19:23).

Share the beauty of the scriptures and the peace, serenity, and assurance that distill from them. Consider David's psalm:

The Lord is my shepherd; I shall not want.

He maketh me to lie down in green pastures: he leadeth me beside the still waters.

He restoreth my soul: he leadeth me in the paths of righteousness for his name's sake.

Yea, though I walk through the valley of the shadow of death, I will fear no evil: for thou art with me; thy rod and thy staff they comfort me.

Thou preparest a table before me in the presence of mine enemies: thou anointest my head with oil; my cup runneth over.

Surely goodness and mercy shall follow me all the days of my life: and I will dwell in the house of the Lord for ever. (Psalm 23)

Help your students appreciate the value of considering the context in which a scripture is given.

As impressive as are the statements of Moroni concerning charity, they are tremendously more meaningful when we consider that for many years he hid from every other living being because of the certainty that his life would be taken if discovered.

There is a power that can change lives in the specific words recorded in the standard works. That power is weakened when we paraphrase or alter the actual wording. I therefore suggest that you encourage students to cite scriptural content with precision. All you do to encourage students to memorize accurately selected scriptures will bring to bear in their lives the power of their content. This experience illustrates what I mean.

Some years ago, I received an assignment to go to another part of the world to investigate allegations that a Church leader had fathered a child out of wedlock. I took with me a very spiritual mission president knowing that the assignment would be difficult. The accused was a close friend. We interviewed him, those who made the accusations, and those who supported him. After two days, I could not honestly say I had an impression of innocence or guilt. Each time there appeared to be damaging evidence, other evidence appeared to confuse or refute it. Late into the night I continued to wrestle with the matter in prayer and meditation. I searched the scriptures and was led to some I felt would be helpful.

We met with him again the next morning. This time I was impressed to take a different approach. I began. "Whoever is responsible for the act has this scripture to face. Would you read it and then explain in your own words its meaning?" He read it perfectly, but as he began to explain, he hesitated and stumbled. I continued, "This verse speaks of those sent by the servants of the Lord. Would you read it and explain its meaning?" Other scriptures followed. By then, his whole attitude had changed, and he was perspiring and nervously shifting. There came a knock at the door, and he said, "I see you have another interview. I'll just wait outside," which he did.

About forty-five minutes later, the phone rang. It was the man. He said, "Can I see you privately?" He entered the room, sat down, and pulled from his pocket a piece of paper and pushed it across the table. It was a signed confession. How grateful I am for the scriptures that penetrated his heart and initiated the full operation of repentance, which in time has brought a full restoration of blessings.

Teach of the power in the written word of God.

Encourage Students to "Come unto Christ"

The fourth fundamental is more easily undertaken as a result of prayerful application of the other three: Encourage your students to "come unto Christ" (Omni 1:26). Persuade each one to make Christ the center of their life.

That is the most vital message of all. Moroni declared: "Come unto Christ, and be perfected in him" (Moroni 10:32).

Sometimes it is easier for a young man or a young woman to understand more fully the meaning of the life of the Savior and to love him by beginning to appreciate the powerful examples of others in the scriptures. This truth is depicted in the following statement by President Spencer W. Kimball. As I read it, consider how the individuals mentioned have potently affected his life.

I'm hoping that you will involve our youngsters heavily in scripture reading. I find that when I get casual in my relationships with divinity and when it seems that no divine ear is listening and no divine voice is speaking, that I am far, far away. If I immerse myself in the scriptures, the distance narrows and the spirituality returns. I find myself loving more intensely those whom I must love with all my heart and mind and strength, and loving them more. I find it easier to abide their counsel. We learn the lessons of life more readily and surely if we see the results of wickedness and righteousness in the lives of others.

To know the patriarchs and prophets of ages past and their faithfulness under stress and temptation and persecution strengthens the resolves of youth.

To come to know Job well and intimately is to learn to keep faith through the greatest of adversities. To know well the strength of Joseph in the luxury of ancient Egypt when he was tempted by a voluptuous woman, and to see this clean young man resist all the powers of darkness embodied in this one seductive person, certainly should fortify the intimate reader against such sin.

To see the forbearance and fortitude of Paul when he was giving his life to his ministry is to give courage to those who feel they have been injured and tried. He was beaten many times, imprisoned frequently for the cause, stoned near to death, shipwrecked three times, robbed, nearly drowned, the victim of false and disloyal brethren. While starving, choking, freezing, poorly clothed, Paul was yet consistent in his service. He never wavered once after the testimony came to him following his supernatural experience. To see the growth of Peter with the gospel as the catalyst moving him from a lowly fisherman—uncultured, unlearned, and ignorant, as they rated him—blossoming out into a great organizer, prophet, leader, theologian, teacher. Thus, youth will take courage and know that nothing can stop their progress but themselves and their weaknesses.

When one follows the devious paths of Saul from a tender of asses to king of Israel and prophet, and then through arrogance and pride and hostilities and ignoring his Lord and the prophet, to watch this madman slip down from his high place to the tent of Endor's witch, and then to see him in defeat in battle, rejected of the prophet, to ignominy and devastation; and then to see his decapitated head placed upon the wall for all his enemies to gloat over and spit at—this will surely teach vital lessons to youth. He

Del Parson, *Joseph Resists Potiphar's Wife*. © 2002 Intellectual Reserve Inc. All rights reserved.

climbed from peasant to king and prophet and then slid back to witchcraft. What a lesson on pride and arrogance.

Our children may learn the lessons of life through the perseverance and personal strength of Nephi; the Godliness of the

55

three Nephites; the faith of Abraham; the power of Moses; the deception and perfidy of Ananias; the courage even to death of the unresisting of the Ammonites; the unassailable faith of the Lamanite mothers transmitted down through their sons, so powerful that it saved Helaman's striplings. Not a single one came to his death in that war.

All through the scriptures every weakness and strength of man has been portrayed, and rewards and punishments have been recorded. One would surely be blind who could not learn to live life properly by such reading. The Lord said, 'Search the scriptures, for in them ye think ye have eternal life and they are they which testify of me.' And it was this same Lord and master in whose life we find every quality of goodness: Godliness, strength, controls, perfection. And how can students study this great story without capturing some of it in their lives? ("What I Hope You Will Teach My Grandchildren," 6–7)

In summary, there are four fundamentals I ask you to consider as underpinnings to your devoted service:

Teach by the Spirit.

Testify of the reality of personal communication from and to God. Help each one understand how to pray and how to receive and recognize answers from God.

Kindle a love of the scriptures in the mind and heart of each of your students.

Strive to persuade each one to "come unto Christ" to make Him and our Father in Heaven the center of life.

Although I have tried, I can never express the gratitude I feel for those who have lifted my vision beyond themselves to the Savior. I can only attempt to share with others some of what fills my heart to overflowing because of their efforts in my behalf. I have sincerely tried to qualify to be led to do that today.

As I have spoken to you, I have felt a spirit emanate from you. I have felt impressed with how the Lord loves you, how he loves others of you around the world, how he loves those who administer to your needs and direct your programs.

This year gives you an opportunity to unfold teachings about the Savior, about His plan of happiness that many do not know that are in the Old Testament, to provide that additional witness of the reality of the living God.

I know He lives. I love Him with every fiber of my being. With you, I want to use my life in service to Him and in lifting Father's children around the world by striving to help them understand and live His teachings.

May you be blessed as you serve, teach, and testify. We need you. We love you. God bless you, I pray sincerely, in the name of Jesus Christ, amen.

President Gordon B. Hinckley (1910–2008) was President of The Church of Jesus Christ of Latter-day Saints. Address to Church Educational System religious educators at the Assembly Hall on Temple Square on September 15, 1978, published in *Religious Educator* 5, no. 3 (2004): 1–7.

5 FOUR IMPERATIVES FOR RELIGIOUS EDUCATORS

IT IS A PLEASURE TO be with you. I appreciate the kind words which have been said.

It was almost foolish of me to try to be here tonight. I was scolded by the stewardess for trying to get off the plane before it stopped. I have had a long and crowded day. I arose early this morning and dictated these notes. I then hurried to the temple to perform a marriage, rushed to the barber to get my hair clipped, hurried to the airport to fly to Seattle, attended two meetings there, then rushed to the airport, flew back, and I am here. It is too much to put that much into one day, and it is symptomatic of the jostling, busy times in which we live.

You are familiar with this tempo because it is of the nature of your lives also. Your days are filled with the duties of teaching, and your nights are crowded with meetings such as this and many others incident to the responsibilities you carry as active and able members of the Church.

I wish it were not necessary to stand here at a pulpit and speak to a congregation. I wish, rather, that we could sit down together in small groups and talk quietly of problems and hopes and dreams. But that is not feasible, and so I come to these circumstances not to lecture but simply to talk with you insofar as the circumstances will permit. I earnestly pray for the direction of the Holy Spirit, for I desire only one thing, and that is to say something that will be helpful.

I was tempted to talk about your students and the responsibility you have toward them. But before undertaking this task, I read the talks given on past occasions by Elder Boyd K. Packer, President Ezra Taft Benson, and President Spencer W. Kimball. If you will read them again, you will have what you need on these matters and stated better than I would have done. And so I think I would like to talk rather informally about you, as men and women, as husbands and wives, as teachers and administrators, as those among us who, with talents large and small, have been given great responsibility and of whom so much is expected.

First, I wish to congratulate you on the tremendously effective work you are doing. I have now lived long enough to observe three generations of youth in the Church. There can be no doubt that those who have come under your direction are far better educated in the history, the doctrine, and the practices of the Church than any other generation in our history. We are making great progress. It is not always apparent to those involved in the day-to-day programs. But when one stands back and looks across fifty or sixty years, it is obvious and it is gratifying. I have no doubt that the seminary and institute of religion program has had more to do with this than has any other single factor. I commend you warmly for what you have done, and with that commendation I wish to thank you. I know that it has taken great faith and prayers and tremendous effort, but I know also that you must derive sweet satisfaction as you witness those who have been under your tutelage flower into effective missionaries and then go on to become faithful and active members of the Church and strong and able citizens who carry responsibilities of leadership in many parts of the earth.

1. Keep on Growing

And now I should like to speak briefly of four imperatives, if I may call them that. The first, *keep on growing*. You are all educated people—highly educated. You who are here tonight are graduates of many universities, with bachelor's, master's, and doctor's degrees. One of the great dangers of higher education is what I call "academic burnout." The earning of a degree is such a grind that once it is earned there is a disposition to say, "I have made it, and now I'll coast for a season." The season sometimes becomes a lifetime. I should like to pass on to you these words written by Dr. Joshua Loth Liebman:

> The great thing is that as long as we live, we have the privilege of growing. We can learn new skills, engage in new kinds of work, devote ourselves to new causes, make new friends. Accepting, then, the truth that we are capable in some directions and limited in others, that genius is rare, that mediocrity is the portion of most of us, let us remember that we can and must change ourselves. Until the day of our death we can and must change ourselves. Until the day of our death we can grow, we can tap hidden resources in our makeup.[1]

None of us, my brethren and sisters, knows enough. The learning process is an endless process. We must read, we must observe, we must assimilate, and we must ponder that to which we expose our minds. I believe in evolution, not organic evolution, as it is called, but in the evolution of the mind, the heart, and the soul of man. I believe in improvement. I believe in growth. I commend to you these marvelous words given by the Lord through revelation to the Prophet Joseph Smith: "That which is of God is light; and he that receiveth light, and continueth in God, receiveth more light; and that light groweth brighter and brighter until the perfect day" (D&C 50:24).

I think this is one of the great and stimulating and promising statements in all of our scripture. It sets forth the pathway to perfection through a process of increase of light and understanding of eternal truths. You cannot afford to stop. You must not rest in your development. You are teaching a generation of youth who are hungry for knowledge and even more hungry for inspiration. You, my beloved associates, need to be constantly drinking of the waters of knowledge and revelation. There is so much to learn and so little time in which to learn it. I confess I am constantly appalled by the scarcity of my knowledge, and the one resentment I think I carry concerns the many pressing demands which limit the opportunity for reading. As we talk of reading, I should like to add a word concerning that which we absorb not only out of the processes of the mind, but something further which comes by the power of the Spirit. Remember this promise given by revelation: "God shall give unto you knowledge by his Holy Spirit, yea, by the unspeakable gift of the Holy Ghost" (D&C 121:26).

Keep on growing, my brothers and sisters, whether you are thirty or whether you are seventy. Your industry in so doing will cause the years to pass faster than you might wish, but they will be filled with a sweet and wonderful zest that will add flavor to your life and power to your teaching. And to all of this you may add the promise that "whatever principle of intelligence we attain unto in this life, it will rise with us in the resurrection" (D&C 130:18).

2. Grow with Balance

My second imperative is *grow with balance*. An old cliché states that modern education leads a man to know more and more about less and less. I want to plead with you to keep balance in your lives. Do not become obsessed with what may be called "a gospel hobby." A good meal always includes more than one course. You ought to have great strength in your chosen and assigned field of expertise. But I warn you against making that your only interest. I glory in the breadth of this commandment to the people of the Church:

> And I give unto you a commandment that you shall teach one another the doctrine of the kingdom.
>
> Teach ye diligently and my grace shall attend you, that you may be instructed more perfectly in theory, in principle, in doctrine, in the law of the gospel, in all things that pertain unto the kingdom of God, that are expedient for you to understand;
>
> Of things both in heaven and in the earth, and under the earth; things which have been, things which are, things which must shortly come to pass; things which are at home, things which are abroad; the wars and the perplexities of the nations, and the judgments which are on the land; and a knowledge also of countries and of kingdoms—
>
> That ye may be prepared in all things. (D&C 88:77–80)

In my life I have had opportunity to serve in many different capacities in the Church. Every time I was released in connection with a new calling, I felt reluctant to leave the old. But every call brought with it an opportunity to learn of another segment of the great program of the Church. I carry in my heart something of pity for those who permit themselves to get locked into one situation and never have an opportunity to experience any other. Missionaries not infrequently plead with their presidents that they be able to extend their missions. This is commendable and is usually indicative of the fact that they have been effective in their work. But a missionary's release usually is as providential as his call, as thereby there is opened to him other opportunities. And out of it all will come a balance in his life.

And beyond the Church there are other experiences to be had in other fields. There is so much work to be done in the communities in which we live. We are urged as citizens to make our contributions through participation in the processes of government. If we are to preserve in our communities those qualities which we so greatly cherish, we must become involved and expend time and effort in that labor. We can develop strength and gain much of experience in so doing while assisting with the pressing social problems that confront our society. We also need to know something about the world of business and science and mechanics in which we live.

It is imperative that we as teachers in the seminary and institute of religion program of the Church read constantly the scriptures and other books related directly to the history, the doctrine, and the practices of the Church. But we ought also to be reading secular history, the great literature that has survived the ages, and the writings of contemporary thinkers and doers. In so doing we will find inspiration to pass on to our students who will need all the balanced strength they can get as they face the world into which they move.

Brethren and sisters, grow in the knowledge of the eternal truths which you are called to teach, and grow in understanding of the great and good men and women who have walked the earth and of the marvelous phenomena with which we are surrounded in the world in which we live. Now and then as I have watched a man become obsessed with a narrow segment of knowledge, I have worried about him. I have seen a few such. They have pursued relentlessly only a sliver of knowledge until they have lost a sense of balance. At the moment I think of two who went so far and became so misguided in their narrow pursuits that they who once had been effective teachers of youth have been found to be in apostasy and have been excommunicated from the Church. Keep balance in your lives. Beware of obsession. Beware of narrowness. Let your interests range over many good fields while working with growing strength in the field of your own profession.

3. LET LOVE BE YOUR LODESTAR

Third, *let love be your lodestar.* It is the greatest force on earth. Love is a word of many meanings, and all of these apply to you. Cultivate love for the subjects you teach. There is a central figure in all of these, and that figure is the Lord Jesus Christ, the Son of the living God. Teach of Him. Bear testimony of Him out of a deep and earnest conviction so that your students will feel the strength of your testimony. Let me read a few words from a letter I received from a missionary who had been in the mission field less than three months:

> I arrived in the mission field, and my love for my family, girl-friend, and home caused me great homesickness, and my feeling of homesickness brought me within inches of returning home. My mission president, with unbelievable love, held me here long enough to have me attend a very special missionary meeting with [one of the General Authorities] who was visiting our mission. He took us through an exercise with the scriptures in which we came to know our Redeemer, Jesus Christ. At the end of the meeting, we all stood and sang "I Am a Child of God" and then "I Know That My Redeemer Lives." As the second song began, I found myself unable to sing. At that time I had the most spiritual experience of my life thus far. Through the entire song I just stood there, visualizing the Savior in my mind, and tears streamed down my face. At that very time I came to the unshakable knowledge that Jesus is the Christ and that He atoned for my sins.

I think such an experience is the privilege and opportunity and responsibility of every young man and woman in this Church. It is conviction of this kind that expressed itself in a great and powerful love that has been the root of the success of our missionary work, as everyone who has been in that work could testify. It has been said that more true love for the Lord has been *caught* than has been *taught*.

I recall hearing in England in a stake conference the testimony of an extremely able young man who had recently joined the Church. He said, "I was trained as a chartered accountant, trained to look for flaws in all that I examined. Because of my critical nature and training, the missionary lessons turned me off. But a good man who was a member, a man of limited education but great faith, talked quietly with me about what the gospel meant to him. He spoke out of a great spirit of love. And somehow that touched my heart, and I am here tonight speaking to you because of it."

I hope that you will cultivate in your hearts not only a love for the Savior of whom you bear testimony, but also a deep love for those you teach and particularly for those who appear to be so difficult to reach. They need you most, and the miracle that will come into their lives as you labor with them in a spirit of encouragement and kindness will bring gladness and satisfaction to you all of your days and strength and faith and testimony to them. Never forget the statement of the Lord concerning the sinner who repented. Read frequently that marvelously beautiful and touching parable of the prodigal son that is set forth in the fifteenth chapter of Luke.

Further, cultivate a spirit of love for your family. We all say we have it. Maybe we do. Hopefully we do. But I should like to remind you that it constantly needs refreshing. Husbands, look for the beauty in your wives. Wives, uphold and sustain and cherish your husbands; and parents, love your children with a great and evident affection. Unless there is love in the home, the work in the classroom will become only an exercise.

4. ENJOY YOUR WORK

And now, finally, *enjoy your work*. Be happy. I meet so many people who constantly complain about the burden of their responsibilities.

Of course the pressures are great. There is much, too much, to do. There are financial burdens to add to all of these pressures, and with all of this are prone to complain, frequently at home, often in public. Turn your thinking around. The gospel is good news. Man is that he might have joy. Be happy! Let that happiness shine through your faces and speak through your testimonies. You can expect problems. There may be occasional tragedies. But shining through all of this is the plea of the Lord: "Come unto me, all ye that labour and are heavy laden, and I will give you rest. Take my yoke upon you, and learn of me; for I am meek and lowly in heart; and ye shall find rest unto your souls. For my yoke is easy, and my burden is light" (Matthew 11:28–30).

I enjoy these words of Jenkins Lloyd Jones, which I clipped from a column in the *Deseret News* some years ago. I pass them on to you as I conclude my remarks. Said he:

> Anyone who imagines that bliss is normal is going to waste a lot of time running around shouting that he's been robbed.
>
> Most putts don't drop. Most beef is tough. Most children grow up to be just people. Most successful marriages require a high degree of mutual toleration. Most jobs are more often dull than otherwise.
>
> Life is like an old-time rail journey—delays, sidetracks, smoke, dust, cinders, and jolts, interspersed only occasionally by beautiful vistas and thrilling bursts of speed. The trick is to thank the Lord for letting you have the ride.[2]

I repeat, my brothers and sisters, the trick is to thank the Lord for letting you have the ride; and really, isn't it a wonderful ride? Enjoy it! Laugh about it! Sing about it! Remember the words of the writer of Proverbs: "A merry heart doeth good like a medicine: but a broken spirit drieth the bones" (Proverbs 17:22).

God bless you, my beloved associates, in this great and sacred work. May you grow in strength and power and capacity and understanding with each passing day. May you cultivate constantly a saving balance in your life. May you speak from hearts filled with love for the Lord, for His children, for your own dear ones. And may there be gladness in your hearts as you reflect on the marvelous kindness of the Lord to you and upon your great and sacred opportunity to touch for everlasting good those who daily come under your direction.

God bless each of you that there may be love and peace in your homes, and in your hearts that satisfaction which comes of work well done in so great a cause, I humbly pray in the name of Jesus Christ, amen.

NOTES

1. Joshua Loth Liebman, in "Peace of Mind," in *Getting the Most Out of Life* (Pleasantville, NY: Reader's Digest, 1948), 120.
2. Jenkins Lloyd Jones, "Big Rock Candy Mountains," *Deseret News*, June 12, 1973, A4.

Elder Bruce R. McConkie (1915–85) was a member of the Quorum of the Twelve Apostles. Address to Church Educational System religious educators at the Assembly Hall on Temple Square on September 18, 1981, published in *Religious Educator* 6, no. 1 (2005): 1–21.

6 THE FOOLISHNESS OF TEACHING

I DESIRE TO BE GUIDED BY the Spirit, and I shall take as my subject "the foolishness of teaching." I do not say "the foolishness of teachers." There may be some of that, but I am not aware of any. I take this expression "the foolishness of teaching" from a similar statement made by the Apostle Paul. But first, I think we ought to set forth the dignity and preeminence of gospel teaching and the eternal worth and everlasting value that comes because of those who teach the gospel in the way the Lord intended that it should be taught.

Yours is a high, a holy, and a glorious work. It was of you, as some of the chief gospel teachers in the Church, that President J. Reuben Clark said:

> You teachers have a great mission. As teachers you stand upon the highest peak in education, for what teaching can compare in priceless value and in far-reaching effect with that which deals with man as he was in the eternity of yesterday, as he is in the mortality of today, and as he will be in the forever of tomorrow. Not only time but eternity is your field. Salvation of yourself not only, but of those who come within the purlieus of your temple, is the blessing you seek, and which, doing your duty, you will gain. How brilliant will be your crown of glory, with each soul saved an encrusted jewel thereon.[1]

Now with that statement setting the tone and conveying the spirit for what, if I am properly guided, I hope to say, I shall turn to that wondrous verse in the twelfth chapter of 1 Corinthians in which Paul speaks of the kind of teachers who are involved in proclaiming the message of salvation to the world. He is identifying the true church. He is giving some of the essential identifying characteristics of the kingdom that has the power to save men. He says, "And God hath set some in the church, first apostles, secondarily prophets, thirdly teachers, after that miracles, then gifts of healings, helps, governments, diversities of tongues" (1 Corinthians 12:28).

That verse tells you some of the proofs or evidences or witnesses that the work is true. It names some of the essential identifying characteristics of the true church. Where there are apostles and prophets and teachers of the sort and kind of whom Paul is speaking, there will be found the true church and kingdom of God on earth. And where any of these are not found, there the church and kingdom of God is not. That makes our living prophet an evidence and a witness that this work is true. The fact we are guided by a prophet shows we have the true Church. That makes all of the Apostles who have been called in this dispensation witnesses and evidences and proofs to the world that the work is true. True Apostles are always found in the true Church. I think this order of priority is perfect: Apostles, prophets, teachers. And that places you, because you are the kind of teachers that Paul is talking about, that makes you the third great group whose very existence establishes the truth and divinity of the work. This means that if you learn how to present the message of salvation, and in fact do it in the way that the Lord intends that it be presented, you stand to all the world as an evidence that this is God's kingdom. As we go forward in this presentation, I think it will be evident to all that no one is or can be a teacher in the divine sense, in the eternal sense of which President Clark is speaking, except a legal administrator in The Church of Jesus Christ of Latter-day Saints—except someone who is so living that he *is* endowed with the gift and power of the Holy Ghost.

We are not talking about worldly teachers. We do not concern ourselves a great deal about those in the various academic or scientific disciplines.

What they do is meritorious and appropriate so long as it conforms to the standards of truth and integrity and virtue. Their work is in no sense to be demeaned. But the kind of teaching that is involved where the Church and kingdom of God on earth is concerned, the kind of teaching that *you* do is as the heavens above the earth when compared to the intellectual type of teaching and learning that is to be had out in the world.

All of us are agents of the Lord. We are the servants of the Lord. In the law there is a branch that is called the law of agency. And in the law of agency there are principals and there are agents. These are something akin to master and servant. An agent represents a principal, and the acts of the agent bind the principal, provided they are performed within the proper scope and authorization, within the authority delegated to the agent. Now, the Lord said to us, "Wherefore, as ye are agents, ye are on the Lord's errand; and whatever ye do according to the will of the Lord is the Lord's business" (D&C 64:29).

We are engaged in our Father's business. Our Father's business is to bring to pass the immortality and eternal life of man. We do not have anything to do with bringing to pass immortality. That comes as a free gift to all men because of the atoning sacrifice of the Lord Jesus. But we have a very great deal to do with bringing to pass eternal life for ourselves and for our brethren and sisters and in offering it to our Father's other children. Eternal life is the kind of life that God our Father lives. It is the name of the life He lives. It is to have exaltation and glory and honor and dominion in His presence everlastingly. And it comes by obedience to the laws and ordinances of the gospel. It is full and complete salvation. And so we bring to pass, in a sense, the eternal life of men by persuading them to conform to the standards that the Lord has set.

Eternal life and immortality both come by the grace of God. They are made available through the Atonement, but in the case of the great gift of eternal life, which is the greatest of all the gifts of God, it comes by conformity, and obedience, and sacrifice—by doing all of the things that are counseled and required in the inspired word.

Now let me point to the source of my text and my title, "The Foolishness of Teaching." It is a paraphrase of Paul's words. "For Christ sent me not to baptize, but to preach the gospel" (1 Corinthians 1:17). And I will use *preach* and *teach,* for our purposes, as synonyms. Preaching is teaching and teaching, in many respects, is a perfected form of preaching.

> [He] sent me . . . to preach [teach] the gospel: not with wisdom of words, lest the cross of Christ should be made of none effect. For the preaching [or teaching] of the cross is to them that perish foolishness; but unto us which are saved it is the power of God. For it is written, I will destroy the wisdom of the wise, and will bring to nothing the understanding of the prudent. Where is the wise? where is the scribe? where is the disputer of this world? hath not God made foolish the wisdom of this world? For after that in the wisdom of God the world by wisdom knew not God, it pleased God by the foolishness of preaching to save them that believe. (1 Corinthians 1:17–21)

Now I turn it to the teaching aspect: "It pleased God by the foolishness of [teaching] to save them that believe. For the Jews require a sign, and the Greeks seek after wisdom: But we preach [meaning we teach] Christ crucified, unto the Jews a stumblingblock, and unto the Greeks foolishness; But unto them which are called, both Jews and Greeks, Christ the power of God, and the wisdom of God. Because the foolishness of God is wiser than men; and the weakness of God is stronger than men" (1 Corinthians 1:21–25).

Now think of yourselves as I read this next scripture. Think of Presidents Wilford Woodruff and Lorenzo Snow. Think of the men who have presided over this dispensation. Think of them as they have been viewed by the worldly wise and the aristocrats and the highly intellectual and by those with great mental capacities. Paul says: "For ye see your calling, brethren, how that not many wise men after the flesh, not many mighty, not many noble, are called: But God hath chosen the foolish things of the world to confound the wise; and God hath chosen the weak things of the world to confound the things which are mighty; And base things of the world, and things which are despised, hath God chosen, yea, and things which are not to bring to nought things that are: That no flesh should glory in his presence" (1 Corinthians 1:26–29).

We are the weak and the simple and the unlearned as far as the intellectual giants of the world are concerned, but our teaching is not in the intellectual field. It is pleasing if we have some intellectual attainments. But basically and fundamentally, as teachers we are dealing with the things of the Spirit.

At general conference in April, I was doing what we are pretty much required to do now. I was reading the expressions that I was making. And then at the end I said a few sentences extemporaneously. As I said them I had in mind the document that had recently come to light purporting to be an account of a prophetic utterance or a blessing given by the Prophet Joseph to one of his sons. And so I felt impressed, after my formal remarks were concluded, to bear a witness of what was involved in succession in the presidency. And I named all of the Presidents from Joseph Smith to Spencer W. Kimball and said that down that line the power and authority and keys of the kingdom had come. Then I said something that highly offended all the intellectuals: "What I am saying is what the Lord would say if he were here."[2] Now the only way you can say a thing like that is to be guided and prompted by the power of the Holy Spirit because the Spirit is a revelator and places in your mind the thoughts that the Lord wants expressed.

Well, our intellectual friends reading that in the account went into a great explosive tizzy, whatever that is. And in decrying the stand I had taken, one of the chief among them said, "Well, what can you expect when they have incompetents like Bruce R. McConkie running loose?"[3] I read about it in one of the semi-anti-Mormon publications. And when I read it, it gave me a great feeling of personal satisfaction. I thought, "This is marvelous. It is just as important to know who your enemies are as your friends." And of course, the intellectuals in the world view our teachings as foolishness, or as Paul calls it, "the foolishness of God" (1 Corinthians 1:25).

Well, there is worldly teaching and there is Church teaching. There is teaching by the power of the intellect alone, and there is teaching by the power of the intellect when quickened and enlightened by the power of the Holy Spirit.

"O that cunning plan of the evil one! [Jacob is speaking] O the vainness, and the frailties, and the foolishness of men! When they are learned they think they are wise, and they hearken not unto the counsel of God, for they set it aside, supposing they know of themselves, wherefore, their wisdom is foolishness and it profiteth them not. And they shall perish. But to be learned is good if they hearken unto the counsels of God" (2 Nephi 9:28–29).

That is our stand in the Church and kingdom.

THE TEACHER'S DIVINE COMMISSION

If I may now, I shall take the heading "The Teacher's Divine Commission" and make it a subtext or a subheading to this matter of the foolishness of teaching. I shall suggest to you five things that compose and comprise the teacher's divine commission. We are talking about divine, inspired, heavenly, Church teaching, the type and kind in which we are, or should be, involved.

1. We are commanded to teach the principles of the gospel. Our revelation says: "And again, the elders, priests and teachers of this church [this language is mandatory] shall teach the principles of my gospel, which are in the Bible and the Book of Mormon, in which is the fulness of the gospel. And they shall observe the covenants and church articles to do them, and these shall be their teachings, as they shall be directed by the Spirit" (D&C 42:12–13).

We are to teach the principles of the gospel. We are to teach the doctrines of salvation. We have some passing interest in ethical principles but not a great deal as far as emphasis in teaching is concerned. If we teach the doctrines of salvation, the ethical concepts automatically follow. We do not need to spend long periods of time or make elaborate presentations in teaching honesty or integrity or unselfishness or some other ethical principle. Any Presbyterian can do that. Any Methodist can do that. But if we teach the doctrines of salvation, which are basic and fundamental, the ethical concepts automatically follow. It is the testimony and knowledge of the truth that causes people to reach high ethical standards in any event. And so our revelation says: "And I give unto you a commandment [again we are using mandatory language;

the Lord is talking] that you shall teach one another the doctrine of the kingdom. Teach ye diligently and my grace shall attend you, that you may be instructed more perfectly in theory, in principle, in doctrine, in the law of the gospel, in all things that pertain unto the kingdom of God, that are expedient for you to understand" (D&C 88:77–78).

That last modifying phrase indicates that we are to leave the mysteries alone. There are some things that are not given us in clarity, and, as of now, do not need to be fully comprehended in order to work out our salvation. We stay away from these; we stay with the basic concepts. Now President Clark's words:

> These students are prepared to believe and understand that all these things are matters of faith, not to be explained or understood by any process of human reason, and probably not by any experiment of known physical science.
>
> These students (to put the matter shortly) are prepared to understand and to believe that there is a natural world and there is a spiritual world; that the things of the natural world will not explain the things of the spiritual world; that the things of the spiritual world cannot be understood or comprehended by the things of the natural world; that you cannot rationalize the things of the spirit, because first, the things of the spirit are not sufficiently known and comprehended, and secondly, because finite mind and reason cannot comprehend nor explain infinite wisdom and ultimate truth.
>
> These students already know that they must be honest, true, chaste, benevolent, virtuous, and do good to all men, and that "if there is anything virtuous, lovely, or of good report or praiseworthy, we seek after these things"—these things they have been taught from very birth. They should be encouraged in all proper ways to do these things which they know to be true, but they do not need to have a year's course of instruction to make them believe and know them.
>
> These students fully sense the hollowness of teachings which would make the Gospel plan a mere system of ethics, they know

that Christ's teachings are in the highest degree ethical, but they also know they are more than this. They will see that ethics relate primarily to the doings of this life, and that to make of the Gospel a mere system of ethics is to confess a lack of faith, if not a disbelief, in the hereafter. They know that the Gospel teachings not only touch this life, but the life that is to come, with its salvation and exaltation as the final goal.

These students hunger and thirst, as did their fathers before them, for a testimony of the things of the spirit and of the hereafter, and knowing that you cannot rationalize eternity, they seek faith, and the knowledge which follows faith. They sense by the spirit they have, that the testimony they seek is engendered and nurtured by the testimony of others and that to gain this testimony which they seek for. . . .[4]

Now notice this. I never heard this better expressed by anyone than President Clark gives it:

[They know that] one living, burning, honest testimony of a righteous God-fearing man that Jesus is the Christ and that Joseph was God's prophet is worth a thousand books and lectures aimed at debasing the Gospel to a system of ethics or seeking to rationalize infinity.[5]

Conversion comes through testimony. We must teach in that way, as I will subsequently, with some particularity, point out.

There is neither reason nor is there excuse for our Church religious teaching and training facilities and institutions, unless the youth are to be taught and trained in the principles of the Gospel, embracing therein the two great elements that Jesus is the Christ and that Joseph was God's prophet. The teaching of a system of ethics to the students is not a sufficient reason for running our seminaries and institutes. The great public school system teaches ethics. The students of seminaries and institutes should of course be taught the ordinary canons of good and righteous living, for these are part, and an essential part, of the Gospel. But there are the great principles involved in eternal life, the Priesthood, the resurrection, and many like other things, that go way beyond these canons of good living. These great fundamental principles also must be taught to the youth; they are the things the youth wish first to know about.[6]

From all this I conclude that we should do as Jesus did. We should teach the gospel. We should teach the gospel only. We should teach nothing but the gospel. Ethics are a part of the gospel, but they will take care of themselves if we preach the gospel. Teach doctrine. Teach sound doctrine. Teach the doctrines of the kingdom. You say, What did Jesus teach? Well, of course we have the great accounts of His teachings about ethical principles, but notice this: "Now after that John was put in prison, Jesus came into Galilee, preaching the gospel of the kingdom of God. And saying, The time is fulfilled, and the kingdom of God is at hand: repent ye, and believe the gospel" (Mark 1:14–15).

Now what did Jesus teach? Jesus taught the gospel. Unfortunately, from our standpoint, there is not very much preserved in the New Testament account of what He taught. I say from our standpoint because we as a people, having the Restoration and the light of heaven, would be able to recognize and glory in the gospel truths He taught had they been recorded and preserved for us. But obviously, in the wisdom of Him who knoweth all things and doeth all things right, it was the intent and design that only the portion of His teachings that are found in Matthew, Mark, Luke, and John should have been preserved for men in this day.

But with our background and understanding, when the revelation says that Jesus preached the gospel, we know thereby what He preached. And we know it simply by answering the questions, What is the gospel? What is the eternal plan of salvation? What truths has God given us which we must believe and understand and obey to gain peace in this life and glory and honor and dignity in the life to come?

The gospel can be defined from two perspectives. We can talk about it in the eternal sense as it was in the mind of God when He ordained and established all things. And we can talk about it in a more restricted sense as it is involved in the lives of people here.

Now, in the eternal and unlimited sense, the gospel that Jesus taught was itself infinite and eternal. It included the creation of all things, the nature of this probationary estate, and the great and eternal plan of redemption. He taught that God was the creator of all things, that He created this earth and all things that on it are. He taught that there was a fall of Adam—that Adam and all forms of life fell, or changed, from their original paradisiacal state to the mortal state that now prevails—and that as a consequence of that Fall, which brought temporal and spiritual death into the world, an atonement of a divine being was required. Someone had to come and ransom men from the effects of the Fall and bring to pass a continuation of temporal life, which is immortality, and make available spiritual life again, which is eternal life.

The great and eternal plan of salvation, from God's viewpoint, is the Creation, the Fall, and the Atonement. If there had been no creation, there would be nothing. If things had not been created in the manner and form and way that they were, there could have been no fall. And as a consequence, no procreation and no mortality and no death. And if there had been no Fall of Adam, which brought temporal and spiritual death into the world, there would be no need for the redemption of the Lord Jesus.

The plan of salvation, to us, is the atoning sacrifice of the Lord Jesus by which immortality and eternal life come. When you talk about the gospel from the standpoint of men, you are talking about the things men must do to work out their own salvation with fear and trembling before the Lord. And what is involved there is faith in the Lord Jesus Christ; repentance from sin; baptism by immersion under the hands of a legal administrator for the remission of sins; the receipt of the gift of the Holy Ghost, which gift is the right to the constant companionship of that member of the Godhead; and then, finally, enduring in righteousness and integrity and devotion and obedience all of one's days. That is the plan of salvation as far as acts on our part are concerned. But that plan of salvation rests on the greater eternal concept of the atoning sacrifice, which grew out of the Fall, which Fall grew out of the Creation.

Jesus preached the gospel. Jesus was a theologian. There has never been a theologian on earth to compare with Him. In this field, as in all others, no man ever spake as He did. In His providences, He let Paul and Peter and some of the others present to us the theological concepts that had to be known in order for people to gain salvation. But Jesus preached the gospel. That, of course, is what we are expected to do; that is the first great concept. Here is the second:

2. We are to teach the principles of the gospel as they are found in the standard works. "And let them [the elders of the kingdom] journey from thence preaching the word by the way, saying none other things than that which the prophets and apostles have written, and that which is taught them by the Comforter through the prayer of faith" (D&C 52:9).

We have a multitude of passages that talk about searching the scriptures, about searching "these commandments." We have counsel to "ponder" the things of the Lord, to "treasure up" the words of truth. He told the Nephites, "Great are the words of Isaiah" (3 Nephi 23:1). He said to them, "Search the prophets" (3 Nephi 23:5).

These and other passages show we should study the standard works of the Church. The scriptures themselves present the gospel in the way that the Lord wants it presented to us in our day. I do not say that it is always presented to men in the same way. There have been civilizations of a higher spiritual standing than ours. I think He did some different kind of teaching among the people in Enoch's day and in that golden Nephite era when for two hundred years everyone was conforming to principles of light and truth and had the Holy Spirit for a guide. We know perfectly well that during the Millennium the teaching processes will change. One of the revelations says of that day: "And they shall teach no more every man his neighbour, and every man his brother, saying, Know the Lord: for they shall all know me, from the least of them unto the greatest of them" (Jeremiah 31:34).

But for *our* day and *our* time and *our* hour, the time of our mortal probation, we are to teach in the way things are recorded in the standard works that we have. And if you want to know what emphasis should be given to gospel principles, you simply teach the whole standard works and, automatically, in the process, you will have given the

Lord's emphasis to every doctrine and every principle. As far as learning the gospel and teaching the gospel is concerned, the Book of Mormon, by all odds, is the most important of the standard works—because in simplicity and in plainness it sets forth in a definitive manner the doctrines of the gospel. If you would like to test that sort of thing, just arbitrarily choose a hundred or so gospel subjects and then put in parallel columns what the Bible says about them and what the Book of Mormon says about them. In about 95 percent of the cases, the clarity and perfection and superlative nature of the Book of Mormon teaching will be so evident that it will be perfectly clear that that is the place to learn the gospel.

I think, in many respects, the literature and the language and the power of expression that is in Paul's writings and Isaiah's writings is superior to what is in the Book of Mormon. But we understand the Bible because we have the knowledge gained out of the Book of Mormon. The epistles of Paul, for instance, were written to members of the Church. I do not think he has any epistles that are intended to be definitive explanations of gospel doctrines. He was writing the portion of the Lord's word that the Corinthians or the Hebrews or the Romans needed, he being aware of the problems and questions and difficulties that confronted them. In effect, he is writing to people who already had the knowledge that is in the Book of Mormon. That means, obviously, that there are no people on earth who can understand the epistles of Paul and the other brethren in the New Testament until they first get the knowledge that we as Latter-day Saints have.

The Book of Mormon is a definitive, all-embracing, comprehensive account. Our scripture says it contains the fulness of the everlasting gospel. What that means is that it is a record of God's dealings with a people who had the fulness of the gospel. It means that in it are recorded the basic principles which men must believe to work out their salvation. After we accept and believe and comprehend the principles therein recorded, we are qualified and prepared to take another step and to begin to acquire a knowledge of the mysteries of godliness.

After somebody gets the basic understanding that is in the Book of Mormon—about salvation, for instance—then he is in a position to envision and comprehend what section 76 is all about. When that section was first given in our dispensation, the Prophet forbade the missionaries to talk about it when they went out into the world and told them that if they did they would heap persecution upon their heads because it was something that was beyond the spiritual capacity of those to whom they were sent. We do not have that type of religious climate today, but it was one that prevailed in that day.

I think this language in the Psalms is about as good as anything that has been written about the scriptures: "The law of the Lord is perfect, converting the soul: the testimony of the Lord is sure, making wise the simple. The statutes of the Lord are right, rejoicing the heart: the commandment of the Lord is pure, enlightening the eyes. The fear of the Lord is clean, enduring for ever: the judgments of the Lord are true and righteous altogether. More to be desired are they than gold, yea, than much fine gold: sweeter also than honey and the honeycomb. Moreover by them is thy servant warned: and in keeping of them there is great reward" (Psalm 19:7–11).

I love these words also that Paul wrote to Timothy: "And that from a child thou hast known the holy scriptures, which are able to make thee wise unto salvation through faith which is in Christ Jesus. All scripture is given by inspiration of God, and is profitable for doctrine, for reproof, for correction, for instruction in righteousness: that the man of God may be perfect, throughly furnished unto all good works" (2 Timothy 3:15–17).

President Clark said on this point:

> You do have an interest in matters purely cultural and in matters of purely secular knowledge; but, I repeat again for emphasis, your chief interest, your essential and all but sole duty, is to teach the Gospel of the Lord Jesus Christ as that has been revealed in these latter days. You are to teach this Gospel using as your sources and authorities the Standard Works of the Church, and the words of those whom God has called to lead His people in these last days. You are not, whether high or low, to intrude into your work your own peculiar philosophy, no matter

what its source or how pleasing or rational it seems to you to be. To do so would be to have as many different churches as we have seminaries—and that is chaos.[7]

3. We are to teach by the power of the Holy Ghost. There are some passages on this matter of teaching by the power of the Holy Ghost that are so strong and so blunt and so plain that unless we understand what is involved, it almost makes us fear ever to teach. And a couple of them I shall read: "And the Spirit shall be given unto you by the prayer of faith: and if ye receive not the Spirit ye shall not teach" (D&C 42:14). That is a mandatory thing, a prohibition. "And all this ye shall observe to do as I have commanded concerning your teaching, until the fulness of my scriptures is given. And as ye shall lift up your voices by the Comforter, ye shall speak and prophesy as seemeth me good; For, behold, the Comforter knoweth all things, and beareth record of the Father and of the Son" (D&C 42:15–17).

We are talking about Church teaching, gospel teaching, teaching spiritual things, teaching by the power of the Holy Ghost. And if you teach by the power of the Holy Ghost, you say the things that the Lord wants said, or you say the things the Lord would say if He Himself were here. The Holy Ghost is a revelator, and you are speaking words of revelation. And that kind of preacher or teacher, as we have seen, is the third great essential identifying officer of God's kingdom.

"First apostles, secondarily prophets, thirdly teachers" (1 Corinthians 12:28).

"And now come, saith the Lord, by the Spirit, unto the elders of his church, and let us reason together, that ye may understand; Let us reason even as a man reasoneth one with another face to face. Now, when a man reasoneth he is understood of man, because he reasoneth as a man; even so will I, the Lord, reason with you that you may understand" (D&C 50:10–12).

Have in mind as we consider these matters from section 50 the law pertaining to principals and agents, to masters and servants. Consider how these apply to a divine being who gives direction to someone else, letting him know what he should teach and what he should say.

Have in mind also that it really does not make a parade of difference to any of you what we teach. I often think as I go around the Church and preach in various meetings that it just does not make a snap of the fingers' difference to me what I am talking about. I do not care what I talk about. All I am concerned with is getting in tune with the Spirit and expressing the thoughts, in the best language and way that I can, that are implanted there by the power of the Spirit. The Lord knows what a congregation needs to hear, and He has provided a means to give that revelation to every preacher and every teacher.

We do not create the doctrines of the gospel. People who ask questions about the gospel, a good portion of the time, are looking for an answer that sustains a view they have expressed. They want to justify a conclusion that they have reached instead of looking for the ultimate truth in the field. Once again, it does not make one snap of the fingers' difference to me what the doctrines of the Church are. I cannot create a doctrine. I cannot originate a concept of eternal truth. The only thing I ought to be concerned with is learning what the Lord thinks about a doctrine. If I ask a question of someone to learn something, I ought *not* to be seeking for a confirmation of a view that I have expressed. I ought to be seeking knowledge and wisdom. It should not make any difference to me whether the doctrine is on the right hand or on the left. My sole interest and my sole concern would be to find out what the Lord thinks on the subject.

And we have the power to do that. I suppose that is part at least of what Paul had in mind when he said of the Saints, "We have the mind of Christ" (1 Corinthians 2:16).

If we have the mind of Christ, we think what Christ thinks and we say what Christ says; and out of those two things come our acts, and so we do what Christ would have done in an equivalent situation. Well, back to section 50 in which the Lord is reasoning with us: "Wherefore, I the Lord ask you this question—unto what were ye ordained?" (D&C 50:13). That is, "What agency did I give you? What commission have I conferred upon you? What authorization is yours? What divine commandment came from me to you?" And then He answers, and His answer tells us what we are ordained to do: "To preach my gospel by the

Spirit, even the Comforter which was sent forth to teach the truth. And then received ye spirits which ye could not understand, and received them to be of God; and in this are ye justified?" (D&C 50:14–15).

I'd like to try that again. "And then received ye spirits [doctrines, tenets, views, theories] which ye could not understand" (D&C 50:15). Then you received something that you could not understand and thought it came from God. And are you justified? "Behold ye shall answer this question yourselves; nevertheless, I will be merciful unto you; he that is weak among you hereafter shall be made strong" (D&C 50:16).

Now, here is some very strong language. If you can italicize words in your mind as it were, when they are read, do it with these words: "Verily I say unto you, he that is ordained of me and sent forth to preach the word of truth by the Comforter [that is our commission], in the Spirit of truth, doth he preach it by the Spirit of truth or some other way? And if it be by some other way it is not of God" (D&C 50:17–18).

Now, let me pick up that last again and give you the antecedent of the pronoun. It said, "If it be by some other way it is not of God" (D&C 50:18).

What is the antecedent of "it"? It is the "word of truth." That is to say, if you teach the word of truth—now note, you're saying what is true, everything you say is accurate and right—by some other way than the Spirit, it is not of God. Now what is the other way to teach than by the Spirit? Well, obviously, it is by the power of the intellect.

Suppose I came here tonight and delivered a great message on teaching, and I did it by the power of the intellect without any of the Spirit of God attending. Suppose that every word that I said was true, no error whatever, but it was an intellectual presentation. This revelation says, "If it be by some other way it is not of God" (D&C 50:18).

That is, God did not present the message through me because I used the power of the intellect instead of the power of the Spirit. Intellectual things—reason and logic—can do some good, and they can prepare the way, and they can get the mind ready to receive the Spirit under certain circumstances. But conversion comes and the truth sinks into the hearts of people only when it is taught by the power of the Spirit.

"And again, he that receiveth the word of truth, doth he receive it by the Spirit of truth or some other way?" (D&C 50:19).

And the answer is: "If it be some other way it is not of God. Therefore, why is it that ye cannot understand and know, that he that receiveth the word by the Spirit of truth receiveth it as it is preached by the Spirit of truth? Wherefore, he that preacheth and he that receiveth, understand one another, and both are edified and rejoice together" (D&C 50:20–22).

That is how you worship. Real, true, genuine, Spirit-born worship, in a sacrament meeting for instance, comes when a speaker speaks by the power of the Holy Ghost, and when a congregation hears by the power of the Holy Ghost. So the speaker gives the word of the Lord, and the congregation receives the word of the Lord. Now that is not the norm, I think, in our sacrament meetings. At least it does not happen anywhere nearly as often as it ought to happen. What happens is this: the congregation comes together in fasting and prayer, pondering the things of the Spirit, desiring to be fed. They bring a gallon jug. The speaker comes in his worldly wisdom, and he brings a little pint bottle, and he pours his pint bottle out, and it rattles around in the gallon jug. Or else, as sometimes happens, the preacher gets his errand from the Lord and gets in tune with the Spirit and comes with a gallon jug to deliver a message, and there is not anybody in the congregation that brought anything bigger than a cup. And he pours out the gallon of eternal truth, and people get just a little sample, enough to quench a moment's eternal thirst, instead of getting the real message that is involved. It takes teacher and student, it takes preacher and congregation, both of them uniting in faith to have a proper preaching or teaching situation.

I suspect that many of you sometime or other, probably in high school, took a course in physics and had laboratory experiments and used a tuning fork. You remember an occasion when two tuning forks were selected which were calibrated to the same wavelength, and one of them was set up in one part of the room and the other thirty or forty feet away. Someone struck the first tuning fork, and people put their ear to the second, and it vibrated and made the same sound that came from the first one. This is an illustration. It is what is involved in speaking by the Spirit. Somebody who is in tune with the Spirit speaks words that are heard by the power of the Spirit, where righteous people are concerned.

4. We are to apply the gospel principles taught to the needs and circumstances of our hearers. The principles are eternal. They never vary. World conditions and personal problems vary. We apply the divine teachings to the present need. Nephi said, "I did liken all scriptures unto us, that it might be for our profit and learning" (1 Nephi 19:23).

What he did was quote Isaiah who was talking about the whole house of Israel. And he, Nephi, applied it to the Nephite portion of Israel. Now President Clark says:

> Our youth are not children spiritually; they are well on towards the normal spiritual maturity of the world. To treat them as children spiritually, as the world might treat the same age group, is therefore and likewise an anachronism. I say once more there is scarcely a youth that comes through your seminary or institute door who has not been the conscious beneficiary of spiritual blessings, or who has not seen the efficacy of prayer, or who has not witnessed the power of faith to heal the sick, or who has not beheld spiritual outpourings, of which the world at large is today ignorant.[8]

Now this next expression pleases me no end.

> You do not have to sneak up behind this spiritually experienced youth and whisper religion in his ears; you can come right out, face to face, and talk with him. You do not need to disguise religious truths with a cloak of worldly things; you can bring these truths to him openly, in their natural guise. Youth may prove to be not more fearful of them than you are. There is no need for gradual approaches, for "bedtime" stories, for coddling, for patronizing, or for any of the other childish devices used in efforts to reach those spiritually inexperienced and all but spiritually dead.[9]

I suppose that has some bearing on games and parties and entertainments and gimmicks which, really, brethren, are poor substitutes for teaching the doctrines of salvation to the students that you have.

5. We must testify that what we teach is true. We are a testimony-bearing people. Everlastingly we are bearing testimony. You pay particular attention to the testimonies that are borne in sacrament meeting. A lot of them will just be expressions of thanksgiving or of appreciation for parents or this or that. Sometimes there will be a testimony that says in words that the work is true and that Jesus is the Lord and Joseph Smith is a prophet. And that raises the level. Now I am going to talk about something different from that.

There are two fields in which we are expected to bear testimony, if we perfect our testimony bearing. Of course, we are to bear testimony of the truth and divinity of the work. We are to say that we know by the power of the Holy Spirit that the work is the Lord's, that the kingdom is His. We get a revelation, and it tells us that Jesus is the Lord and Joseph Smith is a prophet, and we ought to say it. That is testimony bearing. But we are obligated also to bear testimony of the truth of the doctrine that we teach, not simply that the work is true, but that we have taught true doctrine, which of course we cannot do unless we have taught by the power of the Spirit.

The fifth chapter of Alma is a very expressive sermon on being born again. Alma teaches the great truths incident to that doctrine in some language and with some expressions that are not found anywhere else in the revelations. And after he has taught his doctrine about being born again, he says this: "For I am called to speak after this manner, according to the holy order of God, which is in Christ Jesus; yea, I am commanded to stand and testify unto this people the things which have been spoken by our fathers concerning the things which are to come" (Alma 5:44).

He is using the scriptures. He is using the revelations that came to the fathers.

"And this is not all. Do ye not suppose that I know of these things myself? Behold, I testify unto you that I do know that these things whereof I have spoken are true" (Alma 5:45).

He's testifying of the truth of the doctrine that he taught.

"And how do ye suppose that I know of their surety? Behold, I say unto you they [the doctrines he has taught] are made known unto me by the Holy Spirit of God. Behold, I have fasted and prayed many days that I might know these things of myself. And now I do know of myself that they are true; for the Lord God hath made them manifest unto me by his Holy Spirit; and this is the spirit of revelation which is in me" (Alma 5:45–46).

The foolishness of teaching! The foolishness of teaching after the manner we have been describing! The teacher's divine commission!

I repeat: I have no power to create a doctrine. I have no power to manufacture a theory or a philosophy or choose a way in which we must go or a thing we must believe to gain eternal life in our Father's kingdom. I am an agent, a servant, a representative, an ambassador, if you will. I have been called of God to preach what? To preach *His* gospel, not mine. It doesn't matter what I think. The only commission I have is to proclaim *His* word. And if I proclaim *His* word by the power of the Spirit, then everyone involved is bound. People are bound to accept it, or if they reject it, it is at their peril.

Now, my divine commission and your divine commission is (1) to teach the principles of the gospel; (2) to teach them out of the standard works; (3) to teach them by the power of the Holy Ghost; (4) to apply them to the situation at hand; and (5) to bear a personal witness, a witness born of the Spirit, that the doctrine that is taught is true. That is the teacher's divine commission.

I do not always measure up to that by any means. I guess the Brethren, of whom I am one, do as much preaching and speaking in Church congregations as anyone, unless it is the seminary and institute teachers. There are times when I struggle and strive to get a message over and just do not seem to myself to be getting in tune with the Spirit. The fact is, it is a lot harder for me to choose what ought to be said, what subject ought to be considered, than it is for me to get up and preach it. I am always struggling and trying to get the inspiration to know what ought to be said at general conference or in a stake conference or whatever. If we labor at it and if we struggle, the Spirit will be given by the prayer of faith. If we do our part, we will improve and grow in the things of the Spirit until we get to a position where we can, being in tune, say what the Lord wants said. That is what is expected of us. And that is foolishness in the eyes of the world, in the disciplines of science and sociology and so on. But it is the foolishness of God, and the foolishness of God, which is wiser than men, is what brings salvation.

Let me say just a word about false doctrine. We are supposed to teach. Pitfalls we are supposed to avoid are the teaching of false doctrine: teaching ethics in preference to doctrine, compromising our doctrines with the philosophies of the world, entertaining rather than teaching, and using games and gimmicks rather than sound doctrine, coddling students, as President Clark expressed it.

We ought to judge everything by gospel standards, not the reverse. Do not take a scientific principle, so-called, and try to make the gospel conform to it. Take the gospel for what it is, and, insofar as you can, make other things conform to it, and if they do not conform to it, forget them. Forget them; do not worry. They will vanish away eventually. In the true sense of the word, the gospel embraces all truth. And everything that is true is going to conform to the principles that God has revealed.

"O the wise, and the learned, and the rich, that are puffed up in the pride of their hearts, and all those who preach false doctrines, and all those who commit whoredoms, and pervert the right way of the Lord, wo, wo, wo be unto them, saith the Lord God Almighty, for they shall be thrust down to hell!" (2 Nephi 28:15).

I shall repeat the portion of that that deals with teaching. "Those who preach false doctrines, . . . wo, wo, wo be unto them, saith the Lord God Almighty, for they shall be thrust down to hell!" (2 Nephi 28:15).

I want to say something about this. That scripture is talking about people who have a form of godliness, as Paul expressed it, but who deny the power thereof (see 2 Timothy 3:5). And the Lord quoted Paul in the First Vision, using his very language. He is talking about those people of whom Paul said, they are "ever learning, and never able to come to the knowledge of the truth" (2 Timothy 3:7). President Clark said:

> You are not to teach the philosophies of the world, ancient or modern, pagan or Christian, for this is the field of the public schools. Your sole field is the Gospel, and that is boundless in its own sphere.

We pay taxes to support those state institutions whose function and work it is to teach the arts, the sciences, literature, history, the languages, and so on through the whole secular curriculum. These institutions are to do this work. But we use the tithes of the Church to carry on the Church school system, and these are impressed with a holy trust. The Church seminaries and institutes are to teach the Gospel.[10]

You talk about teaching false doctrine and being damned. Here is a list of false doctrines that if someone teaches he will be damned. And there is not one of these that I have ever known to be taught in the Church, but I am giving you the list for a perspective because of what will follow. Teach that God is a spirit, the sectarian trinity. Teach that salvation comes by grace alone, without works. Teach original guilt, or birth sin, as they express it. Teach infant baptism. Teach predestination. Teach that revelation and gifts and miracles have ceased. Teach the Adam-God theory. (That does apply in the Church.) Teach that we should practice plural marriage today. Now any of those are doctrines that damn. They are what I just read about from 2 Nephi 28.

Now here are some doctrines that weaken faith and may damn. It depends on how inured a person gets to them, and how much emphasis he puts on them, and how much the doctrine begins to govern the affairs of his life. Evolution is one of them. Somebody can get so wrapped up in so-called organic evolution that he ends up not believing in the atoning sacrifice of the Lord Jesus. Such a course leads to damnation.

Somebody can teach that God is progressing in knowledge. And if he begins to believe it, and emphasizes it unduly, and it becomes a ruling thing in his life, then, as the *Lectures on Faith* say, it is not possible for him to have faith unto life and salvation. He is required to believe, in the Prophet's language, that God is omnipotent, omniscient, and omnipresent, that He has all power and He knows all things.

If you teach a doctrine that there is a second chance for salvation, you may lose your soul. You will if you believe that doctrine to the point that you do not live right and if you go on the assumption that someday you will have the opportunity for salvation even though you did not keep the commandments here.

And so it is with the paradisiacal creation, with progression from one degree of glory to another, with figuring out what the beasts in the book of Revelation are about or the mysteries in any field. Or maybe you will get talking about the fact that the sons of perdition are not resurrected or where the ten tribes are. Or perhaps you will make a mistake on the true doctrine of the gathering of Israel or some of the events incident to the Second Coming or millennial events and the like.

Now I am not saying that those doctrines will damn in the sense that the first list that I read *will*, but they *may*. They certainly will lead people astray, and they will keep you from perfecting the kind of faith that will enable you to do good and work righteousness and perform miracles. I do not get very troubled about an honest and a sincere person who makes a mistake in doctrine, provided that it is a mistake of the intellect or a mistake of understanding, and provided it is not on a great basic and fundamental principle. If he makes a mistake on the atoning sacrifice of Christ, he will go down to destruction. But if he errs in a lesser way—in a nonmalignant way, if you will—he can still straighten himself out without too much trouble. The Prophet Joseph Smith tells us of an experience he had with a man by the name of Brown in the early days. This man was taken before the high council for teaching false doctrine. He had been explaining the beasts in the book of Revelation. And he came to the Prophet, and the Prophet, with him present in the congregation, then preached a sermon on the subject, and in fact told us what the beasts mean. In the sermon he said: "I did not like the old man being called up for erring in doctrine. It looks too much like the Methodist, and not like the Latter-day Saints. Methodists have creeds which a man must believe or be asked out of their church. I want the liberty of thinking and believing as I please. It feels so good not to be trammelled. It does not prove that a man is not a good man because he errs in doctrine."[11]

That statement applies to doctrines of the lesser sort. If you err in some doctrines, and I have, and all of us have, what we want to do is get the further light and knowledge that we ought to receive and get our souls in tune and clarify our thinking. Now, obviously if you preach one of these great basic doctrines and it is false and you adhere to it, you will lose your soul. You know the Book of Mormon account says that a man goes to hell if he dies believing in infant baptism. Well, he *is* denying the atoning sacrifice of Christ and the goodness of God and the salvation of men if he supposes that infant baptism is needed. It is my hope, obviously, that we will teach sound, true doctrine. And we shall do that if we confine ourselves to the scriptures and if we leave the mysteries alone.

TESTIMONY

The marvelous and wondrous thing about this work that we are engaged in is the simple fact that it is true. There is not anything that you can imagine or conceive in your heart that is more glorious than the simple fact that the work we are engaged in is true. This is the Lord's work. This is the kingdom of God on earth, and He has issued the eternal decree that the work is going to roll on until it covers the earth, until the knowledge of God covers the earth as the waters cover the sea. That will happen because it is true, and truth will prevail. That is the ultimate destiny of the kingdom. And we shall have peace and joy and happiness if we stay with the kingdom, believe its principles, and live its laws.

In addition to the fact that the kingdom is true, the doctrine I have been teaching tonight is true. The points that I have made under the heading "The Teacher's Divine Commission" are true. If we can conform to them and follow them we shall rise to a standard of teaching that will change the lives of people. You do not change anybody's life by teaching them mathematics, but as President Brigham Young told Karl G. Maeser, he was not even to teach the multiplication tables except by the Spirit of God. That is a lesser thing. But you do change the lives of people when you teach them the doctrines of salvation.

"It [pleases] God by the foolishness of preaching to save them that believe" (1 Corinthians 1:21).

We save ourselves by our teaching, and we save those who will get in tune with the same Spirit that we have, when we teach those truths. What a glorious and wondrous thing it is not to have to worry about the doctrines of the kingdom, not to have to defend them and support them and uphold them. They are true, and they sustain and defend and uphold themselves. And they do it because the work is true. God be praised that we have the truths of salvation and that we are members of His kingdom, the Church and kingdom of God on earth. I thank Him for this blessing, and I do it for myself, and I act as mouth for all of you on this occasion, in the name of Jesus Christ, amen.

NOTES

1. J. Reuben Clark Jr., *The Charted Course of the Church in Education* (Salt Lake City: The Church of Jesus Christ of Latter-day Saints, 1980), 10.
2. See Conference Report, April 1981, 104.
3. See Fred Esplin, "The Saints Go Marching On: Learning to Live with Success," *Utah Holiday*, June 1981, 47.
4. Clark, *Charted Course*, 5–6.
5. Clark, *Charted Course*, 6.
6. Clark, *Charted Course*, 6–7.
7. Clark, *Charted Course*, 10–11.
8. Clark, *Charted Course*, 10.
9. Clark, *Charted Course*, 10.
10. Clark, *Charted Course*, 11.
11. *History of the Church of Jesus Christ of Latter-day Saints*, ed. B. H. Roberts, 2nd ed. rev. (Salt Lake City: Deseret Book, 1957), 5:340.

Part 2

LEARNING

President Boyd K. Packer is President of the Quorum of the Twelve Apostles. Address to Church Educational System religious educators at the Salt Lake Tabernacle on February 6, 2004, published in *Religious Educator* 5, no. 2 (2004): 1–11.

7

The One Pure Defense

WORLD WAR II STOPPED AS suddenly as it had begun five years earlier. All at once, I had something I was not sure I would have. I had a future. It was a strange feeling. What does one do with a future?

I was on Ie Shima, a tiny speck of an island off the northwest coast of Okinawa. A few days earlier the island had been destroyed by a typhoon of such ferocious power that large ships went down and planes were blown off the island. The storm was passed, and the war was over, and I had a future.

One calm, clear, moonlit night, I sat alone on a cliff high above the beach. Only a few days before, the ocean, so calm now, sent immense waves crashing over the top of that cliff. I sat for hours pondering and praying. I decided what to do with my future. I would be a teacher.

I had a high school diploma earned with very average grades. I had a burning witness of the restored gospel of Jesus Christ. I had some knowledge of the scriptures from hours and days and weeks and months of study. I did not know what I would teach. I could learn practical and secular subjects.

I struggled through college. That was shortened by a year because of credits in aeronautics granted for service as an Air Force pilot. I had a college degree in education, and of consummate importance, I had a wife and two little boys.

Suddenly I was a seminary teacher hired midyear to replace John P. Lillywhite, who was called out of the classroom to preside over the Netherlands Mission. I knew what to do with my future.

I had no idea that I would be here now speaking to teachers. I was content then, and I would be content now, to be a classroom teacher. And my wife would be content to join me.

Knowing what I know now, I do not expect in the field of destiny to be rewarded for my present calling above those of you I have known who wore out your lives one day at a time teaching in the classroom.

But we are here. I say *we*, for my wife is with me. We do not know how many years are allotted us. Not a great number, I would think. But we have sure testimonies of the Father and the Son and the unspeakable gift of the Holy Ghost.

We know also that the being from the unseen world who confronted the boy Joseph in the Sacred Grove is always near, for as Peter said, "Be sober, be vigilant; because your adversary the devil, as a roaring lion, walketh about, seeking whom he may devour" (1 Peter 5:8).

Now, by moral and social and political and even intellectual standards, we seem to be losing. But mankind also knows that in the final windup scene Satan cannot win.

There are over forty thousand of you here in this meeting. Measured against the need, that really is not a great number. But I remember hearing Sir Winston Churchill say in the darkest hours of World War II, speaking of a handful of Royal Air Force pilots facing almost insurmountable odds, "Never in the field of human conflict was so much owed by so many to so few."[1]

In October of 1983, I returned from South America and left almost immediately for London to join Elder Neal A. Maxwell at the first regional conference as a substitute for one of the First Presidency. This first conference was something of an experiment.

We met in the Hyde Park Chapel for a four-hour priesthood meeting. Elder Maxwell spoke first, quoting King Benjamin, "Brethren, we did not come here to trifle with words" (see Mosiah 2:9). What he said next changed my life: "We come to you today in our true identity as Apostles of the Lord Jesus Christ."

Suddenly my body was filled with warmth and light. The weariness of travel was replaced by confidence and confirmation. What we were doing was approved of the Lord.

I have never forgotten that moment, much like moments of inspiration each of you has experienced. Such moments confirm that the restored gospel of Jesus Christ is true.

BOOK OF MEMORY

As I prepared to meet you here tonight, I had great difficulty in keeping my book of memory closed.

I remember tall, smiling J. Wiley Sessions, who opened the first institute of religion at Moscow, Idaho.

Thomas J. Yates, an engineer at a power plant in the mountains east of Salt Lake City, rode a horse down the canyon each day to teach at the first released-time seminary, Granite. I did not know Brother Yates, but I remember those who replaced him.

Abel S. Rich, an agriculture teacher, was hired to go across the street from the high school in Brigham City to an adobe home to open the second released-time seminary. He was serving as principal when Elder A. Theodore Tuttle and I taught there together.

Brother Tuttle had been a lieutenant in the Marines. At Iwo Jima he returned to the ship to get a large flag. On shore he handed it to a runner who took it to the top of Mount Sirabachi and on to the pages of history.

Before Brother Tuttle and I were called as General Authorities, we taught together in the same building where I had attended seminary and then worked together as supervisors of seminaries and institutes of religion. They were administered by William E. Berrett.

Brother Berrett had opened the seminary in the Uintah Basin. During the summer he walked from town to town recruiting students for his class. Their first child was born and buried there. Brother and Sister Berrett rode to the cemetery in the back seat of a car. On his lap was the little wooden, unpainted casket he had built.

I knew Elijah Hicken, who was sent to the Big Horn Basin in Wyoming to open the seminary. He was not welcomed by a very rough crowd. A group threatened his life. The patriarch came with a blessing and a promise that his life would be protected. On the strength of that blessing, Brother Hicken took off the six-shooter he had worn to class each day.

In the 1950s we established stake boards of education. The story was told, quite possibly true, that one seminary teacher had a little difficulty convincing the stake leaders of the need to study the scriptures.

He decided to give them a quiz to test their scriptural knowledge. The first question was, "Who knocked down the walls of Jericho?" That opened something of a debate.

Finally the stake president said, "Oh, what difference does it make who knocked down the walls? Just get them put back up! We'll pay for it out of stake funds."

In England I attended a sacrament meeting. The seminary teacher, speaking on the subject of the scriptures, said, "I will now turn to Mosiah chapter 3 in the Doctrine and Covenants." No one laughed. I knew we still had work to do.

When I first taught seminary, we had three textbooks—one each for Old Testament, New Testament, and Church history. In Brigham City we added a class in the Book of Mormon.

The Old Testament textbook was out of print and hard to find. When the monthly faculty group meeting was held in our building, we hid our textbooks. If we did not, these precious books would disappear.

We had a record player that played fourteen-inch Bible stories. We did not have a projector in the class.

CURRICULUM

Now you have course outlines, visual aids, equipment, and buildings. All are superior to anything before available.

Your curriculum is the same—the scriptures: the Old Testament, the New Testament, the Book of Mormon, the Doctrine and Covenants, the Pearl of Great Price. Other sources come from the living Prophets and Apostles. We are told in the revelation, when inspired by the Holy Ghost, their words take on the stature of scripture (see D&C 1:38).

BE ON ALERT

Now, again from my book of memories:

In the early 1930s, there grew up in some of the institutes a so-called superior scholarship. Secular approval, they thought, would bring more acceptance from those with whom they associated at the universities.

This attitude infected a number in the seminaries. Some work actually went forward to produce a curriculum focused on contemporary social values rather than revealed doctrine and scripture.

Several of the teachers went to obtain advanced degrees under eminent Bible scholars. They sought learning "out of the best books" (see D&C 88:118; 109:7, 14), but with too little faith. They came back having won their degrees but having lost touch with, and perhaps interest in, the restored gospel of Jesus Christ.

This pulling at the moorings by some teachers of religion did not go unnoticed in the councils of the Church. The Brethren became concerned. In 1938 all seminary and institute personnel were assembled for summer school at Aspen Grove.

President J. Reuben Clark Jr., speaking for the First Presidency, delivered a monumental address, "The Charted Course of the Church in Education."[2] It is as much an anchor today as it was the day that it was given. Surely you have read and do reread that charter. Now tonight as your teacher, I assign you to read it again. That is your homework.

I knew virtually all of those men who drifted off course. They found themselves in conflict with the simple things of the gospel. Some of them left and went on to prominent careers in secular education where they felt more comfortable. One by one they found their way outside Church activity and a few of them outside the Church. With each went a following of students—a terrible price to pay.

Over the years I have watched. Their children and grandchildren and great-grandchildren are not numbered among the faithful in the Church.

That same thing happened again. In 1954 the seminary and institute teachers were called to a summer school at Brigham Young University. Elder Harold B. Lee of the Quorum of the Twelve was our teacher. For two hours a day, five days a week for five weeks, Elder Lee and others of the Twelve taught us. President J. Reuben Clark Jr. spoke to us twice. That pulled us back on course.

Happily, though, most of those who went away to study returned magnified by their experience and armed with advanced degrees. They returned firm in their knowledge that a man can be in the world but not of the world (see John 17:14–19).

Be careful! Without watch care such things can and have happened again. Each of you must be on alert. If you feel drawn to others who regard intellectual achievement to be more important than the fundamental doctrines, or who expose their students to the so-called realities of life, back away.

In Harm's Way

When I was a boy, childhood diseases appeared regularly in every community. When someone had chicken pox or measles or mumps, the county health officer would visit the home and tack on the porch or put in the window a quarantine sign to warn everyone to stay away. In a large family such as ours, those childhood diseases would visit the home by relay, one child getting it from another, so the sign might stay up for many weeks.

When I was in junior high school in a health class, the teacher read an article. A mother learned that the neighbor children had chicken pox. She faced the probability that her children would have it as well, perhaps one at a time. She determined to get it all over with at once.

So she sent her children to the neighbor's to play with their children to let them be exposed, and then be done with it. Imagine her horror when the doctor finally came and announced that it was not chicken pox the children had; it was smallpox.

"Teach Them the Word of God"

Now, I close the book of memories and come to here and now.

I come to you as did Jacob when he taught in the temple, "having first obtained mine errand from the Lord" (Jacob 1:17). Jacob and his brother Joseph had been consecrated priests and teachers over the people.

"And [they] did magnify [their] office unto the Lord, taking upon [themselves] the responsibility, answering the sins of the people upon [their] own heads if [they] did not teach them the word of God with all diligence" (Jacob 1:19).

The world and the Christian churches have discarded the Old Testament, but it is there we find the nuggets of doctrine—such words as *Aaronic, Melchizedek, priesthood, patriarch, Jehovah, ordinance, covenants,* and so many more. They form essential links in our understanding of the plan of redemption.

From the New Testament the students learn the life and teachings of the Master.

Teach your students of the Apostasy and the Restoration of the priesthood, of Joseph Smith and the organization of The Church of Jesus Christ of Latter-day Saints, by the Lord's own declaration, "the only true and living church upon the face of the whole earth" (D&C 1:30).

Immerse them in the truths of the Book of Mormon. That will lead them to the test and to the promise that is there, and then they will be armed with the protective influence of the truth.

Each individual can then "ask God, the Eternal Father, in the name of Christ, if these things are not true," as the Book of Mormon invites them to do. Teach them to ask "with a sincere heart, with real intent, having faith in Christ, [and God] will manifest the truth of it unto [them], by the power of the Holy Ghost. And by the power of the Holy Ghost [they] may know the truth of all things" (Moroni 10:4–5).

With an individual testimony, they will be safe in the world.

Much Depends on You

The world is spiraling downward at an ever-quickening pace. I am sorry to tell you that it will not get better.

It is my purpose to *charge* each of you as *teachers* with the responsibility—to put you on alert. These are days of great spiritual danger for our youth.

Morally Mixed-up World

I know of nothing in the history of the Church or in the history of the world to compare with our present circumstances. Nothing happened in Sodom and Gomorrah which exceeds in wickedness and depravity that which surrounds us now.

Words of profanity, vulgarity, and blasphemy are heard everywhere. Unspeakable wickedness and perversion were once hidden in dark places; now they are in the open, even accorded legal protection.

At Sodom and Gomorrah these things were localized. Now they are spread across the world, and they are among us.

I need not—I will not—identify each evil that threatens our youth. It is difficult for man to get away from it.

The First Line of Defense

You, with the leaders and teachers in the priesthood and auxiliaries, are not the first line of defense. The family holds that line. Satan uses every intrigue to disrupt the family.

The sacred relationship between man and woman, husband and wife, through which mortal bodies are conceived and life is passed to the next generation, is being showered with filth.

Surely you can see what the adversary is about. The first line of defense, the home, is crumbling.

The very purpose for the Restoration centers on the sealing authority, the temple ordinances, baptism for the dead, eternal marriage, eternal increase—centers on the family!

The Lord placed the responsibility upon parents first, saying: "Inasmuch as parents have children in Zion, or in any of her stakes which are organized, that teach them not to understand the doctrine of repentance, faith in Christ the Son of the living God, and of baptism and the gift of the Holy Ghost by the laying on of the hands, when eight years old, the sin be upon the heads of the parents. . . . And they shall also teach their children to pray, and to walk uprightly before the Lord" (D&C 68:25, 28).

There is "the shield of faith wherewith" the Lord said "ye shall be able to quench all the fiery darts of the wicked" (D&C 27:17).

The Armor Is Fitted at Home

This shield of faith is handmade in a cottage industry. What is most worth doing ideally is done at home. It can be polished in the classroom,

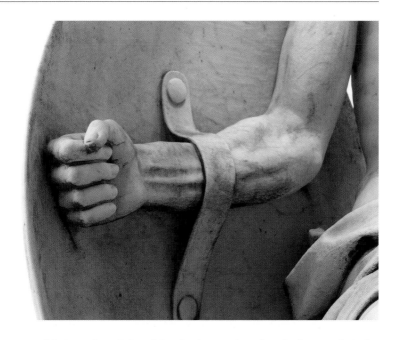

Courtesy of iStockphoto

but it is fabricated and fitted in the home, handcrafted to each individual. Many do not have support in the family. When that shield is not provided at home, we must, and we can, build it. You and the leaders and teachers then become the first line of defense.

THE PROPHETS HAVE WARNED

We are now exactly where the prophets warned we would be.

In preparation for what is coming, the Lord warned, "In consequence of evils and designs which do and will exist in the hearts of conspiring men in the last days, I have warned you, and forewarn you, by giving unto you this word of wisdom by revelation" (D&C 89:4).

Moroni spoke to us: "O ye Gentiles, it is wisdom in God that these things should be shown unto you. . . . Wherefore, the Lord commandeth you, when ye shall see these things come among you that ye shall awake to a sense of your awful situation" (Ether 8:23–24).

Paul prophesied, "In the last days perilous times shall come" (2 Timothy 3:1), then word by word and phrase by phrase, described exactly what our present conditions are now. He spoke of "blasphemers, disobedient to parents, . . . unholy, without natural affection, . . .

incontinent, . . . despisers of those that are good, . . . lovers of pleasures more than lovers of God; . . . ever learning, and never able to come to the knowledge of the truth," and other things (2 Timothy 3:2–4, 7).

Could he have described our plight more accurately? Read the prophecy very carefully.

The Power of Scriptures

Paul prophesied, also, that things will not get better. "Evil men and seducers shall wax worse and worse, deceiving, and being deceived" (2 Timothy 3:13).

Fortunately, he told us what to do about it: "But continue thou in the things which thou hast learned and hast been assured of, knowing of whom thou hast learned them; and that from a child thou hast known the holy scriptures, which are able to make thee wise unto salvation through faith which is in Christ Jesus. All scripture is given by inspiration of God, and is profitable for doctrine, for reproof, for correction, for instruction in righteousness" (2 Timothy 3:14–16). In His supernal prayer for the Apostles, the Lord said, "I pray not that thou shouldest take them out of the world, but that thou shouldest keep them from the evil. They are not of the world, even as I am not of the world. Sanctify them through thy truth: thy word is truth" (John 17:15–17).

A World Spiritually Diseased

Spiritual diseases of epidemic proportion sweep over the world. We are not able to curb them. But we can prevent our youth from being infected by them.

Knowledge and a testimony of the restored gospel of Jesus Christ are like a vaccine. We can inoculate them.

Inoculate: In—"to be within" and *oculate* means "eye to see." We place an eye within them—the unspeakable gift of the Holy Ghost.

Nephi told us that "angels speak by the power of the Holy Ghost; wherefore, they speak the words of Christ. Wherefore, I said unto you, feast upon the words of Christ; for behold, the words of Christ will tell you *all things* what ye should do" (2 Nephi 32:3; emphasis added).

NARROW WAY

It is a very narrow and straight path laid out for you teachers.

"Strait is the gate, and narrow is the way, which leadeth unto life, and few there be that find it" (Matthew 7:14).

Your path as teachers may be broadened to include some worthy activities and cultural events. Activities are like spices and desserts that flavor a balanced meal. These must always be of the standard to reflect the gospel. Do not leave out the nourishing nutrients that build the spirit; it is not the entertainment that protects them.

The teaching of the restored gospel of Jesus Christ *must* not be regarded as just one among your offerings. It is more important than any or all of the activities put together. You may provide them activities, but you must not leave the teaching undone.

The auxiliaries have been organized and have the responsibility for most of the activities. Teach your students to be faithful and active in the wards and branches and stakes, to have a deep regard for the priesthood leaders called to preside over them.

I repeat, the way is straight and narrow. You must not wander from it.

HAVE FAITH—COURAGE

When our youth feel surrounded and outnumbered, remember what Elisha told his servant when he saw that "an host compassed the city both with horses and chariots." The servant was frightened and said, "Alas, my master! how shall we do? [Elisha] answered, Fear not: for they that be with us are more than they that be with them. And Elisha prayed, and said, Lord, I pray thee, open his eyes, that he may see. And the Lord opened the eyes of the young man; and he saw: and, behold, the mountain was full of horses and chariots of fire" (2 Kings 6:15–17).

You are *not* responsible to cure the world's environment. You can, with parents and priesthood and auxiliary leaders and teachers, send young Latter-day Saints out as leaven into the world, spiritually nourished, immunized to the influences of evil.

"The glory of God is intelligence, or, in other words, light and truth. Light and truth forsake that evil one. . . . [You are] commanded . . . to bring up your children in light and truth" (D&C 93:36–37, 40).

A Defense and a Refuge

"The gathering together upon the land of Zion," the Lord said, "and upon her stakes, may be for a defense, and for a refuge from the storm, and from wrath when it shall be poured out without mixture upon the whole earth" (D&C 115:6).

They need not fear. *We* need not fear. Fear is the opposite of faith.

I have been in the councils of the Church and seen many things. I have seen disappointment and shock and concern. Never once have I seen any fear.

Our youth can look forward with hope for a happy life. They shall marry and raise families in the Church and teach their little ones what you have taught them. They, in turn, will teach their children and their grandchildren.

Isaiah and Micah prophesied: "It shall come to pass in the last days, that the mountain of the Lord's house shall be established in the top of the mountains, and shall be exalted above the hills; and all nations shall flow unto it. And many people shall go and say, Come ye, and let us go up to the mountain of the Lord, to the house of the God of Jacob; and he will teach us of his ways, and we will walk in his paths: for out of Zion shall go forth the law, and the word of the Lord from Jerusalem" (Isaiah 2:2–3; see also Micah 4:1–2).

In our day the house of the Lord *has* been established in the tops of the mountains, and nations *do* flow unto it. The word of the Lord—the Old and New Testaments—has gone forth from Jerusalem. Now the law goes forth from Zion. And you are teachers of the law.

We Will Not Fail

We will not fail!

"How long can rolling waters remain impure? What power shall stay the heavens? As well might man stretch forth his puny arm to stop the Missouri river in its decreed course, or to turn it up stream, as to hinder the Almighty from pouring down knowledge from heaven upon the heads of the Latter-day Saints" (D&C 121:33).

It has been fifty-nine years since I sat on that cliff on that tiny speck of an island in the Pacific Ocean and decided to be a teacher. I knew then that a teacher would not be rewarded with wealth; the reward is more lasting.

During those years, whole nations have been born and died as the evil one has worked his will. I have seen the borders of Zion enlarged to cover the whole earth (see D&C 82:14; 107:74).

I do not know now any more surely that Jesus is the Christ, the Son of God, the Only Begotten of the Father, than I did then as a soldier boy sitting on the cliff on that tiny speck of an island. There is one difference—now I know the Lord.

I bear witness of Him and invoke His blessings upon you who teach, as fathers and mothers, as grandfathers and grandmothers, upon your families, upon your classes, upon your work. I bless you that His power and inspiration will follow you in such a way that those who come within your influence will have that protective testimony born within them. I invoke this blessing upon you as a servant of the Lord and in the name of Jesus Christ, amen.

Notes

1. Extract from speech by Winston Churchill, August 20, 1940 (Churchill Papers).
2. See J. Reuben Clark Jr., *The Charted Course of the Church in Education*, rev. ed. (Salt Lake City: The Church of Jesus Christ of Latter-day Saints, 1994).

Elder Dallin H. Oaks is a member of the Quorum of the Twelve Apostle. Address at a Brigham Young University devotional assembly on September 29, 1981, published in *Sperry Symposium Classics: The Doctrine and Covenants* (Provo, UT: Religious Studies Center, Brigham Young University, 2004), 10–22.

8 REVELATION

EVELATION IS COMMUNICATION FROM GOD to man. It can occur in many different ways. Some prophets, like Moses and Joseph Smith, have talked with God face to face. Some persons have had personal communication with angels. Other revelations have come, as Elder James E. Talmage described it, "through the dreams of sleep or in waking visions of the mind."[1]

In its more familiar forms, revelation or inspiration comes by means of words or thoughts communicated to the mind (see D&C 8:2–3; Enos 1:10), by sudden enlightenment (see D&C 6:14–15), by positive or negative feelings about proposed courses of action, or even by inspiring performances, as in the performing arts. As President Boyd K. Packer has stated, "Inspiration comes more as a feeling than as a sound."[2]

Assuming you are familiar with these different forms of revelation or inspiration, I have chosen to discuss this subject in terms of a different classification—the purpose of the communication. I can identify eight different purposes served by communication from God: (1) to testify, (2) to prophesy, (3) to comfort, (4) to uplift, (5) to inform, (6) to restrain, (7) to confirm, and (8) to impel. I will describe each of these in that order, giving examples.

My purpose in suggesting this classification and in giving these examples is to persuade each of you to search your own experience and to conclude that you have already received revelations and that you can receive more revelations, because communication from God to men and women is a reality. President Lorenzo Snow declared that it is "the grand privilege of every Latter-day Saint . . . to have the manifestations of the spirit every day of our lives."[3]

President Harold B. Lee taught that "every man has the privilege to exercise these gifts and these privileges in the conduct of his own affairs; in bringing up his children in the way they should go; in the management of his business, or whatever he does. It is his right to enjoy the spirit of revelation and of inspiration to do the right thing, to be wise and prudent, just and good, in everything that he does."[4]

As I review the following eight purposes of revelation, I hope you will recognize the extent to which you have already received revelation or inspiration and resolve to cultivate this spiritual gift for more frequent use in the future.

1. The Holy Ghost *testifies* or reveals that Jesus is the Christ and that the gospel is true.

When the Apostle Peter affirmed that Jesus Christ was the Son of the living God, the Savior called him blessed, "for flesh and blood hath not revealed it unto thee, but my Father which is in heaven" (Matthew 16:17). This precious revelation can be part of the personal experience of every seeker after truth and, once received, becomes a polestar to guide in all the activities of life.

2. *Prophecy* is another purpose or function of revelation.

Speaking under the influence of the Holy Ghost and within the limits of his or her responsibility, a person may be inspired to predict what will come to pass in the future.

The one who holds the office of the prophet, seer, and revelator prophesies for the Church, as when Joseph Smith prophesied concerning the Civil War (see D&C 87) and foretold that the Saints would become a mighty people in the Rocky Mountains. Prophecy is part of the calling of a patriarch. Each of us is also privileged occasionally to receive prophetic revelation illuminating future events in our lives, like a Church calling we are to receive. To cite another example, after our fifth child was born, my wife and I did not have any more children. After more than ten years, we concluded that our family would not be any larger, which grieved us. Then one day, while my wife was in the temple, the Spirit whispered to her that she would have another child. That prophetic revelation was fulfilled about a year and a half later with the birth of our sixth child, for whom we had waited thirteen years.

3. A THIRD PURPOSE OF REVELATION IS TO GIVE *COMFORT.*

Such a revelation came to the Prophet Joseph Smith in Liberty Jail. After many months in deplorable conditions, he cried out in agony and loneliness, pleading for the Lord to remember him and the persecuted Saints. The comforting answer came:

"My son, peace be unto thy soul; thine adversity and thine afflictions shall be but a small moment; and then, if thou endure it well, God shall exalt thee on high; thou shalt triumph over all thy foes" (D&C 121:7–8).

In that same revelation the Lord declared that no matter what tragedies or injustices should befall the Prophet, "Know thou, my son, that all these things shall give thee experience, and shall be for thy good" (D&C 122:7).

Each of us knows of other examples of revelations of comfort. Some have been comforted by visions of departed loved ones or by feeling their presence. The widow of a good friend told me that she had felt the presence of her departed husband, giving her assurance of his love and concern for her. Others have been comforted in adjusting to the loss of a job or a business advantage or even a marriage. A revelation of comfort can also come in connection with a blessing of the priesthood, either from the words spoken or simply from the feeling communicated in connection with the blessing.

Another type of comforting revelation is the assurance received that a sin has been forgiven. After praying fervently for an entire day and night, a Book of Mormon prophet recorded that he heard a voice, which said, "Thy sins are forgiven thee, and thou shalt be blessed.

Liz Lemon Swindle, *Joseph Smith in Liberty Jail*. Used by permission.

"Wherefore," Enos wrote, "my guilt was swept away" (see Enos 1:5–6; see also D&C 61:2). This assurance, which comes when a person has completed all the steps of repentance, gives assurance that the price has been paid, that God has heard the repentant sinner, and that his or her sins are forgiven. Alma described that moment as a time when he was no longer "harrowed up by the memory" of his sins. "And oh, what joy, and what marvelous light I did behold; yea, my soul was filled with joy. . . . There can be nothing so exquisite and sweet as was my joy" (Alma 36:19–21).

4. CLOSELY RELATED TO THE FEELING OF COMFORT IS THE FOURTH PURPOSE OR FUNCTION OF REVELATION, TO *UPLIFT*.

At some time in our lives each of us needs to be lifted up from a depression, from a sense of foreboding or inadequacy, or just from a plateau of spiritual mediocrity. Because it raises our spirits and helps us resist evil and seek good, I believe that the feeling of uplift that is communicated by reading the scriptures or by enjoying wholesome music, art, or literature is a distinct purpose of revelation.

5. THE FIFTH PURPOSE OF REVELATION IS TO *INFORM*.

This may consist of inspiration giving a person the words to speak on a particular occasion, such as in the blessings pronounced by a patriarch or in sermons or other words spoken under the influence of the Holy Ghost. The Lord commanded Joseph Smith and Sidney Rigdon to lift up their voices and speak the thoughts that would be put into their hearts, "for it shall be given you in the very hour, yea, in the very moment, what ye shall say" (D&C 100:5–6; see also D&C 84:85; D&C 124:97).

On some sacred occasions, information has been given by face-to-face conversations with heavenly personages, such as in the visions related in ancient and modern scripture. In other circumstances, needed information is communicated by the quiet whisperings of the Spirit. A child loses a treasured possession, prays for help, and is inspired to find it; an adult has a problem at work, at home, or in genealogical research, prays, and is led to the information necessary to resolve it; a Church leader prays to know who the Lord would have him call to fill a position, and the Spirit whispers a name. In all of these examples—familiar to each of us—the Holy Ghost acts in His office as a teacher and revelator, communicating information and truths for the edification and guidance of the recipient.

Revelation from God serves all five of these purposes: testimony, prophecy, comfort, uplift, and information. I have spoken of these only briefly, giving examples principally from the scriptures. I will speak at greater length about the remaining three purposes of revelation, giving examples from my personal experience.

6. The sixth type or purpose of revelation is to *restrain* us from doing something.

Thus, in the midst of a great sermon explaining the power of the Holy Ghost, Nephi suddenly declares, "And now I . . . cannot say more; the Spirit stoppeth mine utterance" (2 Nephi 32:7). The revelation that restrains is one of the most common forms of revelation. It often comes by surprise, when we have not asked for revelation or guidance on a particular subject. But if we are keeping the commandments of God and living in tune with His Spirit, a restraining force will steer us away from things we should not do.

One of my first experiences in being restrained by the Spirit came soon after I was called as a counselor in a stake presidency in Chicago. In one of our first stake presidency meetings, our stake president made a proposal that our new stake center be built in a particular location. I immediately saw four or five good reasons why that was the wrong location. When asked for my counsel, I opposed the proposal, giving each of those reasons. The stake president wisely proposed that each of us consider the matter prayerfully for a week and discuss it further in our next meeting. Almost perfunctorily I prayed about the subject and immediately received a strong impression that I was wrong, that I was standing in the way of the Lord's will, and that I should remove myself from opposition to it. Needless to say, I was restrained and promptly gave my approval to the proposed construction. Incidentally, the wisdom of constructing the stake center at that location was soon evident, even to me. My reasons to the contrary turned out to be short-sighted, and I was soon grateful to have been restrained from relying on them.

Several years ago I picked up the desk pen in my office at Brigham Young University (BYU) to sign a paper that had been prepared for my signature, something I did at least a dozen times each day. That document committed the university to a particular course of action we had decided to follow. All the staff work had been done, and all appeared to be in order. But as I went to sign the document, I was filled with such negative thoughts and forebodings that I put it to one side and asked for the entire matter to be reviewed again. It was, and within a few days additional facts came to light which showed that the proposed course of action would have caused the university serious problems in the future.

On another occasion the Spirit came to my assistance as I was editing a casebook on a legal subject. A casebook consists of several hundred court opinions, together with explanatory material and text written by the editor. My assistant and I had finished almost all of the work on the book, including the necessary research to assure that these court opinions had not been reversed or overruled. Just before sending it to the publisher, I was leafing through the manuscript and a particular court opinion caught my attention. As I looked at it, I had a profoundly uneasy feeling. I asked my assistant to check that opinion again to see if everything was in order. He reported that it was. In a subsequent check of the completed manuscript, I was again stopped at that case, again with great feelings of uneasiness. This time I went to the law library myself. There, in some newly received publications, I discovered that this case had just been reversed on appeal. If that opinion had been published in my casebook, it would have been a serious professional embarrassment. I was saved by the restraining power of revelation.

7. A COMMON WAY TO SEEK REVELATION IS TO PROPOSE A PARTICULAR COURSE OF ACTION AND THEN TO PRAY FOR INSPIRATION TO *CONFIRM* IT.

The Lord explained the confirming type of revelation when Oliver Cowdery failed in his efforts to translate the Book of Mormon: "Behold, you have not understood; you have supposed that I would give it unto you, when you took no thought save it was to ask me. But, behold, I say unto you, that you must study it out in your mind; then you must ask me if it be right, and if it is right I will cause that your bosom shall burn within you; therefore, you shall feel that it is right" (D&C 9:7–8).

Similarly, the prophet Alma likens the word of God to a seed and tells persons studying the gospel that if they will give place for the seed to be planted in their heart, the seed will enlarge their souls and enlighten their understanding and begin to be delicious to them (see Alma 32). That feeling is the Holy Ghost's confirming revelation of the truth of the word.

When he spoke on the BYU campus some years ago on the subject "Agency or Inspiration," Elder Bruce R. McConkie stressed our responsibility to do all that we can before we seek a revelation. He gave a very personal example. When he set out to choose a companion for eternity, he did not go to the Lord and ask whom he ought to marry. "I went out and found the girl I wanted," he said. "She suited me; . . . it just seemed . . . as though this ought to be. . . . [Then] all I did was pray to the Lord and ask for some guidance and direction in connection with the decision that I'd reached."[5]

Elder McConkie summarized his counsel on the balance between agency and inspiration as follows: "We're expected to use the gifts and talents and abilities, the sense and judgment and agency with which we are endowed. . . . Implicit in asking in faith is the precedent requirement that we do everything in our power to accomplish the goal that we seek. . . . We're expected to do everything in our power that we can, and then to seek an answer from the Lord, a confirming seal that we've reached the right conclusion."[6]

As a regional representative I was privileged to work with four different members of the Quorum of the Twelve and with other General Authorities as they sought revelation in the calling of stake presidents. All proceeded in the same manner. They interviewed persons residing in the stake—counselors in the stake presidency, members of the high council, bishops, and others who had gained special experience in Church administration—asking them questions and hearing their counsel. As these interviews were conducted, the servants of the Lord gave prayerful consideration to each person interviewed and mentioned. Finally, they reached a tentative decision on the new stake president. This proposal was then prayerfully submitted to the Lord. If confirmed, the call was issued. If not confirmed, or if restrained, that proposal was tabled and the process continued until a new proposal was formed and the confirming revelation was received.

Sometimes confirming and restraining revelations are combined. For example, during my service at BYU I was invited to give a speech before a national association of attorneys. Because it would require many days to prepare, this was the kind of speaking invitation I had routinely declined. But as I began to dictate a letter declining this particular invitation, I felt restrained. I paused and reconsidered my action. I then considered how I might accept the invitation, and as I came to consider it in that light, I felt the confirming assurance of the Spirit and knew that this was what I must do.

The speech that resulted, "A Private University Looks at Government Regulation," opened the door to a host of important opportunities. I was invited to repeat that same speech before several other nationally prominent groups. It was published in *Vital Speeches*, in a professional journal, and in several other periodicals and books, from which it was used as a leading statement of the private university's interest in freedom from government regulation. This speech led to BYU's being consulted by various church groups on the proper relationship between government and a church-related college. These consultations in turn contributed to the formation of a national organization of church-related colleges and universities that has provided a significant coalition to oppose unlawful or unwise government regulation in the future. I have no doubt, as I look back on the event, that this speaking invitation I almost declined was one of those occasions when a seemingly insignificant act made a great deal of difference.

Those are the times when it is vital for us to receive the guidance of the Lord, and those are the times when revelation will come to aid us if we will hear and heed it.

8. The eighth purpose or type of revelation consists of those instances where the Spirit *impels* a person to action.

This is not a case where a person proposes to take a particular action and the Spirit either confirms or restrains. This is a case where revelation comes when it is not being sought and impels some action not proposed. This type of revelation is obviously less common than other types, but its rarity makes it all the more significant.

A scriptural example is recorded in the first book of Nephi. After Nephi obtained the precious records from the treasury in Jerusalem, the Spirit of the Lord directed him to kill Laban as he lay drunk in the street. This act was so far from Nephi's heart that he recoiled and wrestled with the Spirit, but he was again directed to slay Laban, and he finally followed that revelation (see 1 Nephi 4).

Students of Church history will recall Wilford Woodruff's account of an impression that came to him in the night telling him to move his carriage and mules away from a large tree. He did so, and his family and livestock were saved when the tree crashed to the ground in a tornado that struck thirty minutes later.[7]

As a young girl, my grandmother Chasty Olsen Harris had a similar experience. She was tending some children who were playing in a dry riverbed near their home in Castle Dale, Utah. Suddenly she heard a voice that called her by name and directed her to get the children out of the riverbed and up on the bank. It was a clear day, and there was no sign of rain. She saw no reason to heed the voice and continued to play. The voice spoke to her again, urgently. This time she heeded the warning. Quickly gathering the children, she made a run for the bank. Just as they reached it, an enormous wall of water, originating with a cloudburst in the mountains many miles away, swept down the canyon and roared across where the children had played. Except for this impelling revelation, she and the children would have been lost.

For nine years Professor Marvin Hill and I had worked on the book *Carthage Conspiracy*, which concerns the 1845 court trial of the murderers of Joseph Smith. We had several different sources of minutes on the trial, some bearing their author's name and others unsigned. The fullest set of minutes was unsigned, but because we had located them in the Church Historian's Office, we were sure they were the minutes kept by George Watt, the Church's official scribe who was sent to record the proceedings of the trial. We so stated in seven drafts of our manuscript and analyzed all of our sources on that assumption.

Finally, the book was completed, and within a few weeks the final manuscript would be sent to the publisher. As I sat in my office at BYU one Saturday afternoon, I felt impelled to go through the pile of unexamined books and pamphlets accumulated on the table behind my desk. At the very bottom of a pile of fifty or sixty publications, I found a printed catalog of the contents of the Wilford C. Wood Museum, which Professor LaMar C. Berrett, the author, had sent to me a year and a half earlier. As I quickly flipped through the pages of this catalog of Church history manuscripts, my eyes fell on a page describing the manuscript of the trial minutes we had attributed to George Watt. This catalog page told how Wilford Wood had purchased the original of that set of minutes in Illinois and had given the Church the typewritten version we had obtained from the Church historian.

We immediately visited the Wilford Wood Museum in Woods Cross, Utah, and obtained additional information which enabled us to determine that the minutes we had thought were the official Church source had been prepared by one of the lawyers for the defense. With this knowledge we returned to the Church Historian's Office and were able to locate for the first time George Watt's official and highly authentic set of minutes on the trial. This discovery saved us from a grievous error in the identification of one of our major sources and also permitted us to enrich the contents of our book significantly. The impression I received that day in my office is a cherished example of the way the Lord will help us in our righteous professional pursuits when we qualify for the impressions of His Spirit.

I had another choice experience with impelling revelation a few months after I began my service at BYU. As a new and inexperienced president, I had many problems to analyze and many decisions to reach. I was very dependent on the Lord. One day in October I drove up Provo Canyon to ponder a particular problem. Although alone and without any interruption, I found myself unable to think of the problem at hand. Another pending issue I was not yet ready to consider kept thrusting itself into my mind: should we modify BYU's academic calendar to complete the fall semester before Christmas?

After ten or fifteen minutes of unsuccessful efforts to exclude thoughts of this subject, I realized what was happening. The issue of the calendar did not seem timely to me, and I was certainly not seeking any guidance on it, but the Spirit was trying to communicate on that subject. I immediately turned my full attention to that question and began to record my thoughts on a piece of paper. Within a few minutes I had recorded the details of a three-semester calendar, with all of its powerful advantages.

Hurrying back to the campus, I reviewed this with my colleagues and found them enthusiastic. A few days later the Board of Trustees approved our proposed new calendar, and we published its dates, barely in time to make them effective in the fall of 1972. Since that time I have reread these words of the Prophet Joseph Smith and realized that I had had the experience he described: "A person may profit by noticing the first intimation of the spirit of revelation; for instance, when you feel pure intelligence flowing into you, it may give you sudden strokes of ideas . . . and thus by learning the Spirit of God and understanding it, you may grow into the principle of revelation."[8]

I have now described eight different purposes or types of revelation: (1) testifying, (2) prophesying, (3) comforting, (4) uplifting, (5) informing, (6) restraining, (7) confirming, and (8) impelling. Each of these refers to revelations that are received. Before concluding, I will suggest a few ideas about revelations that are not received.

First, we should understand what can be called the principle of "responsibility in revelation." Our Heavenly Father's house is a house of order, where His servants are commanded to "act in the office in which [they are] appointed" (D&C 107:99). This principle applies to revelation. Only the President of the Church receives revelation to guide the entire Church. Only the stake president receives revelation for the special guidance of the stake. The person who receives revelation for the ward is the bishop. For a family, it is the priesthood leadership of the family. Leaders receive revelation for their own areas of responsibility. Individuals can receive revelation to guide their own lives.

But when one person purports to receive revelation for another person outside his or her own area of responsibility—such as a Church member who claims to have revelation to guide the entire Church or a person who claims to have a revelation to guide another person over whom he or she has no presiding authority according to the order of the Church—you can be sure that such revelations are not from the Lord. "There are counterfeit signals."[9] Satan is a great deceiver, and he is the source of some of these spurious revelations. Others are imagined.

If a revelation is outside the limits of your specific responsibility, you know it is not from the Lord and you are not bound by it. I have heard of cases where a young man told a young woman she should marry him because he had received a revelation that she was to be his eternal companion. If this is a true revelation, it will be confirmed directly to the woman if she seeks to know. In the meantime, she is under no obligation to heed it. She should seek her own guidance and make up her own mind. The man can receive revelation to guide his own actions, but he cannot properly receive revelation to direct hers. She is outside his jurisdiction.

What about those times when we seek revelation and do not receive it? We do not always receive inspiration or revelation when we request it. Sometimes we are delayed in the receipt of revelation, and sometimes we are left to our own judgment. We cannot force spiritual things. It must be so. Our life's purpose to obtain experience and to develop faith would be frustrated if our Heavenly Father directed us in every act, even in every important act. We must make decisions and experience the consequences in order to develop self-reliance and faith.

Even in decisions we think very important, we sometimes receive no answer to our prayers. This does not mean that our prayers have not been heard. It only means that we have prayed about a decision which, for one reason or another, we should make without guidance by revelation. Perhaps we have asked for guidance in choosing between alternatives that are equally acceptable or equally unacceptable. I suggest that there is not a right and wrong to every question. To many questions, there are only two wrong answers or two right answers. Thus, a person who seeks guidance on which of two different ways he should pursue to get even with a person who has wronged him is not likely to receive a revelation. Neither is a person who seeks guidance on a choice he will never have to make because some future event will intervene, such as a third alternative that is clearly preferable. On one occasion, my wife and I prayed earnestly for guidance on a decision that seemed very important. No answer came. We were left to proceed on our own best judgment. We could not imagine why the Lord had not aided us with a confirming or restraining impression. But it was not long before we learned that we did not have to make a decision on that question because something else happened that made a decision unnecessary. The Lord would not guide us in a selection that made no difference.

No answer is likely to come to a person who seeks guidance in choosing between two alternatives that are equally acceptable to the Lord. Thus, there are times when we can serve productively in two different fields of labor. Either answer is right. Similarly, the Spirit of the Lord is not likely to give us revelations on matters that are trivial. I once heard a young woman in testimony meeting praise the spirituality of her husband, indicating that he submitted every question to the Lord. She told how he accompanied her shopping and would not even choose between different brands of canned vegetables without making his selection a matter of prayer. That strikes me as improper. I believe the Lord expects us to use the intelligence and experience He has given us to make these kinds of choices. When a member asked the Prophet Joseph Smith for advice on a particular matter, the Prophet stated: "It is a great thing to inquire at the hands of God, or to come into His presence: and we feel fearful to approach Him on subjects that are of little or no consequence."[10]

Of course, we are not always able to judge what is trivial. If a matter appears of little or no consequence, we should proceed on the basis of our own judgment. If the choice is important for reasons unknown to us, such as the speaking invitation I mentioned earlier or a choice between two cans of vegetables when one contains a hidden poison, the Lord will intervene and give us guidance. Where a choice will make a real difference in our lives—obvious or not—and where we are living in tune with the Spirit and seeking its guidance, we can be sure that we will receive the guidance we need to attain our goal. The Lord will not leave us unassisted when a choice is important to our eternal welfare.

Notes

1. James E. Talmage, *Articles of Faith*, 12th ed. (Salt Lake City: The Church of Jesus Christ of Latter-day Saints, 1924), 229.

2. Boyd K. Packer, "Prayers and Answers," *Ensign*, November 1979, 19–20.

3. Lorenzo Snow, in Conference Report, April 1899, 52.

4. Harold B. Lee, *Stand Ye in Holy Places* (Salt Lake City: Deseret Book, 1974), 141–42.

5. Bruce R. McConkie, "Agency or Inspiration—Which?" in *Speeches of the Year: BYU Devotional Addresses 1972–1973* (Provo, UT: Brigham Young University Press, 1973), 107, 111.

6. See McConkie, "Agency and Inspiration—Which?" 108, 110, 113.

7. See Matthias F. Cowley, *Wilford Woodruff: History of His Life and Labors* (Salt Lake City: Bookcraft, 1964), 31–32.

8. *Teachings of the Prophet Joseph Smith*, comp. Joseph Fielding Smith (Salt Lake City: Deseret Book, 1976), 151.

9. Packer, "Prayers and Answers," 19–20.

10. *History of the Church of Jesus Christ of Latter-day Saints*, ed. B. H. Roberts, 2nd ed. rev. (Salt Lake City: Deseret Book, 1957), 1:339

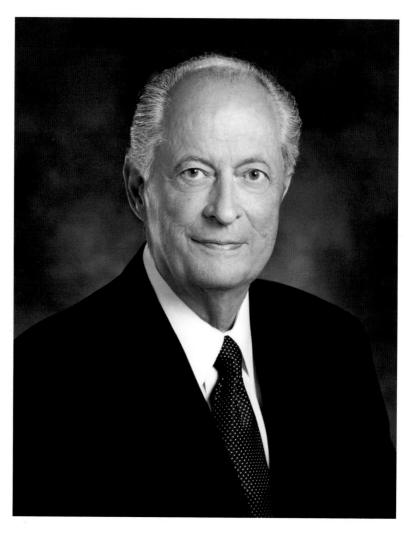

Elder Robert D. Hales is a member of the Quorum of the Twelve Apostles. Address at the Brigham Young University Campus Education Week on August 19, 2008, published in *Religious Educator* 10, no. 2 (2008): 1–13.

9 THE JOURNEY OF LIFELONG LEARNING

Today in this devotional I am honored to be addressing those committed to lifelong learning.

Our quest for knowledge and our journey of eternal progression began long before our mortal existence. We are given a clear understanding that during the Council in Heaven we used our agency, choosing to come to earth and participate in mortality. In choosing to come to this earth, we were choosing the opportunity to progress, to grow, and to gain more knowledge. And in that process of learning and coming to earth, taking upon us a mortal body to gain knowledge and to experience mortality is an essential part of our eternal learning and progression.

The theme of lifelong learning is important because for Latter-day Saints the lifelong pursuit of knowledge is not only secular but spiritual. We understand that gaining knowledge is essential to gaining eternal salvation. Brigham Young said, "Should our lives be extended to a thousand years, still we may live and learn."[1]

For most worldly and temporal possessions, the old adage is true: You can't take it with you. However, the intellectual treasures of knowledge and spiritual values hold a promise of eternal significance. We read in the Doctrine and Covenants, "Whatever principle of intelligence we attain unto in this life, it will rise with us in the resurrection. And if a person gains more knowledge and intelligence in this life through his diligence and obedience than another, he will have so much the advantage in the world to come" (D&C 130:18–19).

So while mortality is only a small moment in eternity, learning throughout our mortal lives is an essential part of our eternal education. Here on earth, as Brigham Young once observed, "we are in a great school."²

When we see our learning here as part of our eternal education, we raise our sights for learning. As children, we might have begun learning because our parents coaxed or cajoled us. They wanted us to acquire a formal education with college degrees or technical labor skills, knowing that at the end of our labors we would be rewarded by being self-sufficient, productive, and able to survive in the real world. Some of us studied hard as we became interested in the stiff competition for grades and honors.

While these motivations for learning played important roles at different times in our lives, if they are our only motivations, we will stop learning when our parents or teachers are gone and our degrees are earned. Lifelong learners are driven by more eternal motives. One of the giant steps in maturing and acquiring knowledge and experience is when we learn for the joy of being edified rather than for the pleasure of being entertained. The goal of the wisest lifelong learners is not so much to impress others but to improve themselves and to help others. Their desire is to learn and to change their behavior by following the sound counsel and example imparted from great teachers around them.

Sometimes our learning is limited if we think of it as only one course at a time or getting one degree. But as we look to the scriptures, they give us the curriculum of the lifetime learner: "Things both in heaven and in the earth, and under the earth; things which have been, things which are, things which must shortly come to pass; things which are at home, things which are abroad; the wars and the perplexities of the nations, and the judgments which are on the land; and a knowledge also of countries and of kingdoms" (D&C 88:79).

The first verse of the Book of Mormon reads, "I, Nephi, having been born of goodly parents, therefore I was taught somewhat in all the learning of my father" (1 Nephi 1:1). Just as Nephi's field of study was all that his father knew, lifelong learners know no disciplinary boundaries in their quest for greater knowledge.

Lifelong learners have an insatiable inner desire to acquire knowledge in a broad range of subjects and disciplines. Thus the reward for lifelong learners is simply the joy of learning and acquiring knowledge in a wide spectrum of subjects that interest them.

Some may wonder whether it is possible to teach lifelong learning or if it is simply a genetic gift. Just as some are born with greater speed, some of us may naturally have a greater desire for learning. Yet just as wise coaches can improve anyone willing to pay the price, in like manner Heavenly Father is eager to bless us with the drive and determination to become lifelong learners if we are willing to pay the price.

Oftentimes it takes a great teacher to motivate us and to instill that desire in us. How can we improve our desire and increase the desire of others to gain more knowledge over a lifetime of learning experiences?

Attributes of Lifelong Learners

It is important to consider the attributes that one must acquire to become a lifelong learner. A few of the basic attributes needed to become a lifelong learner are courage, faithful desire, humility, patience, curiosity, and a willingness to communicate and share the knowledge that we gain. Let's take a moment to pause and reflect in more depth how each of these attributes may contribute to our becoming a lifelong learner. And the other side of the coin would be to consider how we may be able to instill lifelong learning in those around us, especially our children.

Courage. "Be of good courage, and he shall strengthen your heart, all ye that hope in the Lord" (Psalm 31:24).

Lifelong learners have the courage to overcome the fear of leaving the outer limits of their educational comfort zone and entering into the unknown and the unfamiliar. The scriptures say, "For God hath not given us the spirit of fear; but of power, and of love, and of a sound mind" (2 Timothy 1:7).

Too often we dwell in the comfort of our educational strengths and avoid overcoming our educational weaknesses. Thus our greatest strengths can become our greatest weaknesses. We may dwell in the security of the past, unwilling to venture into the future because of the fear of ignorance or the lack of knowledge about a subject we desire to study or to research. We need the courage to take a long step of faith into a fearful darkness, not knowing how deep the educational cave is that we are about to enter.

Fear is only dispelled by the amount of intellectual light we are willing to shine on the dark educational abyss that is a void in our understanding. We must find the courage to go forward—to press on. We read in the Doctrine and Covenants, "There were fears in your hearts, and verily this is the reason that ye did not receive" (D&C 67:3). Despite our fears, courage in acquiring new learning is essential for lifelong learners.

Faithful desire. "Seek ye diligently and teach one another words of wisdom; yea, seek ye out of the best books words of wisdom; seek learning, even by study and also by faith" (D&C 88:118).

Next is faithful desire. Lifelong learners have an insatiable, unselfish inner desire to acquire a wide spectrum of knowledge across many disciplines for the mere joy of attaining and sharing the increased knowledge without any recognition or rewards. Oftentimes the motivation and desire for learning is stimulated by a perceived need to help others. For example, a concerned mother who feels there is a lack of a medical diagnosis concerning a family physical or mental health problem researches medical books and journals to assist in the solution.

A lifelong learner may have a desire for self-improvement to have a happier or more benevolent life. Lifelong learners have a desire for knowledge that will help them to be better helpmeets, better mothers, better fathers, better citizens, and better servants in the Lord's kingdom so "that [they] may learn and glorify the name of [their] God" (2 Nephi 6:4).

Humility. "Let him that is ignorant learn wisdom by humbling himself and calling upon the Lord his God, that his eyes may be opened that he may see, and his ears opened that he may hear" (D&C 136:32).

Next is the quality of humility. Lifelong learners recognize the source of all knowledge is a gift from God. "He that truly humbleth himself . . . , the same shall be blessed" (Alma 32:15).

Because lifelong learners recognize that intelligence is a gift of God, they do not dwell on it or become prideful about their personal intelligence quotient or accomplishments. Each new discovery of knowledge is metered out from on high in the Lord's time and in the Lord's way "line upon line, precept upon precept" (2 Nephi 28:30).

When we are truly humble, we remember that knowledge and wisdom are given to us by the Lord and that we are to use that knowledge and wisdom in lifting and strengthening others: "To every man is given a gift by the Spirit of God. To some is given one, and to some is given another, that all may be profited thereby" (D&C 46:11–12). We gain knowledge to better serve.

Patience. "Add to your faith virtue; and to virtue knowledge; and to knowledge temperance; and to temperance patience; and to patience godliness" (2 Peter 1:5–6).

Lifelong learners acquire an inordinate degree of patience in their quest for learning. They understand through their diligent search for learning that it takes a great deal of energy and a great deal of time to find pure knowledge.

What a feeling! Have you ever sought for something—searched, pondered, and prayed—until *finally* there it was, right before you? Sometimes what we learn today may not seem valuable until months or even years into the future. We not only learn but we ponder that knowledge so that in the right place, at the right time, we can put it to the best use.

Curiosity. "I applied mine heart to know, and to search, and to seek out wisdom, and the reason of things" (Ecclesiastes 7:25).

The next quality is curiosity. My sister used to say to me, "Curiosity killed the cat, but satisfaction brought him back."

Lifelong learners are curious at heart. As children, our curiosity is instinctive, but our formal education is more confining and systematic. Lifelong learners develop personalized learning techniques that surpass what is taught in school. The key learning element is that they never lose their God-given inherent curiosity. They are simply detectives or sleuths in the image of Sherlock Holmes, solving a case by putting together the facts that they have gathered. They do it by asking the question "why" and then finding the answers. The thrill of investigating and researching a new concept or discovering the answer to something previously unknown to us is an exhilarating moment of joy and satisfaction.

Lifelong learners learn "line upon line" and "precept upon precept" but also have personal "aha" moments when they see all at once the larger picture. The lifelong learner does not give up. Thomas Edison was a lifelong learner. He was attributed as saying, "I have not failed, I've just found ten thousand ways that won't work."

Communication. "Wherefore, he that preacheth and he that receiveth, understand one another, and both are edified and rejoice together" (D&C 50:22).

Lifelong learners are teachers at heart, reveling in the communication of learning and knowledge. They find joy when those whom they teach by sharing their knowledge are uplifted and strengthened. They communicate with God through prayer for guidance and knowledge. They communicate with God to give thanks and gratitude for the knowledge they have received. They communicate with other lifelong learners, listening intensively in a two-way exchange of learning that is mutually beneficial to all.

Great teachers are not only great communicators but also great listeners. When we are communicating, we can learn something from every individual we meet.

Great teachers produce lifelong learners. Great teachers do not provide all the answers to their students. They lead them to the fountain of knowledge and instill in them a desire to drink. Great teachers motivate students to seek knowledge.

One educator was in a meeting with President Packer in a question-and-answer period. President Packer was asked about his teachings on the Atonement. What did he teach? They wanted a testimony and a full dissertation from him on the Atonement. That's what they expected from this great teacher. His answer taught everyone there about lifelong learning. President Packer replied, "Read the Book of Mormon a few times, searching for teachings about the Atonement. Then write a one-page summary of what you have learned. Then, my dear brother, you will have your answer."

SCRIPTURE STUDY AND LIFELONG LEARNING

Scripture study is a lifelong learning experience. Perhaps nowhere can we see the need for lifelong learning more clearly than with scripture study. No matter how many times we may read the scriptures, through the power and inspiration of the Holy Ghost we learn new truths and gain valuable counsel and insights to meet life's challenges. President Ezra Taft Benson taught, "Yesterday's meal is not enough to sustain today's needs. So also an infrequent reading of [the Book of Mormon,] 'the most correct of any book on earth,' as Joseph Smith called it, is not enough."[3]

The primary purposes of scripture study are to gain gospel understanding and to strengthen us spiritually. One reason we need to continually feast on the words of Christ is that, like all learning, gospel understanding and spiritual insights come one precept at a time.

Scripture study is a unique form of learning. It requires literacy—the ability to read. King Mosiah taught his sons "in all the language of his fathers, that thereby they might become men of understanding; and that they might know concerning the prophecies which had been spoken by the mouths of their fathers, which were delivered them by the hand of the Lord" (Mosiah 1:2).

Mosiah wasn't just teaching his sons how to read so they could get ahead in the world; he was teaching them to read so they could immerse themselves in the scriptures and become spiritually wise.

The brass plates were preserved and taken to the promised land so that Lehi's family and his posterity would not forget who they were, "a chosen people," and would be reminded how they were to live as children of God. It is for the same purpose that the scriptures have been preserved for us in this day and at this time.

But gaining knowledge through scripture study requires some attributes and actions that most formal educational endeavors do not: sincere desire, unwavering faith, prayer, and the will and obedience to follow the Spirit's promptings. Virtually all humans upon earth, no matter what their mental capacity, can experience the joy and rewards of lifetime gospel study.

Scripture study does not require years of formal education to gain an understanding of essential gospel principles. This is illustrated by

Peter and John in the book of Acts. The Jewish rulers were surprised. They assumed that gospel knowledge required some exhaustive, formal course of training. The scriptures tell us: "Now when they saw the boldness of Peter and John, and perceived that they were unlearned and ignorant men, they marvelled; and they took knowledge of them, that they had been with Jesus" (Acts 4:13).

Unlearned and ignorant in the eyes of the world, Peter and John had gained great gospel knowledge from listening and hearkening to the words of our Savior. The same can be true for each of us and for every member of our family. In gospel study, a master's degree in theology is far less valuable than the degree of knowledge we can all obtain from the Master Himself.

A critical component in gaining knowledge from the Savior is acting upon the principles He taught. In order to gain the greatest insights the scriptures have to offer, our study will focus not so much on places and names as on principles and doctrines. It is not simply book knowledge we are after but insights that will change the way we live and that will actually make a difference in our lives. We must see the scriptures for what they are: an instruction manual for becoming like our Savior.

Lifelong scripture study is an unending quest for spiritual insights and understanding and for the growth that results when we apply such insights in our lives. As Latter-day Saints, we understand that acquiring spiritual knowledge, having spiritual experiences, and developing our gifts and aptitudes are important to our mortal growth. In addition, we must develop our spiritual dispositions in relation to God, our Father, and His Son, Jesus Christ, and cultivate the qualities of faith and obedience that will invite the Holy Ghost into our lives. We also grow in spirit as we serve and care for our neighbors and the world around us. All of these elements of lifelong learning have eternal consequences, and their rewards are the essence of our mortal goal to obtain spiritual qualities and achievements. The results of our most important lifelong learning are not reflected in grades or degrees or honors but in who we become. Our aim is to develop eternal character values such as knowledge, hope, faith, charity, and love. This is the most important quest we have in learning.

Studying the scriptures helps us develop and progress as individuals. The scriptures are uniquely suited for lifelong study.

As we increase our spiritual, emotional, and mental capacity through the years, we qualify to gain new insights from the scriptures. How many times have you paused and pondered on a passage of scripture that you have read and passed over many times before and then, in a *revelatory* moment, have a *new awareness*, a *new understanding*, brought to your heart and mind granting additional insight—and that added insight solves a question, a problem, or one of life's challenges. That, my brothers and sisters, is the sweet mystery of lifelong learning—a sweet instant in a blessed moment in time when you experience a leap of faith and understanding.

It is for this reason that we have prayer before and after scripture study. The prayer before scripture study is to prepare us spiritually to receive the *revelatory moments* and a spiritual uplift. The prayer after scripture study is to give thanks and gratitude for that which has been given us.

The knowledge of the truths of the restored gospel of Jesus Christ is the most valuable knowledge we will ever possess. That knowledge is found in the word of God in the scriptures, through living prophets, and in the temple. The endowment is the eternal curriculum. In it we are taught where we came from and why we are here on earth, and we are even given the promise of achieving life eternal in the celestial kingdom if we obey the commandments and covenants we've taken upon ourselves.

Lifelong Learning—Past, Present, and Future

In addition to all the attributes we have talked about, lifelong learners see the connection between what we have learned in the past, what we are learning now, and what we can learn in the future. Lifelong learners are cumulative learners. They put together all that they have learned to help them. They will never dwell in the past because they are eager to explore the future. They will always be open to new concepts, being blessed with inquisitive minds that seek new knowledge on a daily basis.

Lifelong learners spend their lives doing better than their best! Sometimes our best is not good enough. Being challenged to do better than our best may seem unreasonable or defy intuitive logic, but personal progress is just simply that! The reality is that sometimes our best of today is not good enough to succeed in tomorrow's world.

For example, in the 2004 Olympics, American swimmer Michael Phelps, who we've heard a lot about lately, won the bronze medal in the men's 200-meter freestyle with a time of one minute forty-five seconds. Four years ago that was his best. But he knew that to win the gold medal in that event in 2008 he would have to do better than his best, so he set about training to meet that goal. Millions have had the opportunity to watch the Olympic saga that has unfolded as he did better than his previous best, setting a new world record of one minute forty-two seconds and winning a gold medal. In Beijing he shattered his own previous world record by a full second and improved upon Mark Spitz's winning time of 1972 by ten seconds. Think how fast that is! In fact, he shaved off over a full minute from the gold medal winning time in 1904 of two minutes forty-four seconds. Just imagine, today in just a minute they swim two laps of the pool! That's how far he would have finished ahead of the winner in 1904. It is remarkable that of Michael Phelps's 2008 gold medals, seven of his times beat world records; they were not only his own records but world records. The other, his eighth medal, set an Olympic record. Can you imagine being able to do that, and doing better than your best? What an example for us!

The reality is that if we do not improve our efforts and our achievements each day, our best in yesterday's past will not meet the demands of tomorrow's future. This principle of doing better than our best each day applies to both spiritual and temporal demands in our mortal lifetime of learning as we prepare, covenant, and meet the requirements of eternal salvation.

Sometimes the magnificent vista of learning is not limited by the capacity of our mind but rather by the artificial limitations we place upon ourselves and our ability to learn. We must expand the capacity of our mind. Just think of what our learning limitations were before the computer became a universal tool for research, learning, and Internet communication. It is hard for our grandchildren to imagine how we were educated without computers. (Or, for that matter, how we lived without a cell phone or survived without pizza as a diet staple. The list is endless.)

I would like to share with you a unique personal learning experience spanning over thirty years that relates to the emerging computer technology benefits in family history research. In the 1970s I observed Elder Theodore H. Burton presenting the future concept of computers being used for family records and research. He was even bold enough to teach and proclaim that the computer technology was given to man for use to hasten the day of family history, genealogy, and temple work.

Elder Burton's initial computer proclamation was met with understandable reservations: "Computers will always be too big and too expensive for personal use." "There will never be enough Church members with computers." "So few of the members are able to operate computers." "The detail and explanation required and the examination required to make personal research compatible with temple records are too complex." All seemed reasonable reservations for their time, but what of the future computer developments?

Today we are embarking on a new era of family history computer technology. With the upcoming release of the new system—already available in half of the temple districts around the world—we will be able to prepare and submit names of our ancestors for temple work from our homes using a new Internet-based system. This new system will help you readily see which ancestors need proxy temple ordinances and make it possible to print a summary page with a bar code that when scanned in the temple will print out a card for use in temple sessions. After an ordinance is completed, a record of the completed ordinance is typically available on this secure Web site within twenty-four hours.

Now, why do I tell this story to you as lifelong learners? I have a simple message. Never dwell on the past or attempt to protect your comfort zone against the inevitable changes required to meet the future advancements that will be needed. When Jesus said "It is finished"

(John 19:30) as He died on the cross, it was the end of only one mission—the Atonement. He then went on to see those in eternity to shore them up and to give them hope (see D&C 138). We read in 3 Nephi that in yet another mission experience He also visited the faithful at the temple in the New World as a resurrected being, blessing them for their faithfulness. In our lives, as in the Savior's example, our endings only usher in new beginnings. The ending of one era ushers in a new era. Lifelong learners do not dwell on the past.

Past learning creates a valuable foundation of experience upon which to build, not a comfortable place to dwell for a lifetime.

Sometimes when we reach a milestone we viewed as an ultimate goal, we may find ourselves once the elation has passed almost depressed—for example, when you finish a mission or when the honeymoon is over. There is a moment of shocking, stark reality when you ask yourself, "What next? What do I do now?" At such times, remember the end is only the dawn of a new beginning.

As you stand atop any peak you have climbed, enjoy the moment of satisfaction in the present to look at the remarkable view and the progress you have made from the past. But then turn around to see what new peaks are now in sight and set a course to climb higher into the future. When you do this, the achievement of one goal set in the past will eventually pave the way to a higher goal of achievement in the future. As we contemplate the sacrifice and hard work that was required to achieve past goals, let us muster the confidence and determination needed to move on to greater heights.

Let me pause once again and talk to you from the depths of my heart about one of the unique experiences of learning. The real meaning of lifelong learning takes shape in the circle of past, present, and future—progressing as time moves on in its swift, inevitable pace. Time stops for no man. In fact, one of the few common possessions we all share is time. What we do with our time will determine the degree of lifelong learning and spiritual values we take to the eternities following our mortal test.

Also, let me spend a moment or two talking about a unique lifelong learning experience for a woman—*motherhood*.

MOTHERHOOD: THE IDEAL OPPORTUNITY FOR LIFELONG LEARNING

Motherhood is the ideal opportunity for lifelong learning. A mother's learning grows as she nurtures the child in his or her development years. They are both learning and maturing together at a remarkable pace. It's exponential, not linear. Just think of the learning process of a mother throughout the lifetime of her children. Each child brings an added dimension to her learning because their needs are so varied and far-reaching.

For example, in the process of rearing her children, a mother studies such topics as child development; nutrition; health care; physiology; psychology; nursing with medical research and care; and educational tutoring in many diverse fields such as math, science, geography, literature, English, and foreign languages. She develops gifts such as music, athletics, dance, and public speaking. The learning examples could continue endlessly. Just think of the spiritual learning that is required as a mother teaches about gospel principles and prepares for teaching family home evening and auxiliary lessons in Primary, Relief Society, Young Women, and Sunday School.

My point is, my dear sisters—as well as for the brethren, who I hope are listening carefully—a mother's opportunity for lifelong learning and teaching is universal in nature. My dear sisters, don't ever sell yourself short as a woman or as a mother.

It never ceases to amaze me that the world would state that a woman is in a form of servitude that does not allow her to develop her gifts and talents. Nothing, absolutely nothing, could be further from the truth. Do not let the world define, denigrate, or limit your feelings of lifelong learning and the values of motherhood in the home—both here mortally and in the eternal learning and benefits you give to your children and to your companion.

Lifelong learning is essential to the vitality of the human mind, body, and soul. It enhances self-worth and self-actuation. Lifelong learning is invigorating mentally and is a great defense against aging, depression, and self-doubt. When we stand still in seeking new knowledge, our forward learning progress ceases and mental stagnation begins.

Progress and improvement are the essence of lifelong learning. You will not be surprised to know that there is only one ultimate goal: living a faithful life and enduring to the end worthy of eternal salvation and glory. All other goals and achievements are corollary to faithfully enduring to the end. Indeed, it is the plan of life set forth in the scriptures for our eternal benefit.

The learning process taught by Solomon in the Holy Bible in the book of Proverbs is helpful to aid us in understanding the nature of lifelong learning. "Happy is the man that findeth wisdom, and the man that getteth understanding" (Proverbs 3:13).

To further explain, we start with basic intelligence, or an IQ, which is God-given as one of the gifts bestowed on mankind. "The glory of God is intelligence, or, in other words, light and truth" (D&C 93:36).

To basic intelligence we add knowledge, which comes to us through learning and experience.

The sum of basic intelligence plus knowledge and experience equals wisdom. "Wisdom is the principal thing; therefore get wisdom: and with all thy getting get understanding" (Proverbs 4:7).

The world stops at wisdom's level of learning, but the scriptures teach "The Lord by *wisdom* hath founded the *earth*; by *understanding* hath he established the *heavens*" (Proverbs 3:19; emphasis added).

Wisdom plus the gifts of the Holy Ghost provide an understanding in our hearts. When we truly have an understanding and our hearts are softened, we will "no more desire to do evil" (Alma 19:33).

We will have "an eye single to the glory of God" (D&C 82:19) and desire to return with honor into the presence of our Heavenly Father and His Son, Jesus Christ.

Here is a lifetime homework assignment for you! Ponder and seek to acquire the remarkable attributes of a lifelong learner: courage, faithful desire, curiosity, humility, patience, and willingness to communicate. These are desirable character qualities. Ponder and ask yourself these questions: "What is the meaning and value of each of these qualities to me?" "How do these qualities apply to me?" "How am I going to have each of these qualities be part of my life?" Then for a few minutes ponder these qualities and ask yourself what you can do to enhance them in your character and in your life. Even if you only take one of the qualities and seek to improve yourself, it will make a difference. The reward will be great in your future for you and for those around you.

I hope you can see the value of reviewing your ultimate goals with an eye to lifelong learning perspectives and to life's cycle of past, present, and future. May your life be one of learning—growing in knowledge, intelligence, and wisdom while seeking spiritual values and characteristics that will bless you with the rewards of eternal life.

Seek to Know That God Lives

I give you my testimony that God lives and that we can learn not just to believe but to know that God lives. Seek that knowledge. It will be granted to you. Seek to know and to have those around you know, through your testimony, that Joseph Smith was a prophet of God and that in this last dispensation of the fulness of time we have had restored to us all that has ever been restored to mankind. Learn all that you can within our temples and our scriptures. Learn and conduct your life in such a way that you may return to the presence of our Father and His Son. I pray that our desires and goals will be to become lifelong learners to accomplish that end, in the name of Jesus Christ, amen.

Notes

1. Brigham Young, in *Journal of Discourses* (London: Latter-day Saints' Book Depot, 1854–86), 9:292.
2. Brigham Young, in *Journal of Discourses*, 12:124.
3. Ezra Taft Benson, "A New Witness for Christ," *Ensign*, November 1984, 6–7; quoting Joseph Smith, *History of the Church of Jesus Christ of Latter-day Saints*, ed. B. H. Roberts, 2nd ed. rev. (Salt Lake City: Deseret News, 1957), 4:461.

Elder Jeffrey R. Holland is a member of the Quorum of the Twelve Apostles. Address at the Sidney B. Sperry Symposium at Brigham Young University on October 7, 1995, published in *A Book of Mormon Treasury: Gospel Insights from General Authorities and Religious Educators* (Provo, UT: Religious Studies Center, Brigham Young University, 2003), 47–66.

10 RENDING THE VEIL OF UNBELIEF

I F ONE WERE TO ASK a casual reader of the Book of Mormon to name the principal character in that book, the responses would undoubtedly vary. For one thing, any record covering more than a thousand years of history—with all the persons such a history would include—is unlikely to have any single, central figure emerge over such an extended period as the principal character. Nonetheless, after acknowledging that limitation, perhaps some might list any one of several favorite, or at least memorable, persons. Such names as Mormon, the abridger for whom the book is named; or Nephi, the book's early and very recognizable young prophet; or Alma, to whom so many pages are devoted; or Moroni, the fearless captain who flew the title of liberty; or his namesake, who concluded the book and delivered it some fourteen hundred years later to the young Joseph Smith—these would undoubtedly be among some of those figures mentioned.

All of these responses would be provocative, but they would also be decidedly incorrect. The principal and commanding figure in the Book of Mormon, from first chapter to last, is the Lord Jesus Christ, of whom the book is truly "another testament." From the first page—indeed, from the book's title page—to the last declaration in the text, this testament reveals, demonstrates, examines, and underscores the divine mission of Jesus Christ as recorded in the sacred accounts of two New World dispensations, accounts written for the benefit of a third dispensation, the last and greatest of all dispensations, the dispensation of the fulness of times. This sacred record, written by prophets and preserved by angels, was written for one crucial, fundamental, eternally essential reason: "to the convincing of the Jew and Gentile that Jesus is the Christ, the Eternal God, manifesting himself unto all nations" (Book of Mormon, title page).

In a remarkable vision recorded early in the Book of Mormon, the young prophet Nephi sees the eventual preparation and circulation of the Holy Bible, "a record of the Jews, which contains the covenants of the Lord, which he hath made unto the house of Israel" (1 Nephi 13:23). But, alarmingly, he also sees the abuse and doctrinal decimation of that book as it moves down through the ages and passes through many hands.

It was foretold in this vision that the Bible record would be clear and untarnished in the meridian of time, that in its beginning "it contained the fulness of the gospel of the Lord," with both Old and New Testaments going "from the Jews in purity unto the Gentiles" (1 Nephi 13:24–25). But over time, through both innocent error and malicious design, many doctrines and principles, especially those emphasizing covenantal elements of "the gospel of the Lamb," were lost—and sometimes were simply willfully expunged—from "the book of the Lamb of God" (1 Nephi 13:26, 28). Unfortunately, these missing elements were both "plain and precious" (1 Nephi 13:28)—plain, we presume, in their clarity and power and ability to be understood; precious surely in their profound worth, gospel significance, and eternal importance. Whatever the reason for or source of the loss of these truths from the biblical record, that loss has resulted in "pervert[ing] the right ways of the Lord, . . . blind[ing] the eyes and harden[ing] the hearts of the children of men" (1 Nephi 13:27). In painful understatement, "an exceedingly great many do stumble" (1 Nephi 13:29). Honest women and men are less informed of gospel truths and less secure in the salvation of Christ than they deserve to be because of the loss of vital truths from the biblical canon as we have it in modernity (see 1 Nephi 13:21–29).

But in His love and foreknowledge, the great Jehovah, the premortal Christ, promised Nephi, and all who have received Nephi's record, that after the Gentiles do stumble exceedingly, because of the most plain and precious parts of the gospel of the Lamb which have been kept back . . . I will be merciful unto the Gentiles in that day, insomuch that I will bring forth unto them, in mine own power, much of my gospel, which shall be plain and precious, saith the Lamb.

For, behold, saith the Lamb: I will manifest myself unto thy seed, that they shall write many things which I shall minister unto them, which shall be plain and precious. . . .

And in them shall be written my gospel, saith the Lamb, and my rock and my salvation. (1 Nephi 13:34–36)

This promised record, now known to the world as the Book of Mormon, along with "other books" that have now come forth by the revelatory power of the Lamb,

shall make known the plain and precious things which have been taken away from [the Bible]; and shall make known to all kindreds, tongues, and people, *that the Lamb of God is the Son of the Eternal Father, and the Savior of the world; and that all men must come unto him, or they cannot be saved.*

And they must come according to the words which shall be established by the mouth of the Lamb; and the words of the Lamb shall be made known in the records of thy seed, as well as in [the Bible]; wherefore they both shall be established in one; for there is one God and one Shepherd over all the earth. (1 Nephi 13:39–41; emphasis added)

Surely the most plain and precious of all truths lost from the Bible, particularly the Old Testament, are the clear, unequivocal, and extensive declarations regarding the coming of Christ and the eternal, essential covenantal elements of His gospel that have been taught beginning with Adam and continuing in each dispensation of time. Thus, the highest and most revered purpose of the Book of Mormon is to restore to Abraham's seed that crucial message declaring Christ's divinity, convincing all who read its pages "with a sincere heart, with real intent" that Jesus is the Christ (Moroni 10:4).

The fact that four-fifths of this record comes out of a period *before* Christ's birth, the fact that it is a record of an otherwise unknown people, the fact that inspiring insights and deep doctrines regarding Jesus are revealed here and found nowhere else in the biblical canon—or all of Christendom, for that matter—and the fact that the Book of Mormon reaffirms the truthfulness and divinity of that Bible insofar as the latter has been translated correctly are just a few of the reasons that the book should rightly be considered the most remarkable and important religious text produced since the New Testament gospels were compiled nearly two millennia ago. Indeed, in light of the plain and precious portions that have been lost from the New Testament as well as the Old Testament, it could be said that in restoring ancient biblical truths and adding scores of new ones about the Only Begotten Son of the Living God of us all, the Book of Mormon links with the Holy Bible to form the most remarkable and important religious text ever given to the world in any age of time.

The Book of Mormon has many purposes, and it contains many true and stimulating principles, but one purpose transcends all others in both kind and degree. That purpose is "the convincing of the Jew and Gentile that Jesus is the Christ" (Book of Mormon, title page).

A very special contribution the Book of Mormon makes in this matter is to our knowledge of the *premortal* Christ. Christ as Jehovah, Christ as the God of Lehi and Nephi and the brother of Jared before His birth as well as the Redeemer of Mormon and Moroni after it, is one of the prominent messages of this record.

In modern times many students of religion have great difficulty in linking Old Testament theology and divinity with that which is presented in the New Testament. The Book of Mormon does so very much to bridge that gap, not only in terms of actual history, beginning six hundred years before Christ and ending four hundred years afterward, but also in the continuity of doctrine and consistent image of divinity that is taught through that period. We talk about the two sticks of Judah and Joseph coming together, as prophesied by Ezekiel, as one of the great latter-day contributions of the Book of Mormon (see Ezekiel 37:15–28); however, I think it is nearly as important to note, in bringing "sticks" together, what the Book of Mormon does to unite the Old Testament with the New Testament in a way that is not recognized or sometimes even seen as a possibility in other religious traditions.

Early Witnesses of Christ

Nephi, Jacob, and Isaiah—all living and prophesying before Christ—are positioned where they are at the beginning of the book to serve as the three ancient witnesses of the Book of Mormon or, more specifically, three special Book of Mormon witnesses of Christ, which surely they are. But that role of witness is shared by many, many others in the Book of Mormon, most of them prior to Christ's birth and ministry in mortality.

Amulek says to his fellow citizens of Ammonihah (about 74 BC), "My brethren, I think that it is impossible that ye should be ignorant of the things which have been spoken concerning the coming of Christ, who is taught by us to be the Son of God; yea, *I know that these things were taught unto you bountifully* before your dissension from among us" (Alma 34:2; emphasis added).

The coming of Christ and the particulars of His mission and message were taught bountifully throughout the entire course of the Book of Mormon. It should not be surprising that the book as we now have it begins with a vision of "One descending out of the midst of heaven, and [Lehi] beheld that his luster was above that of the sun at noon-day" (1 Nephi 1:9). This vision of the premortal Christ, accompanied in spirit by "twelve others," brought forth a book in which Lehi was bidden to read. The book spoke of "many great and marvelous things," including the plain declaration "of the coming of a Messiah, and also the redemption of the world" (1 Nephi 1:14, 19).

From these opening passages onward, the Book of Mormon speaks continually of Christ before His mortal birth, during His sojourn among both the Jews and the Nephites, and in His postmortal rule and reign in the eternities that follow. Even though His contemporaries in Jerusalem rejected that message given by Lehi, that great prophet nevertheless continued his prophecies of "a Messiah, or, in other words, a Savior of the world" (1 Nephi 10:4). Included in Lehi's very specific knowledge of the coming of Christ to mortality were such revelatory details as a vision that the Messiah would be slain and "should rise from the dead, and should make himself manifest, by the Holy Ghost, unto the Gentiles" (1 Nephi 10:11).

Whether it was this kind of revelation or something even more definitive (a personal appearance of Christ?) we do not know, but Lehi obviously had some very special manifestations regarding the Son of God. Shortly before his death, he testified to his sons, "Behold, the Lord hath redeemed my soul from hell; *I have beheld his glory,* and I am encircled about eternally in the arms of his love" (2 Nephi 1:15; emphasis added).

As early as Nephi's writings we learn the name which the Messiah shall carry, but that same Nephi is quick to acknowledge that other ancient prophets knew the name as well. "For according to the words of the prophets," he writes, "the Messiah cometh in six hundred years from the time that my father left Jerusalem; and according to the words of the prophets, and also the word of the angel of God, his name shall be Jesus Christ, the Son of God" (2 Nephi 25:19).

Nephi's brother Jacob follows that acknowledgment with a powerful testimony of the breadth of revelation and widespread knowledge of Christ that had been given to those ancient prophets. He writes:

> For this intent have we written these things, that they may know that we knew of Christ, and we had a hope of his glory many hundred years before his coming; and not only we ourselves had a hope of his glory, but also all the holy prophets which were before us.
>
> Behold, they believed in Christ and worshiped the Father in his name, and also we worship the Father in his name. And for this intent we keep the law of Moses, it pointing our souls to him. . . .
>
> Wherefore, we search the prophets, and we have many revelations and the spirit of prophecy; and having all these witnesses we obtain a hope, and our faith becometh unshaken, insomuch that

we truly can command in the name of Jesus and the very trees obey us, or the mountains, or the waves of the sea. (Jacob 4:4–6)

In that bold and persuasive spirit he pleads with his brethren: "Behold, will ye reject these words? Will ye reject the words of the prophets; and will ye reject all the words which have been spoken concerning Christ, after so many have spoken concerning him; and deny the good word of Christ, and the power of God, and the gift of the Holy Ghost, and quench the Holy Spirit, and make a mock of the great plan of redemption, which hath been laid for you?" (Jacob 6:8).

But soon enough one came doing exactly those things: Sherem, the first of the anti-Christs in the Book of Mormon. Sherem came declaring "that there should be no Christ" and in every way attempted to "overthrow the doctrine of Christ" (Jacob 7:2). Knowing that Jacob "had faith in Christ who should come," Sherem sardonically made particular effort to confront and challenge him on the practice of what Sherem called "preaching that which ye call the gospel, or the doctrine of Christ" (Jacob 7:3, 6). His argument was based on the feeble and tediously predictable reasoning of all anti-Christs—that "no man knoweth of such things; for he cannot tell of things to come" (Jacob 7:7).

Of Sherem, Jacob asks: "Believest thou the scriptures? And he said, Yea. And I said unto him: Then ye do not understand them; for they truly testify of Christ. Behold, I say unto you that none of the prophets have written, nor prophesied, save they have spoken concerning this Christ" (Jacob 7:10–11).

THE BROTHER OF JARED

One of the greatest of those prophets in the Book of Mormon—indeed, a very strong case could be made for calling him *the* greatest of the prophets in the Book of Mormon—goes unnamed in the record that documents Christ's remarkable life. That prophet is identified to the modern reader only as "the brother of Jared." Yet even in such near anonymity, the revelation that unfolded before this man's eyes was so extraordinary that his life and legacy to us have become synonymous with bold, consummate, perfect faith.

In the dispersion required of them at the time of the Tower of Babel, the people of Jared arrived at "the great sea which divideth the lands" (Ether 2:13), where they pitched their tents, awaiting further revelation regarding the crossing of a mighty ocean. For four years they awaited divine direction, but apparently they waited too casually—without supplication and exertion. Then this rather remarkable moment presented itself:

"And it came to pass at the end of four years that the Lord came again unto the brother of Jared, and stood in a cloud and talked with him. And for the space of three hours did the Lord talk with the brother of Jared, and chastened him because he remembered not to call upon the name of the Lord" (Ether 2:14).

It is difficult to imagine what a three-hour rebuke from the Lord might be like, but the brother of Jared endured it. With immediate repentance and immediate prayer, this prophet once again sought guidance for the journey they had been assigned and for those who were to pursue it. God accepted his repentance and lovingly gave further direction for this crucial mission.

For such an oceanic crossing, these families and their flocks needed seaworthy crafts similar to the barges they had constructed for earlier water travel—small, light, dish-shaped vessels identical in design above and beneath so that they were capable of staying afloat even when facing overwhelming waves or, worse yet, when they might be overturned by them. These "exceedingly tight" crafts (Ether 2:17) were obviously boats of unprecedented design and undiminished capability, made under the direction of Him who ruled the seas and the winds that rend them, to the end that the vessels might travel with the "lightness of a fowl upon the water" (Ether 2:16).

These were miraculously designed and meticulously constructed ships. But they had one major, seemingly insoluble limitation. In such a tight, seaworthy design, there was no means of allowing light for the seafarers who would travel in them. The brother of Jared "cried again unto the Lord saying: O Lord, behold I have done even as thou hast commanded me; and I have prepared the vessels for my people, and behold there is no light in them. Behold, O Lord, wilt thou suffer that we shall cross this great water in darkness?" (Ether 2:22).

Then comes an extraordinary and unexpected response from the Creator of heaven and earth and all things that in them are, He who boldly declared to Abraham, "Is anything too hard for the Lord?" (Genesis 18:14): "And the Lord said unto the brother of Jared: *What will ye that I should do* that ye may have light in your vessels?" (Ether 2:23; emphasis added).

Then, as if such a disarming inquiry from omnipotent deity is not enough, the Lord proceeds to verbalize the very problems that the brother of Jared already knows only too well.

> For behold, ye cannot have windows, for they will be dashed in pieces; neither shall ye take fire with you, for ye shall not go by the light of fire.
> For behold, ye shall be as a whale in the midst of the sea; for the mountain waves shall dash upon you. . . . *Therefore what will ye that I should prepare for you* that ye may have light when ye are swallowed up in the depths of the sea? (Ether 2:23–25; emphasis added)

Clearly the brother of Jared was being tested. The Lord had done His part—miraculously, profoundly, ingeniously. Unique, resolutely seaworthy ships for crossing the ocean had been provided. The brilliant engineering had been done. The hard part of this construction project was over. Now He wanted to know what the brother of Jared would do about incidentals.

After what has undoubtedly been a great deal of soul-searching and head-scratching, the brother of Jared comes before the Lord—perhaps red-faced but not empty-handed. In a clearly apologetic tone, he says:

> Now behold, O Lord, and do not be angry with thy servant because of his weakness before thee; for we know that thou art holy and dwellest in the heavens, and that we are unworthy before thee; because of the fall our natures have become evil continually; nevertheless, O Lord, thou hast given us a commandment that we must call upon thee, that from thee we may receive according to our desires.

> Behold, O Lord, thou hast smitten us because of our iniquity, and hast driven us forth, and for these many years we have been in the wilderness; nevertheless, thou hast been merciful unto us. O Lord, look upon me in pity, and turn away thine anger from this thy people, and suffer not that they shall go forth across this raging deep in darkness; but behold these things which I have molten out of the rock. (Ether 3:2–3)

Things—the brother of Jared hardly knows what to call them. *Rocks* probably doesn't sound any more inspiring. Here, standing next to the Lord's magnificent handiwork, these *ne plus ultra*, impeccably designed, and marvelously unique seagoing barges, the brother of Jared offers for his contribution: *rocks*. As he eyes the sleek ships the Lord has provided, it is a moment of genuine humility.

He hurries on:

> And I know, O Lord, that thou hast all power, and can do whatsoever thou wilt for the benefit of man; therefore touch these stones, O Lord, with thy finger, and prepare them that they may shine forth in darkness; and they shall shine forth unto us in the vessels which we have prepared, that we may have light while we shall cross the sea.
>
> Behold, O Lord, thou canst do this. We know that thou art able to show forth great power, which looks small unto the understanding of men. (Ether 3:4–5)

For all of his self-abasement, the faith of the brother of Jared is apparent. In fact, we might better say *transparent* in light of the purpose for which these stones will be used. Surely God, as well as the reader, feels something very striking in the childlike innocence and fervor of this man's faith. *"Behold, O Lord, thou canst do this."* Perhaps there is no more powerful single line of faith spoken by man in scripture. It is almost as if he is encouraging God, emboldening Him, reassuring Him. Not "Behold, O Lord, I am sure that thou canst do this." Not "Behold, O Lord, thou hast done many greater things than this." However uncertain the prophet is about his own ability, he has *no* uncertainty about God's power. There is nothing here but a single, clear, bold, and assertive declaration with no hint or element of vacillation. It is encouragement to Him who needs no encouragement but who surely must have been touched by it. "Behold, O Lord, thou canst do this."

THE RENDING OF THE VEIL

What happened next ranks among the greatest moments in recorded history, surely among the greatest moments in recorded faith. It forever established the brother of Jared among the greatest of God's prophets. As the Lord reaches forth to touch the stones one by one with His finger—a response, it would seem, coming in undeniable response to the commanding faith of the brother of Jared—"the veil was taken from off the eyes of the brother of Jared, and he saw the finger of the Lord; and it was as the finger of a man, like unto flesh and blood; and the brother of Jared fell down before the Lord, for he was struck with fear" (Ether 3:6).

The Lord, seeing the brother of Jared fall to the earth, commands him to rise and asks, "Why hast thou fallen?" (Ether 3:7).

The reply: "I saw the finger of the Lord, and I feared lest he should smite me; for I knew not that the Lord had flesh and blood" (Ether 3:8).

Then this marvelous declaration from the Lord: "Because of thy faith thou hast seen that I shall take upon me flesh and blood; and never has man come before me with such exceeding faith as thou hast; for were it not so ye could not have seen my finger. Sawest thou more than this?" (Ether 3:9).

The brother of Jared answers, "Nay; Lord, show thyself unto me"

Arnold Friberg, *The Brother of Jared Sees the Finger of the Lord.* © Intellectual Reserve Inc. All rights reserved.

(Ether 3:10). The Lord removed the veil completely from the eyes of the brother of Jared and came into full view of this resolutely faithful man.

Then this most remarkable revelation of the premortal Jehovah: "Behold, I am he who was prepared from the foundation of the world to redeem my people," He said.

> Behold, I am Jesus Christ. I am the Father and the Son. In me shall all mankind have life, and that eternally, even they who shall believe on my name; and they shall become my sons and my daughters.
>
> And never have I showed myself unto man whom I have created, for never has man believed in me as thou hast. Seest thou that ye are created after mine own image? Yea, even all men were created in the beginning after my own image.
>
> Behold, this body, which ye now behold, is the body of my spirit; and man have I created after the body of my spirit; and even as I appear unto thee to be in the spirit will I appear unto my people in the flesh. (Ether 3:14–16)

Before examining the doctrinal truths taught in this divine encounter, it will be useful to note two seemingly problematic issues here, issues that would seem to have reasonable and acceptable resolutions.

The first issue is suggested in two questions the Lord asks the brother of Jared during the vision as it unfolds: "Why hast thou fallen?" and "Sawest thou more than this?" It is a basic premise of Latter-day Saint theology that God "knoweth all things, and there is not anything save he knows it" (2 Nephi 9:20). The scriptures, both ancient and modern, are replete with this assertion of omniscience. Nevertheless, God has frequently asked questions of men, usually as a way to test their faith, measure their honesty, or allow their knowledge greater development. For example, he called unto Adam in the Garden of Eden, "Where art thou?" and later asked Eve, "What is this that thou hast done?" (Genesis 3:9, 13), yet an omniscient parent clearly knew the answer to both questions, for He could see where Adam was and He had watched what Eve had done. It is obvious that the questions are for the children's sake, giving Adam and Eve the responsibility of replying honestly. Later, in trying Abraham's faith, God repeatedly called out regarding Abraham's whereabouts, to which the faithful patriarch would answer: "Here am I" (Genesis 22:11). The purpose in this scriptural moment was not to provide God with information He already knew but to reaffirm Abraham's fixed faith and unwavering position in the most difficult of all parental tests. These kinds of rhetorical questions are frequently used by God, particularly in assessing faith, honesty, and the full measure of agency, allowing the "students" the freedom and opportunity to express themselves as revealingly as they wish, even though God knows the answer to His own and all other questions.

The second issue that requires preliminary comment stems from the Lord's exclamation, "Never has man come before me with such exceeding faith as thou hast; for were it not so ye could not have seen my finger" (Ether 3:9). And later, "Never have I showed myself unto man whom I have created, for never has man believed in me as thou hast" (Ether 3:15). The potential for confusion here comes with the realization that many—indeed, we would assume all—of the major prophets living prior to the brother of Jared had seen God. How then does one account for the Lord's declaration? Adam's face-to-face conversations with God in the Garden of Eden can be exempted because of the paradisiacal, prefallen state of that setting and relationship. Furthermore, other prophets' visions of God, such as those of Moses and Isaiah in the Bible, or Nephi and Jacob in the Book of Mormon, came after this "never before" experience of the brother of Jared. But before the era of the Tower of Babel, the Lord did appear unto Adam and "the residue of his posterity who were righteous" in the valley of Adam-ondi-Ahman three years before Adam's death (see D&C 107:53–55). And we are left with Enoch, who said very explicitly, "I saw the Lord; and he stood before my face, and he talked with me, even as a man talketh one with another, face to face" (Moses 7:4). We assume there would have been other prophets living in the period between Adam's leaving the Garden of Eden and the building of the Tower of Babel who also saw God in a similar manner, including Noah, who "found grace in the eyes of the Lord" and "walked with God" (Genesis 6:8–9), the same scriptural phrase used to describe Enoch's relationship with the Lord (see Genesis 5:24).

This issue has been much discussed by Latter-day Saint writers, and there are several possible explanations, any one—or all—of which may cast some light upon the larger truth of this passage. Nevertheless, without additional scriptural revelation or commentary on the matter, any conjecture is only that—conjecture—and as such is inadequate and incomplete.

One possibility is that this is simply a comment made in the context of one dispensation and as such applies only to the Jaredites and Jaredite prophets—that Jehovah has never before revealed Himself to one of their seers and revelators. Obviously this theory has severe limitations when measured against such phrases as "never before" and "never has man" and combined with the realization that Jared and his brother are the fathers of this dispensation, the first to whom God could have revealed Himself in their era.

Another suggestion is that the lowercase reference to "man" is the key to this passage, suggesting that the Lord has never revealed Himself to the unsanctified, to the nonbeliever, to temporal, earthy, natural man. The implication here is that only those who have put off the natural man, only those who are untainted by the world—in short, the sanctified (such as Adam, Enoch, and now the brother of Jared)—are entitled to this privilege.

Some have believed that the Lord here means He has never before revealed Himself to this degree or to this extent. This theory would suggest that divine appearances to earlier prophets had not been with this same "fulness," that never before had the veil been lifted to give such a complete revelation of Christ's nature and being.

A further possibility is that this is the first time Jehovah has appeared and identified Himself as Jesus Christ, the Son of God, thus the interpretation of the passage being "never have I showed myself [as Jesus Christ] unto man whom I have created" (Ether 3:15). This possibility is reinforced by one way of reading Moroni's later editorial comment: "Having this perfect knowledge of God, he could not be kept from within the veil; therefore he saw *Jesus*" (Ether 3:20; emphasis added).

Yet another interpretation of this passage is that the faith of the brother of Jared was so great he saw not only the *spirit* finger and body of the premortal Jesus (which presumably many other prophets had also seen) but also had some distinctly more revealing aspect of Christ's body of flesh, blood, and bone. Exactly what insight into the flesh-and-blood nature of Christ's future body the brother of Jared might have had is not clear, but Jehovah does say to him, "Because of thy faith thou hast seen that I shall take upon me flesh and blood" (Ether 3:9), and Moroni does say that Christ revealed Himself in this instance "in the likeness of the same body even as he showed himself unto the Nephites" (Ether 3:17). Some have taken that to mean literally "the same body" the Nephites would see—a body of flesh and blood. A safer position would be that it was at least the exact spiritual likeness of that future body. Jehovah says, "Behold, this body, which ye now behold, is the body of my spirit . . . and even as I appear unto thee to be in the spirit will I appear unto my people in the flesh" (Ether 3:16), and Moroni says, "Jesus showed himself unto this man in the spirit" (Ether 3:17).

A final—and in terms of the faith of the brother of Jared (which is the issue at hand) surely the most persuasive—explanation for me is that Christ is saying to the brother of Jared, "Never have I showed myself unto man *in this manner, without my volition, driven solely by the faith of the beholder.*" As a rule, prophets are invited into the presence of the Lord, are bidden to enter His presence by Him and only with His sanction. The brother of Jared, on the other hand, stands alone then (and we assume now) in having thrust himself through the veil, not as an unwelcome guest but perhaps technically an uninvited one. Says Jehovah, *"Never has man come before me with such exceeding faith as thou hast; for were it not so ye could not have seen my finger. . . . Never has man believed in me as thou hast"* (Ether 3:9, 15; emphasis added). Obviously the Lord Himself is linking unprecedented faith with this unprecedented vision. If the vision is not unique, then it has to be the faith— and how the vision is obtained—that is so remarkable. The only way this faith could be so remarkable would be in its ability to take this prophet, uninvited, where others had only been able to go by invitation.

Indeed it would appear that this is Moroni's own understanding of the circumstance, for he later writes, "Because of the knowledge [which has come as a result of faith] of this man *he could not be kept from beholding within the veil.* . . . Wherefore, having this perfect knowledge of God, *he could not be kept from within the veil;* therefore he saw Jesus" (Ether 3:19–20; emphasis added).

This may be one of those very provocative examples (except that it is real life and not hypothetical) about God's power. Schoolboy philosophers sometimes ask, "Can God make a rock so heavy that He cannot lift it?" or "Can God hide an item so skillfully that He cannot find it?" Far more movingly and importantly we may ask here, "Could God have stopped the brother of Jared from seeing through the veil?" At first blush one is inclined to say, "Surely God could block such an experience if He wished to." But think again. Or, more precisely, read again. "This man . . . *could not be kept from beholding within the veil; . . . he could not be kept from within the veil*" (Ether 3:19–20; emphasis added).

No, this may be an absolutely unprecedented case of a prophet's will and faith and purity so closely approaching that of heaven's that the man moves from understanding God to being actually like Him, with His same thrust of will and faith, at least in this one instance. What a remarkable doctrinal statement about the power of a mortal man's faith! And not an ethereal, unreachable, select category of a man, either. This is one who once forgot to call upon the Lord, one whose best ideas focused on rocks, and one who doesn't even have a traditional name in the book that has immortalized his remarkable feat of faith. Given such a man with such faith, it should not be surprising that the Lord would show this prophet much, show him visions that would be relevant to the mission of all the Book of Mormon prophets and to the events of the latter-day dispensation in which the book would be received.

After the prophet stepped through the veil to behold the Savior of the world, he was not limited in seeing the rest of what the eternal world revealed. Indeed, the Lord showed him "all the inhabitants of the earth which had been, and also all that would be; and he withheld them not from his sight, even unto the ends of the earth" (Ether 3:25). The staying power for such an experience was once again the faith of the brother of

Jared, for "the Lord could not withhold anything from him, for he knew that the Lord could show him all things" (Ether 3:26).

A Remarkable Vision

This vision of "all the inhabitants of the earth which had been, and also all that would be, . . . even unto the ends of the earth" (Ether 3:25) was similar to that given to Moses and others of the prophets (see Moses 1:27–29). In this case, however, it was written down in great detail and then sealed up. Moroni, who had access to this recorded vision, wrote on his plates "the very things which the brother of Jared saw" (Ether 4:4). Then he, too, sealed them up and hid them again in the earth before his death and the final destruction of the Nephite civilization. Of this vision given to the brother of Jared, Moroni wrote, "There never were greater things made manifest than those which were made manifest unto the brother of Jared" (Ether 4:4).

Those sealed plates constitute the sealed portion of the Book of Mormon which Joseph Smith did not translate. Furthermore, they will remain sealed, literally as well as figuratively, until "they shall exercise faith in me, saith the Lord, even as the brother of Jared did, that they may become sanctified in me, then will I manifest unto them the things which the brother of Jared saw, even to the unfolding unto them all my revelations, saith Jesus Christ, the Son of God, the Father of the heavens and of the earth, and all things that in them are" (Ether 4:7).

The full measure of this unprecedented and unexcelled vision—"there never were greater things made manifest"—is yet to be made known to the children of men. But consider what was made known in one man's experience in receiving it, consider that the time was approximately two thousand years before Christ's birth, and consider what is *not* presently contained in the Old Testament canon of that period regarding Jehovah and His true characteristics. These twenty-five items are all drawn from Ether 3 and 4:

1. Jehovah, the God of the pre-Christian era, was the premortal Jesus Christ, identified here by that name (see Ether 3:14).

2. Christ is both a Father and a Son in His divine relationship with the children of men (see Ether 3:14).

3. Christ was "prepared from the foundation of the world to redeem [his] people" (Ether 3:14), knowledge which had been shared before with Enoch and later would be shared with John the Revelator (see Moses 7:47; Revelation 13:8).

4. Christ had a spirit body, which looked like and was in the premortal form of His physical body, "like unto flesh and blood," including fingers, voice, face, and all other physical features (Ether 3:6).

5. Christ assisted in the creation of man, fashioning the human family "after the body of my spirit" (Ether 3:16).

6. With a spirit body and the divinity of His calling, the premortal Christ spoke audibly, in words and language understood by mortals (see Ether 3:16).

7. Christ is a God, acting for and with His Father, who is also a God (see Ether 3:14; 4:7).

8. Christ reveals some truths to some that are to be kept from others until an appointed time—His "own due time" (Ether 3:24).

9. Christ uses a variety of tools and techniques in revelation, including the interpreting power of "two stones": the Urim and Thummim (see Ether 3:23–24; D&C 17:1).

10. Christ's later atoning, redeeming role is clearly stated even before it has been realized in His mortal life. Furthermore, in a most blessed way for the brother of Jared, it is immediately efficacious. "I am he who was prepared from the foundation of the world to redeem my people," Christ says. "In me shall all mankind have life, and that eternally, even they who shall believe on my name; and they shall become my sons and my daughters" (Ether 3:14).

Then the brother of Jared has his redemption pronounced, as though the Atonement had already been carried out. "Because thou knowest these things ye are redeemed from the fall," Christ promises him, "therefore ye are brought back into my presence; therefore I show myself unto you" (Ether 3:13).

This statement underscores the eternal nature of the Atonement, its effects reaching out to all those who lived before the Savior's birth as well as all those living after it. All who in Old Testament times were baptized in Christ's name had the same claim upon eternal life that the brother of Jared had, even though Christ had not yet even been born. In matters of the Atonement, as in all other eternal promises, "time only is measured unto men" (Alma 40:8).

11. Christ had past knowledge of "all the inhabitants of the earth which had been" and foreknowledge of "all that would be," showing all of these to the brother of Jared (Ether 3:25).

Moroni, in recording the experience of the brother of Jared, adds these insights and revelations which come from the same encounter:

12. Future Saints will need to be sanctified in Christ to receive all of His revelations (see Ether 4:6).

13. Those who reject the vision of the brother of Jared will be shown "no greater things" by Christ (Ether 4:8).

14. At Christ's command "the heavens are opened and are shut," "the earth shall shake," and "the inhabitants thereof shall pass away, even so as by fire" (Ether 4:9).

15. Believers in the vision of the brother of Jared will be given manifestations of Christ's spirit. Because of such spiritual experience, belief shall turn to knowledge and they "shall know that these things are true" (Ether 4:11).

16. "Whatsoever thing persuadeth men to do good" is of Christ. Good comes of none except Christ (Ether 4:12).

17. Those who do not believe Christ's words would not believe Him personally (see Ether 4:12).

18. Those who do not believe Christ would not believe God the Father, who sent Him (see Ether 4:12).

19. Christ is the light and the life and the truth of the world (see Ether 4:12).

20. Christ will reveal "greater things" (Ether 4:13), "great and marvelous things" (Ether 4:15), and knowledge hidden "from the foundation of the world" (Ether 4:14) to those who rend the veil of unbelief and come unto Him.

21. Believers are to call upon the Father in the name of Christ "with a broken heart and a contrite spirit" if they are to "know that the Father hath remembered the covenant which he made" unto the house of Israel (Ether 4:15).

22. Christ's revelations to John the Revelator will be "unfolded in the eyes of all the people" in the last days, even as they are about to be fulfilled (Ether 4:16).

23. Christ commands all the ends of the earth to come unto Him, believe in His gospel, and be baptized in His name (see Ether 4:18).

24. Signs shall follow those who believe in Christ's name (see Ether 4:18).

25. Those faithful to Christ's name at the last day shall be "lifted up to dwell in the kingdom prepared for [them] from the foundation of the world" (Ether 4:19).

Indeed, an appeal like that of the brother of Jared is given by the Father to both Gentile and Israelite, to whom this record is sent. Asking the latter-day reader to pierce the limits of shallow faith, Christ cries:

> Come unto me, O ye Gentiles, and I will show unto you the greater things, the knowledge which is hid up because of unbelief.
>
> Come unto me, O ye house of Israel, and it shall be made manifest unto you how great things the Father hath laid up for you, from the foundation of the world; and it hath not come unto you, because of unbelief.
>
> Behold, *when ye shall rend that veil of unbelief* which doth cause you to remain in your awful state of wickedness, and hardness of heart, and blindness of mind, then shall the great and marvelous things which have been hid up from the foundation of the world from you—yea, when ye shall call upon the Father in my name, with a broken heart and a contrite spirit, then shall ye know that the Father hath remembered the covenant which he made unto your fathers, O house of Israel. (Ether 4:13–15; emphasis added)

The Book of Mormon is predicated on the willingness of men and women to "rend that veil of unbelief" in order to behold the revelations—and the Revelation—of God (Ether 4:15). It would seem that the humbling experience of the brother of Jared in his failure to pray and his consternation over the sixteen stones were included in this account to show just how mortal and just how normal he was—so very much like the men and women we know and at least in some ways so much like ourselves. His belief in himself and his view of himself may have been limited—much like our view of ourselves. But his belief in God was unprecedented. It was without doubt or limit: "I know, O Lord, that thou hast all power, and can do whatsoever thou wilt for the benefit of man; therefore touch these stones, O Lord, with thy finger" (Ether 3:4).

And from that command given to the Lord, for it does seem to be something of a command, the brother of Jared and the reader of the Book of Mormon would never be the same again. Ordinary individuals with ordinary challenges could rend the veil of unbelief and enter the realms of eternity. And Christ, who was prepared from the foundation of the world to redeem His people, would be standing at the edge of that veil to usher the believer through.

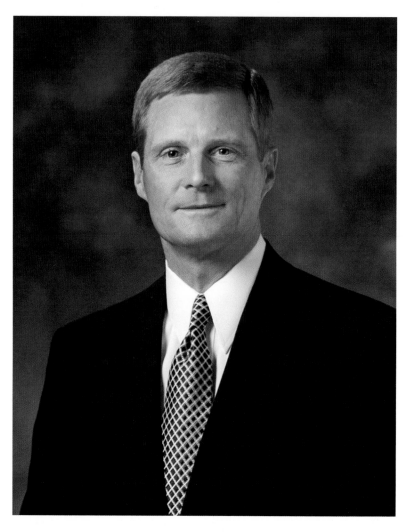

Elder David A. Bednar is a member of the Quorum of the Twelve Apostles. Address to Church Educational System religious educators at the Jordan Institute of Religion on February 3, 2006, published in *Religious Educator* 7, no. 3 (2006): 1–11.

11

Seek Learning
by Faith

I EXPRESS MY LOVE TO AND for you—and the gratitude of the Brethren for the righteous influence you have upon the youth of the Church throughout the world. Thank you for blessing and strengthening the rising generation. I pray that the Holy Ghost will bless and edify us as we share this special time together.

Companion Principles: Preaching by
the Spirit and Learning by Faith

We are admonished repeatedly in the scriptures to preach the truths of the gospel by the power of the Spirit (see D&C 50:14). I believe the vast majority of us as parents and teachers in the Church are aware of this principle and generally strive appropriately to apply it. As important as this principle is, however, it is only one element of a much larger spiritual pattern. We also frequently are taught to seek learning by faith (see D&C 88:118). Preaching by the Spirit and learning by faith are companion principles that we should strive to understand and apply concurrently and consistently.

I suspect we emphasize and know much more about a teacher teaching by the Spirit than we do about a learner learning by faith. Clearly, the principles and processes of both teaching and learning are spiritually essential. However, as we look to the future and anticipate the ever more confused and turbulent world in which we will live, I believe it will be essential for all of us to increase our capacity to seek learning by faith. In our personal lives, in our families, and in the Church, we can and will receive the blessings of spiritual strength, direction, and protection as we seek by faith to obtain and apply spiritual knowledge.

Nephi teaches us, "When a man speaketh by the power of the Holy Ghost the power of the Holy Ghost carrieth [the message] unto the hearts of the children of men" (2 Nephi 33:1). Please notice how the power of the Spirit carries the message *unto* but not necessarily *into* the heart. A teacher can explain, demonstrate, persuade, and testify, and do so with great spiritual power and effectiveness. Ultimately, however, the content of a message and the witness of the Holy Ghost penetrate into the heart only if a receiver allows them to enter.

Brothers and sisters, learning by faith opens the pathway *into* the heart. We will focus upon the individual responsibility each of us has to seek learning by faith. We also will consider the implications of this principle for us as teachers.

The Principle of Action: Faith in the Lord Jesus Christ

The Apostle Paul defined faith as "the substance of things hoped for, [and] the evidence of things not seen" (Hebrews 11:1). Alma declared that faith is not a perfect knowledge; rather, if we have faith, we "hope for things which are not seen, [but] are true" (Alma 32:21). Additionally, we learn in the *Lectures on Faith* that faith is "the first principle in revealed religion, and the foundation of all righteousness" and that it is also "the principle of action in all intelligent beings."[1]

These teachings of Paul and of Alma and from the *Lectures on Faith* highlight three basic elements of faith: (1) faith as the *assurance* of things hoped for which are true, (2) faith as the *evidence* of things not seen, and (3) faith as the principle of *action* in all intelligent beings. I describe these three components of faith in the Savior as simultaneously facing the future, looking to the past, and initiating action in the present.

Faith as the assurance of things hoped for looks to the future. This assurance is founded upon a correct understanding about and trust in God and enables us to "press forward" (2 Nephi 31:20) into uncertain and often challenging situations in the service of the Savior. For example, Nephi relied upon precisely this type of future-facing spiritual assurance as he returned to Jerusalem to obtain the plates of brass— "not knowing beforehand the things which [he] should do. Nevertheless [he] went forth" (1 Nephi 4:6–7).

Faith in Christ is inextricably tied to and results in hope in Christ for our redemption and exaltation. And assurance and hope make it possible for us to walk to the edge of the light and take a few steps into the darkness—expecting and trusting the light to move and illuminate the way.[2] The combination of assurance and hope initiates action in the present.

Faith as the evidence of things not seen looks to the past and confirms our trust in God and our confidence in the truthfulness of things not seen. We stepped into the darkness with assurance and hope, and we received evidence and confirmation as the light in fact moved and provided the illumination we needed. The witness we obtained after the trial of our faith (see Ether 12:6) is evidence that enlarges and strengthens our assurance.

Assurance, action, and evidence influence each other in an ongoing process. This helix is like a coil, and as it spirals upward it expands and grows wider. These three elements of faith—assurance, action, and evidence—are not separate and discrete; rather, they are interrelated and continuous and cycle upward. And the faith that fuels this ongoing process develops and evolves and changes. As we again turn and face forward toward an uncertain future, assurance leads to action and produces evidence, which further increases assurance. Our confidence waxes stronger, line upon line, precept upon precept, here a little and there a little.

We find a powerful example of the interaction among assurance, action, and evidence as the children of Israel transported the ark of the covenant under the leadership of Joshua (see Joshua 3:7–17). Recall how the Israelites came to the river Jordan and were promised the waters would part, or "stand upon an heap" (Joshua 3:13), and they would be able to cross over on dry ground. Interestingly, the waters did not part as the children of Israel stood on the banks of the river waiting for something to happen; rather, the soles of their feet were wet before the water parted. The faith of the Israelites was manifested in the fact that they walked into the water *before* it parted. They walked into the river

Jordan with a future-facing assurance of things hoped for. As the Israelites moved forward, the water parted, and as they crossed over on dry land, they looked back and beheld the evidence of things not seen. In this episode, faith as assurance led to action and produced the evidence of things not seen which were true.

True faith is focused in and on the Lord Jesus Christ and always leads to action. Faith as the principle of action is highlighted in many scriptures with which we are all familiar:

"For as the body without the spirit is dead, so *faith without works is dead* also" (James 2:26; emphasis added).

"But be ye *doers of the word,* and not hearers only" (James 1:22; emphasis added).

"But behold, if ye will awake and arouse your faculties, even to an *experiment upon my words,* and exercise a particle of faith" (Alma 32:27; emphasis added).

And it is faith as the principle of action that is so central to the process of learning and applying spiritual truth.

Learning by Faith: To Act and Not to Be Acted Upon

How is faith as the principle of action in all intelligent beings related to gospel learning? And what does it mean to seek learning by faith?

In the grand division of all of God's creations, there are things to act and things to be acted upon (see 2 Nephi 2:13–14). As sons and daughters of our Heavenly Father, we have been blessed with the gift of agency—the capacity and power of independent action. Endowed with agency, we are agents, and we primarily are to act and not only to be acted upon—especially as we seek to obtain and apply spiritual knowledge.

Learning by faith and from experience are two of the central features of the Father's plan of happiness. The Savior preserved moral agency through the Atonement and made it possible for us to act and to learn by faith. Lucifer's rebellion against the plan sought to destroy the agency of man, and his intent was that we as learners would only be acted upon.

Consider the question posed by Heavenly Father to Adam in the Garden of Eden, "Where art thou?" (Genesis 3:9). Obviously the Father knew where Adam was hiding, but He, nonetheless, asked the question.

Why? A wise and loving Father enabled His child to act in the learning process and not merely be acted upon. There was no one-way lecture to a disobedient child, as perhaps many of us might be inclined to deliver. Rather, the Father helped Adam as a learner to act as an agent and appropriately exercise his agency.

Recall how Nephi desired to know about the things his father, Lehi, had seen in the vision of the tree of life. Interestingly, the Spirit of the Lord begins the tutorial with Nephi by asking the following question, "Behold, what desirest thou?" (1 Nephi 11:2). Clearly the Spirit knew what Nephi desired. So why ask the question? The Holy Ghost was helping Nephi to act in the learning process and not simply be acted upon. (I encourage you at a later time to study chapters 11–14 in 1 Nephi and notice how the Spirit both asked questions and encouraged Nephi to "look" as active elements in the learning process.)

From these examples we recognize that as learners, you and I are to act and be doers of the word and not simply hearers who are only acted upon. Are you and I agents who act and seek learning by faith, or are we waiting to be taught and acted upon? Are the students we serve acting and seeking to learn by faith, or are they waiting to be taught and acted upon? Are you and I encouraging and helping those whom we serve to seek learning by faith? You and I and our students are to be anxiously engaged in asking, seeking, and knocking (see 3 Nephi 14:7).

A learner exercising agency by acting in accordance with correct principles opens his or her heart to the Holy Ghost—and invites His teaching, testifying power, and confirming witness. Learning by faith requires spiritual, mental, and physical exertion and not just passive reception. It is in the sincerity and consistency of our faith-inspired action that we indicate to our Heavenly Father and His Son, Jesus Christ, our willingness to learn and receive instruction from the Holy Ghost. Thus, learning by faith involves the exercise of moral agency to act upon the assurance of things hoped for and invites the evidence of things not seen from the only true teacher, the Spirit of the Lord.

Consider how missionaries help investigators to learn by faith. Making and keeping spiritual commitments, such as studying and praying about the Book of Mormon, attending Church meetings, and keeping the commandments, require an investigator to exercise faith and to act. One of the fundamental roles of a missionary is to help an investigator make and honor commitments—to act and learn by faith. Teaching, exhorting, and explaining, as important as they are, can never convey to an investigator a witness of the truthfulness of the restored gospel. Only as an investigator's faith initiates action and opens the pathway to the heart can the Holy Ghost deliver a confirming witness. Missionaries obviously must learn to teach by the power of the Spirit. Of equal importance, however, is the responsibility missionaries have to help investigators learn by faith.

The learning I am describing reaches far beyond mere cognitive comprehension and the retaining and recalling of information. The type of learning about which I am speaking causes us to put off the natural man (see Mosiah 3:19), to change our hearts (see Mosiah 5:2), and to be converted unto the Lord and to never fall away (see Alma 23:6). Learning by faith requires both "the heart and a willing mind" (D&C 64:34). Learning by faith is the result of the Holy Ghost carrying the power of the word of God both unto and into the heart. Learning by faith cannot be transferred from an instructor to a student through a lecture, a demonstration, or an experiential exercise; rather, a student must exercise faith and act in order to obtain the knowledge for himself or herself.

The young boy Joseph Smith instinctively understood what it meant to seek learning by faith. One of the most well-known episodes in the life of Joseph Smith was his reading of verses about prayer and faith in the book of James in the New Testament (see James 1:5–6). This text inspired Joseph to retire to a grove of trees near his home to pray and to seek for spiritual knowledge. Please note the questions Joseph had formulated in his mind and felt in his heart—and which he took into the grove. He clearly had prepared himself to "ask in faith" (James 1:6) and to act.

> In the midst of this war of words and tumult of opinions, I often said to myself: What is to be done? Who of all these parties are right; or, are they all wrong together? If any one of them be right, which is it, and how shall I know it? . . .

My object in going to inquire of the Lord was to know which of all the sects was right, that I might know which to join. No sooner, therefore, did I get possession of myself, so as to be able to speak, than I asked the Personages who stood above me in the light, which of all the sects was right . . . and which I should join. (Joseph Smith—History 1:10, 18)

Notice that Joseph's questions focused not just on what he needed to know but also on what he needed to do. And his very first question centered on action and what was to be *done*! His prayer was not simply which church is right. His question was which church should he join. Joseph went to the grove to learn by faith. He was determined to act.

Ultimately, the responsibility to learn by faith and apply spiritual truth rests upon each of us individually. This is an increasingly serious and important responsibility in the world in which we do now and will yet live. What, how, and when we learn is supported by—but is not dependent upon—an instructor, a method of presentation, or a specific topic or lesson format.

Jerry Harston, *First Vision*. Church History Museum, Salt Lake City.

Truly, one of the great challenges of mortality is to seek learning by faith. The Prophet Joseph Smith best summarizes the learning process and outcomes I am attempting to describe. In response to a request by the Twelve Apostles for instruction, Joseph taught, "The best way to obtain truth and wisdom is not to ask it from books, but to go to God in prayer, and obtain divine teaching."[3]

And on another occasion, the Prophet Joseph explained that "reading the experience of others, or the revelation given to *them*, can never give *us* a comprehensive view of our condition and true relation to God."[4]

Implications for Us as Teachers

The truths about learning by faith we have discussed thus far have profound implications for us as teachers. Let us now consider together three of these implications.

Implication 1. The Holy Ghost is the only true teacher. The Holy Ghost is the third member of the Godhead, and He is *the* teacher and witness of all truth. Elder James E. Talmage explained: "The office of the Holy Ghost in His ministrations among men is described in scripture. He is a teacher sent from the Father; and unto those who are entitled to His tuition He will reveal all things necessary for the soul's advancement."[5]

We should always remember that the Holy Ghost is the teacher who, through proper invitation, can enter into a learner's heart. Indeed, you and I have the responsibility to preach the gospel by the Spirit, even the Comforter, as a prerequisite for the learning by faith that can be achieved only by and through the Holy Ghost (see D&C 50:14). In this regard, you and I are much like the long, thin strands of glass used to create the fiber-optic cables through which light signals are transmitted over very long distances. Just as the glass in these cables must be pure to conduct the light efficiently and effectively, so we should become and remain worthy conduits through whom the Spirit of the Lord can operate.

But brothers and sisters, we must be careful to remember in our service that we are conduits and channels; we are not the light. "For it is not ye that speak, but the Spirit of your Father which speaketh in you" (Matthew 10:20). It is never about me and it is never about you. In fact, anything you or I do as an instructor that knowingly and intentionally draws attention to self—in the messages we present, in the methods we use, or in our personal demeanor—is a form of priestcraft that inhibits the teaching effectiveness of the Holy Ghost. "Doth he preach it by the Spirit of truth or some other way? And if it be by some other way it is not of God" (D&C 50:17–18).

Implication 2. We are most effective as instructors when we encourage and facilitate learning by faith. We are all familiar with the adage that giving a man a fish feeds him for one meal. Teaching the man to fish, on the other hand, feeds him for a lifetime. As gospel instructors, you and I are not in the business of distributing fish; rather, our work is to help individuals learn to "fish" and to become spiritually self-reliant. This important objective is best accomplished as we encourage and facilitate learners acting in accordance with correct principles—as we help them to learn by doing. "If any man will do his will, he shall know of the doctrine, whether it be of God" (John 7:17).

Please notice this implication in practice in the counsel given to Junius F. Wells by Brigham Young as Brother Wells was called in 1875 to organize the young men of the Church:

> At your meetings you should begin at the top of the roll and call upon as many members as there is time for to bear their testimonies and at the next meeting begin where you left off and call upon others, so that all shall take part and get into the practice of standing up and saying something. Many may think they haven't any testimony to bear, but get them to stand up and they will find the Lord will give them utterance to many truths they had not thought of before. More people have obtained a testimony while standing up trying to bear it than down on their knees praying for it.[6]

President Boyd K. Packer has given similar counsel in our day:

> Oh, if I could teach you this one principle. A testimony is to be *found* in the *bearing* of it! Somewhere in your quest for

spiritual knowledge, there is that "leap of faith," as the philosophers call it. It is the moment when you have gone to the edge of the light and stepped into the darkness to discover that the way is lighted ahead for just a footstep or two. "The spirit of man," as the scripture says, indeed "is the candle of the Lord." (Prov. 20:27.)

It is one thing to receive a witness from what you have read or what another has said; and that is a necessary beginning. It is quite another to have the Spirit confirm to you in your bosom that what *you* have testified is true. Can you not see that it will be supplied as you share it? As you give that which you have, there is a replacement, with increase![7]

I have observed a common characteristic among the instructors who have had the greatest influence in my life. They have helped me to seek learning by faith. They refused to give me easy answers to hard questions. In fact, they did not give me any answers at all. Rather, they pointed the way and helped me take the steps to find my own answers. I certainly did not always appreciate this approach, but experience has enabled me to understand that an answer given by another person usually is not remembered for very long, if remembered at all. But an answer we discover or obtain through the exercise of faith, typically, is retained for a lifetime. The most important learnings of life are caught—not taught.

The spiritual understanding you and I have been blessed to receive, and which has been confirmed as true in our hearts, simply cannot be given to another person. The tuition of diligence and learning by faith must be paid to obtain and personally "own" such knowledge. Only in this way can what is known in the mind be transformed into what is felt in the heart. Only in this way can a person move beyond relying upon the spiritual knowledge and experience of others and claim those blessings for himself or herself. Only in this way can we be spiritually prepared for what is coming. We are to "seek learning, even by study and also by faith" (D&C 88:118).

Implication 3. An instructor's faith is strengthened as he or she helps others seek learning by faith. The Holy Ghost, who can "teach [us] all things, and bring all things to [our] remembrance" (John 14:26), is eager to help us learn as we act and exercise faith in Jesus Christ. Interestingly, this divine learning assistance is perhaps never more apparent than when we are teaching, either at home or in Church assignments. As Paul made clear to the Romans, "Thou therefore which teachest another, teachest thou not thyself?" (Romans 2:21).

Please notice in the following verses from the Doctrine and Covenants how teaching diligently invites heavenly grace and instruction: "And I give unto *you* a commandment that *you* shall teach one another the doctrine of the kingdom. Teach ye diligently and my grace shall attend *you*, that *you* may be instructed more perfectly in theory, in principle, in doctrine, in the law of the gospel, in all things that pertain unto the kingdom of God, that are expedient for *you* to understand" (D&C 88:77–78; emphasis added).

Consider that the blessings described in these scriptures are intended specifically for the teacher: "Teach . . . diligently and my grace shall attend you"—that you, the teacher, may be instructed! The same principle is evident in verse 122 from the same section of the Doctrine and Covenants: "Appoint among yourselves a teacher, and let not *all* be spokesmen at once; but let one speak at a time and let *all* listen unto his sayings, that when *all* have spoken that *all* may be edified of *all*, and that every man may have an equal privilege" (D&C 88:122; emphasis added).

As all speak and as all listen in a dignified and orderly way, all are edified. The individual and collective exercise of faith in the Savior invites instruction and strength from the Spirit of the Lord.

SEEK LEARNING BY FAITH: A RECENT EXAMPLE

All of us were blessed by the challenge from the First Presidency last August to read the Book of Mormon by the end of 2005. In extending the challenge, President Gordon B. Hinckley promised that faithfully observing this simple reading program would bring into our lives and into our homes "an added measure of the Spirit of the Lord, a strengthened resolution to walk in obedience to His commandments, and a stronger testimony of the living reality of the Son of God."[8]

Please note how this inspired challenge is a classic example of learning by faith. First, you and I were not commanded, coerced, or required to read. Rather, we were invited to exercise our agency as agents and act in accordance with correct principles. President Hinckley, as an inspired teacher, encouraged us to act and not just be acted upon. Each of us, ultimately, had to decide if and how we would respond to the challenge—and if we would endure to the end of the task.

Second, in proffering the invitation to read and to act, President Hinckley was encouraging each of us to seek learning by faith. No new study materials were distributed to members of the Church, and no additional lessons, classes, or programs were created by the Church. Each of us had our copy of the Book of Mormon—and a pathway into our heart opened wider through the exercise of our faith in the Savior as we responded to the First Presidency challenge. Thus, we were prepared to receive instruction from the only true teacher, the Holy Ghost.

In recent weeks I have been greatly impressed by the testimonies of so many members concerning their recent experiences reading the Book of Mormon. Important and timely spiritual lessons have been learned, lives have been changed for the better, and the promised blessings have been received. The Book of Mormon, a willing heart, and the Holy Ghost—it really is that simple. My faith and the faith of the other Brethren have been strengthened as we have responded to President Hinckley's invitation and as we have observed so many of you acting and learning by faith.

As I stated earlier, the responsibility to seek learning by faith rests upon each of us individually, and this obligation will become increasingly important as the world in which we live grows more confused and troubled. Learning by faith is essential to our personal spiritual development and for the growth of the Church in these latter days. May each of us truly hunger and thirst after righteousness and be filled with the Holy Ghost (see 3 Nephi 12:6)—that we might seek learning by faith.

I witness that Jesus is the Christ, the Only Begotten Son of the Eternal Father. He is our Savior and Redeemer. I testify that as we learn of Him, listen to His words, and walk in the meekness of His Spirit (see D&C 19:23), we will be blessed with spiritual strength, protection, and peace.

As a servant of the Lord, I invoke this blessing upon each of you: even that your desire and capacity to seek learning by faith—and to appropriately help others to seek learning by faith—will increase and improve. This blessing will be a source of great treasures of spiritual knowledge in your personal life, for your family, and to those whom you instruct and serve. In the sacred name of Jesus Christ, amen.

Notes

1. Joseph Smith, comp., *Lectures on Faith* (Salt Lake City: Deseret Book, 1985), 1.
2. See Boyd K. Packer, "The Candle of the Lord," *Ensign*, January 1983, 54.
3. Joseph Smith, *History of the Church of Jesus Christ of Latter-day Saints*, ed. B. H. Roberts, 2nd ed. rev. (Salt Lake City: Deseret Book, 1957), 4:425.
4. Smith, *History of the Church*, 6:50.
5. James E. Talmage, *The Articles of Faith*, 12th ed. (Salt Lake City: Deseret Book, 1924), 162.
6. Brigham Young, in Junius F. Wells, "Historic Sketch of the YMMIA," *Improvement Era*, June 1925, 715.
7. Boyd K. Packer, "The Candle of the Lord," *Ensign*, January 1983, 54–55.
8. Gordon B. Hinckley, "A Testimony Vibrant and True," *Ensign*, August 2005, 6.

Part 3

SCRIPTURE

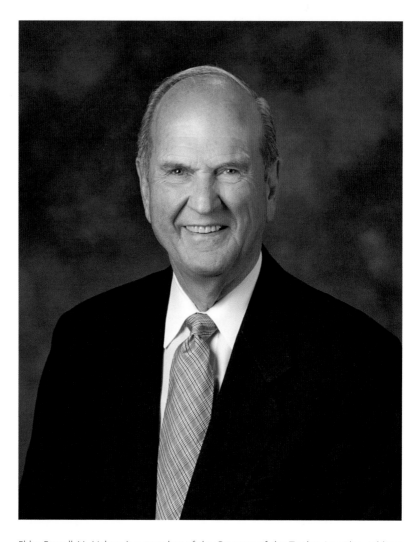

Elder Russell M. Nelson is a member of the Quorum of the Twelve Apostles. Address at the Sidney B. Sperry Symposium at Brigham Young University on October 11, 1997, published in *Sperry Symposium Classics: The Old Testament* (Provo, UT: Religious Studies Center, Brigham Young University, 2005), 1–17.

12 Remnants Gathered, Covenants Fulfilled

T HE TITLE OF MY MESSAGE is "Remnants Gathered, Covenants Fulfilled." It comes from the Book of Mormon. There the Lord speaks of fulfilling "the covenant which the Father hath made unto his people," the house of Israel. "Then," He continues, "shall the remnants, which shall be scattered abroad upon the face of the earth, be gathered in from the east and from the west, and from the south and from the north; and they shall be brought to the knowledge of the Lord their God, who hath redeemed them" (3 Nephi 20:12–13).

The gathering of those remnants and the fulfilling of that divine covenant are occurring in our day. Yet this big picture is obscure to the eye of many who focus upon bargains at supermarkets and rankings of favorite football teams. Let us examine our place in God's plan for His children and for The Church of Jesus Christ of Latter-day Saints. We are part of a destiny known by relatively few people upon the earth.[1]

During the year 1997, attention across the world was attracted to the history of the Church. Its pioneers arrived at the valley of the Great Salt Lake 150 years ago. Replications of handcarts have been featured from Siberia to Swaziland, from Scandinavia and South America to the isles of the South Pacific. Through theater and stage, printed and electronic media, stories of early converts to the Church have been told.

Generally, writers of these accounts have done well in reporting what these pioneers did. But only a few have captured the reasons why.

Even fewer have understood that history in context of the voices of prophets of the Old Testament that link with the great latter-day work that is now being accomplished.

Connections with the New Testament would be no surprise to any who understand the deep commitment to Jesus Christ held by members of this Church that bears His holy name. Its stalwart pioneers opened the period of the Restoration of all things—the promised dispensation of the fulness of times—as prophesied by Peter and Paul (see Acts 3:21; Ephesians 1:10). Those apostolic records and other scriptures of the New Testament are an integral part of the legacy of the restored Church. Its name describes members as Latter-day Saints to distinguish them from those of the Church in the meridian of time. Members were then called *saints,* as they are now. Paul addressed an epistle "to the saints which are at Ephesus, and to the faithful in Christ Jesus" (Ephesians 1:1).[2] To recent converts of that time and place, Paul said, "Now therefore ye are no more strangers and foreigners, but fellowcitizens with the saints, and of the household of God" (Ephesians 2:19; see also 3:17–19).

In that epistle Paul used the word *saint* at least once in every chapter! The term *saint* does not connote beatification or perfection in this life. It simply describes each member of the Church as a believer in Jesus the Christ. It means that members are committed to love God and their neighbor. They are to sacrifice, to serve, and to build the Church as directed by its inspired leaders.

But the connection between the Church and the Old Testament is less apparent. This symposium, which focuses on the voices of the prophets in the Old Testament, is an opportune time to speak of the strong and significant links between ancient and modern Israel. I would like to limit my discussion to five major links that are of immense importance.

As I speak to this theme, you will doubtless think of additional connections. You will also recognize that much more could be said on each segment that I will discuss. That is good. You can explore these interrelationships later without the limitations of time and talent that press upon me now.

THE LINK OF JOSEPH

The first link I shall label as the link of Joseph. This link applies both to Joseph who was sold into Egypt and to the Prophet Joseph Smith. Few men in the Old Testament are of greater importance to Latter-day Saints than is Joseph of Egypt. Many Bible commentators have described him as a type, or shadow, for the Savior. But we also know him as a specific type for the Prophet Joseph Smith and a generic type for all members of The Church of Jesus Christ of Latter-day Saints. Many of the Church's members claim descent from Joseph through his sons, Ephraim or Manasseh.

The importance of Joseph in the book of Genesis is signified by the fact that he figures prominently in sixteen of its fifty chapters (see Genesis 30; 33; 35; 37; 39–50). Joseph's life span from cradle to grave[3] represents only 4 percent of the twenty-seven hundred years covered by the book of Genesis. Yet his life is reported in nearly one-third of its chapters.[4]

In the King James Version, Genesis 50 ends with verse 26, which records the death of Joseph. In the Joseph Smith Translation (JST), that chapter not only adds important information to verses 24 through 26 but provides twelve additional verses that enrich our knowledge of the link of Joseph (see JST, Genesis 50:27–38). Those additions include the following insights, which I paraphrase:

1. A righteous branch would be raised up later out of Joseph's loins (see JST, Genesis 50:24).

2. Israel would be scattered. A branch would be broken off and carried into a far country (see JST, Genesis 50:25).

3. A choice seer would be raised up from Joseph's loins to do work for the fruit of his loins (see JST, Genesis 50:26–29).

4. Writings from the fruit of Joseph's loins would grow together with writings from the fruit of Judah's loins to bring knowledge of their fathers and of everlasting covenants. That knowledge would come in the last days (see JST, Genesis 50:30–32).

5. The promised seer would be called Joseph, after the name of his father, and he would be like unto Joseph, son of Jacob, bringing salvation to the children of the Lord (see JST, Genesis 50:33).

These additions are good examples of "plain and precious" truths that have been restored through the Prophet Joseph Smith (see 1 Nephi 13:40).

He and the ancient Joseph had much in common, as shown by other scriptures that I will cite. From the Book of Mormon we read: "A part of the remnant of the coat of Joseph was preserved and had not decayed. . . . Even as this remnant of garment . . . hath been preserved, so shall a remnant of [Joseph's] seed . . . be preserved by the hand of God" (Alma 46:24).

We are remnants of that precious seed. Joseph Smith had been chosen by the Lord to take up the labors of the tribe of Joseph, son of Jacob. Centuries ago that same Joseph had prophesied of Joseph Smith and described their linkage. Again I quote from the Book of Mormon: "Yea, Joseph truly said: Thus saith the Lord unto me: A choice seer will I raise up out of the fruit of thy loins; and he shall be esteemed highly among the fruit of thy loins. And unto him will I give commandment that he shall do a work for the fruit of thy loins, his brethren, which shall be of great worth unto them, even to the bringing of them to the knowledge of the covenants which I have made with thy fathers. And I will give unto him a commandment that he shall do none other work, save the work which I shall command him. And I will make him great in mine eyes; for he shall do my work" (2 Nephi 3:7–8).

The link of Joseph applied not only to Joseph Smith Jr. but to his father as well. Again I quote from Joseph who was sold into Egypt: "Behold, that seer [Joseph Smith] will the Lord bless; . . . for this promise, which I have obtained of the Lord, of the fruit of my loins, shall be fulfilled. . . . And his name shall be called after me; and it shall be after the name of his father. And he shall be like unto me; for the thing, which the Lord shall bring forth by his hand, by the power of the Lord shall bring my people unto salvation" (2 Nephi 3:14–15).

Joseph and Joseph Smith had more in common than their lineage linking. At age seventeen, Joseph, son of Jacob, was informed of his great destiny (see Genesis 37:2). At that same age, Joseph Smith was informed of his destiny regarding the Book of Mormon: He was seventeen when first visited by the angel Moroni, who told the boy prophet that "God had a work for [him] to do." He was to translate a book written upon golden plates containing the fulness of the everlasting gospel.

His "name should be had for good and evil among all nations, kindreds, and tongues" (Joseph Smith—History 1:33; see also 1:34–41).

Both Josephs were persecuted. Joseph in Egypt was falsely accused of a crime he did not commit and was put into prison (see Genesis 39:11–20). Joseph Smith was incarcerated on trumped-up charges and false accusations.[5]

Joseph's coat of many colors was taken from him by his brothers in a cruel attempt to convince their father that Joseph had been killed (see Genesis 37:2–33). Joseph Smith's life was taken from him, largely because of betrayals by false brethren.

Anciently, "when all the land of Egypt was famished, the people cried to Pharaoh for bread: and Pharaoh said unto all the Egyptians, Go unto Joseph; what he saith to you, do" (Genesis 41:55). In the latter days, people starving for nourishment that only the gospel can provide are again to be fed—by Joseph. The Lord declared that "this generation shall have my word through [Joseph Smith]" (D&C 5:10). Today we "feast upon the words of Christ" because of Joseph Smith (2 Nephi 32:3).

This link of Joseph is summarized in lines from the book of Ether:

> The Lord brought a remnant of the seed of Joseph out of the land of Jerusalem, that he might be merciful unto the seed of Joseph that they should perish not. . . .
>
> Wherefore, the remnant of the house of Joseph shall be built upon this land [of America]; and it shall be a land of their inheritance; and they shall build up a holy city unto the Lord, like unto the Jerusalem of old. . . .
>
> . . . and blessed are they who dwell therein, for it is they whose garments are white through the blood of the Lamb; and they are they who are numbered among the remnant of the seed of Joseph, who were of the house of Israel.
>
> . . . and they are they who were scattered and gathered in from the four quarters of the earth, and from the north countries, and are partakers of the fulfilling of the covenant which God made with their father, Abraham. (Ether 13:7–8, 10–11)

The Link of the Book of Mormon

Link number two I shall identify as the link of the Book of Mormon. In September 1997 I had the extraordinary privilege of seeing portions of the original manuscript and virtually all of the printer's manuscript of the Book of Mormon.[6] That was an incredible experience!

Voices of prophets in the Old Testament foretold of this great book. You are familiar with the prophecy of Isaiah: "Thou shalt be brought down, and shalt speak out of the ground, and thy speech shall be low out of the dust, and thy voice shall be, as of one that hath a familiar spirit, out of the ground, and thy speech shall whisper out of the dust" (Isaiah 29:4).

Could any words have been more descriptive of the Book of Mormon, coming as it did "out of the ground" to "whisper out of the dust" to people of our day?

Other Old Testament passages foretold the Book of Mormon. One such came to mind last January when I attended a prayer breakfast at the White House in Washington DC, hosted by President Bill Clinton. During an informal reception that preceded the breakfast, I was chatting with a distinguished and scholarly Jewish rabbi from New York. Our conversation was interrupted by another rabbi who asked his colleague from New York if he could recall the scriptural reference to the stick of Judah and the stick of Joseph that would come together one day. My friend paused for a moment, stroked his chin pensively, and then replied, "I think you will find that in the book of Ezekiel."

I could not restrain myself. "You might look in the thirty-seventh chapter of Ezekiel," I interjected. "There you will find the scriptures that you seek."

My rabbi friend was surprised. "How did *you* know that?"

"This doctrine," I said, "is very important in our theology."

Indeed it is. You know it, and I know it. I would like to read it: "Moreover, thou son of man, take thee one stick, and write upon it, For Judah, and for the children of Israel his companions: then take another stick, and write upon it, For Joseph, the stick of Ephraim, and for all the house of Israel his companions: and join them one to another into one stick; and they shall become one in thine hand" (Ezekiel 37:16–17).

Saints of modern Israel in 160 nations across the world are blessed to hold the Bible and the Book of Mormon as one in their hands. The worth of this privilege must never be underestimated.

Keys of authority for the Book of Mormon—the stick of Ephraim— were held by the angel Moroni (see D&C 27:5). The Book of Mormon is the great amplifying, clarifying, and converting scripture. It is indeed "Another Testament of Jesus Christ" (Book of Mormon, title page).

Children of the Lord have ever been admonished to "search the scriptures" (John 5:39; Alma 14:1; 33:2; 3 Nephi 10:14). In addition, we of modern Israel have been specifically commanded to study one particular voice and prophet of the Old Testament. Which one? Isaiah! (see 3 Nephi 20:11; 23:1). The importance of that commandment is underlined by the fact that 433 verses of Isaiah appear in the Book of Mormon. Studying them is not repetitious. Sidney B. Sperry reported that 234 of those verses differ from their biblical counterparts.[7] In addition, the Doctrine and Covenants has more than seventy quotations from or paraphrases of Isaiah.[8] Study the words of Isaiah! Do we get the message?

Other prophets of the Old Testament were quoted to our modern prophets. Malachi's teachings have been repeated.[9] Elijah,[10] Moses,[11] and others have taught people of both ancient and modern Israel (see D&C 27:5–13).

Isaiah described the spirit of the Book of Mormon as "familiar." It resonates with people who know the Old Testament, especially with those who are conversant with its Hebrew language. The Book of Mormon is filled with Hebraisms—traditions, symbolisms, idioms, and literary forms. It is familiar because more than 80 percent of its pages come from Old Testament times.[12]

THE LINK OF THE HOUSE OF ISRAEL

Link number three I shall designate as the link of the house of Israel. It includes doctrines of the Abrahamic covenant and of the scattering and gathering of Israel.

About four thousand years ago, Abraham received a promise from the Lord that blessings would be offered to all of his mortal posterity (see D&C 132:29–50; Abraham 2:6–11). Included were promises that the Son of God would come through Abraham's lineage, that certain lands would be inherited by his posterity, that nations and kindreds of the earth would be blessed through his seed, and more. Knowledge of and reaffirmations of this covenant are evident in scriptures of the Old Testament (see Genesis 26:1–4, 24; 28; 35:9; 48). Although certain aspects of that covenant have already been fulfilled, many have not. The Book of Mormon teaches that we of modern Israel are among the covenant people of the Lord (see 1 Nephi 14:14; 15:14; 2 Nephi 30:2; Mosiah 24:13; 3 Nephi 29:3; Mormon 8:15). And, most remarkably, it teaches that the Abrahamic covenant will be fulfilled only in these latter days (see 1 Nephi 15:12–18). The Lord bestowed this Abrahamic covenant upon the Prophet Joseph Smith for the blessing of him and posterity after him (see D&C 124:56–59). Did you know that Abraham is mentioned in more verses of modern revelation than in all the verses of the Old Testament?[13] Abraham—this great patriarch of the Old Testament—is inextricably linked to all who join The Church of Jesus Christ of Latter-day Saints.[14]

Doctrines relating to the scattering and gathering of the house of Israel were also among the earliest lessons taught in the Book of Mormon. I quote from the first book of Nephi: "After the house of Israel should be scattered they should be gathered together again; . . . the natural branches of the olive-tree, or the remnants of the house of Israel, should be grafted in, or come to the knowledge of the true Messiah, their Lord and their Redeemer" (1 Nephi 10:14).

The Old Testament is replete with prophecies that relate to the scattering of Israel. May I cite one from the book of First Kings: "For the Lord shall smite Israel, as a reed is shaken in the water, and he shall root up Israel out of this good land, which he gave to their fathers, and shall scatter them" (1 Kings 14:15).

In this citation, the word "scatter" was translated from the Hebrew verb *zarah,* which means "to scatter, cast away, winnow, or disperse." The richness of the Hebrew language provides other verbs to describe similar actions. For example, from the book of First Kings we also read: "I saw all Israel scattered upon the hills, as sheep that have not a shepherd" (1 Kings 22:17).

In this instance, "scattered" was translated from the Hebrew verb *puwts,* which also means "to scatter" or "to be dispersed."

Isaiah used yet another verb in this prophecy: "He shall set up an ensign for the nations, and shall assemble the outcasts of Israel, and gather together the *dispersed* of Judah from the four corners of the earth" (Isaiah 11:12; emphasis added).

In this case "dispersed" was translated from the Hebrew verb *naphats,* which means "to shatter, break, dash, or beat in pieces."

References to the scattering were also recorded in the New Testament. For example, the book of James begins with these words: "James, a servant of God and of the Lord Jesus Christ, to the twelve tribes which are scattered abroad, greeting" (James 1:1).

In this reference, "scattered" was translated from the Greek feminine noun *diaspora,* which means "dispersed" or "scattered." You may wish to look up the word *diaspora* in the Bible Dictionary (Bible Dictionary, "Diaspora," 657). There the scattering of the house of Israel is succinctly summarized.

Saints of modern Israel know that Peter, James, and John were sent by the Lord with "the keys of [His] kingdom, and a dispensation of the gospel for the last times; and for the fulness of times," in which He would "gather together in one all things, both which are in heaven, and which are on earth" (D&C 27:13).[15]

The travels and travail of our pioneers were of eternal consequence. Their mission was not limited to an international immigration or a transcontinental migration with wagons and handcarts. They were to lay the foundation of an endless work that would "fill the world."[16] They were essential to Jeremiah's prophecy: "Hear the word of the Lord, O ye nations, and declare it in the isles afar off, and say, He that scattered Israel will gather him, and keep him, as a shepherd doth his flock" (Jeremiah 31:10).[17]

They got the message. Missionaries were sent very early to "the isles afar off" to commence the work of the Lord. As a result, the Church was established in the British Isles and in the islands of French Polynesia years before the pioneers entered the valley of the Great Salt Lake. It has been my privilege to participate in sesquicentennial celebrations in the British Isles in 1987 and in French Polynesia in 1994. Now in 1997, I celebrate this one with you in Utah.

Another aspect of the gathering of Israel reflects back to our first link regarding Joseph. The word *Joseph* comes from the Hebrew masculine personal noun *Yowceph,* the literal meaning of which is "Jehovah has added." *Joseph* also relates to the Hebrew root *yasaph,* which means "to add," and "to *asaph,*" which means both "to take away" and "to gather" (see Genesis 30:24, footnote a).

The Hebrew verbs *yacaph* and *acaph*[18] are used in the Hebrew text of the Old Testament 186 and 180 times respectively. Both words were usually translated into English as "gather" in one of its several forms. For example, in the verse, "David *gathered* together all the chosen men of Israel" (2 Samuel 6:1; emphasis added), the Hebrew verb *yacaph* was used.

Another scripture from Genesis deserves special comment. It reports the naming of Jacob and Rachel's firstborn son: "She called his name *Joseph;* and said, The Lord shall *add* to me another son" (Genesis 30:24; emphasis added).[19] In that verse both the words "Joseph" and "add" were derived from the Hebrew root *yacaph.*

The lineage of Joseph—through Ephraim and Manasseh—is the seed appointed to lead in the gathering of Israel.[20] The pioneers knew—through their patriarchal blessings and from doctrines of the Old Testament, amplified by scriptures and revelations of the Restoration—that the long-awaited gathering of Israel was to commence with them.

THE LINK OF EXODUS

The fourth link connecting ancient and modern Israel I shall name the link of the Exodus. At a Church Educational System fireside satellite broadcast in September 1997, I spoke to the subject of "The Exodus Repeated." Then I spoke of some connections between ancient and modern Israel that will also be relevant to a more comprehensive coverage of the topic, "Remnants Gathered, Covenants Fulfilled." Fascinating are the many parallels between the exodus from Egypt of the Israelites under Moses and the exodus from the United States of the pioneers under Brigham Young.

Both peoples were oppressed by their governments. The ancient Israelites were "bondmen" (Deuteronomy 6:21). The Latter-day Saints were persecuted by their own government.[21]

Moses had been prepared in the courts of Egypt and had gained much experience in military and other responsibilities (see Hebrews 11:24, 27). Brigham Young was likewise prepared for his leadership role. In the march of Zion's Camp, he observed the leadership of the Prophet Joseph Smith under difficult conditions.[22] Brigham Young aided in the removal of the Saints from Kirtland and directed the move of the persecuted Saints from Missouri to Nauvoo.[23]

God preserved ancient Israel from plagues that He sent upon Egypt (see Exodus 15:26). God preserved the Saints from the plague of the United States Civil War that caused more American deaths due to war than any other war.

Both groups had to leave their homes and earthly possessions. Both had to learn to rely wholly upon the Lord and be sustained by Him during their travels. Both traversed deserts, mountains, and valleys of untamed wilderness. Ancient Israelites left Egypt via the waters of the Red Sea "as by dry land" (Hebrews 11:29). Some pioneers left the United States by crossing the wide waters of the Mississippi River—frozen to become a highway of ice.[24] Both groups endured trials of their faith during which the weak were winnowed away and the strong were empowered to endure to the end (see Ether 12:6; D&C 101:4–5; 105:19).

The children of ancient Israel had a portable tabernacle wherein covenants were made and ordinances were performed to strengthen them on their journey.[25] Originally the tabernacle was intended to be a portable temple, before the Israelites lost the higher law (see D&C 84:23–26; 124:38; JST, Exodus 34:1–2). Similarly, many Latter-day Saints were endowed in the Nauvoo Temple before their trek.

The journey from Egypt to Mount Sinai took about three months (see Exodus 12:2, 3, 6, 18; 13:4; 19:1). The journey from Winter Quarters to the valley of the Great Salt Lake also took about three months.[26]

The promised land for each group also bore similarities. That of ancient Israel had an inland sea of salt water, the inlet to which was the River Jordan. That for the pioneers also had an inland sea of salt water, fed by the Jordan River. The destination of each group was described by the Lord as a land "flowing with milk and honey."²⁷ The pioneers turned their wilderness into a fruitful field (see Isaiah 32:15–16) and made the desert blossom as a rose (see Isaiah 35:1)—precisely as prophesied by Isaiah.

For both the Israelites and the Saints, civil and ecclesiastical law were unified under one head. Moses bore that responsibility for the early Israelites.²⁸ Brigham Young—a modern Moses²⁹ (see D&C 103:16)—led the Latter-day Saints' movement west, with the Lord's blessing (see D&C 136:1–42). Moses and Brigham Young followed parallel patterns of governance (see Exodus 18:17–21; D&C 136:1–4). And each of them endured dissension from their close associates.³⁰ Nevertheless, that same unified pattern of government will again prevail when the Lord shall be "King over all the earth" (Psalm 47:2; Zechariah 14:9), and He shall govern from Zion and Jerusalem (see Isaiah 2:1–4).

The Israelites celebrated their exodus from Egypt. The Latter-day Saints commemorated their exodus with the establishment of the world headquarters of the restored Church in the tops of the mountains. Both celebrations acclaimed their miraculous deliverance by God (see Jeremiah 16:15; 23:7).³¹ The link of the exodus reminds us of an Old Testament scripture of gratitude: "Moses said unto the people, Remember this day, in which ye came out from Egypt, out of the house of bondage; for by strength of hand the Lord brought you out from this place" (Exodus 13:3).

The Link of the Timeless Truths of the Gospel

The fifth connection between ancient and modern Israel I shall denote as the link of the timeless truths of the gospel. Those truths are included in the unending priesthood order of Melchizedek, though he is mentioned but twice in the Old Testament (see Genesis 14:18; Psalm 110:4). The Melchizedek Priesthood was removed from ancient Israel shortly after the exodus from Egypt (see JST, Exodus 34:1–2; D&C 84:23–25). Thereafter, ancient Israel functioned under the Levitical Priesthood and the law of carnal commandments (see D&C 84:27).

Timeless truths and principles of the gospel were and are important to people of ancient and modern Israel. The Sabbath day, for example, was honored for different reasons through the generations. From the time of Adam to Moses, the Sabbath was observed as a day of rest from the labor of creation (see Exodus 20:8–11; 31:13; Mosiah 13:16–19). From the time of Moses to the Resurrection of the Lord, the Sabbath also commemorated the liberation of the Israelites from their bondage in Egypt (see Deuteronomy 5:12–15; Isaiah 58:13; Ezekiel 20:20–22; 44:24). In latter days, Saints keep the Sabbath day holy in memory of the Atonement of Jesus Christ.[32]

The restoration of the priesthood rejuvenated the principle of tithing, linking to the Old Testament teachings of Genesis and Malachi (see Genesis 14:20; Malachi 3:8–12). Saints of modern Israel know how to calculate their own tithing from this simple instruction: "Those who have thus been tithed shall pay one-tenth of all their interest annually; and this shall be a standing law unto them forever, for my holy priesthood, saith the Lord" (D&C 119:4).

In contrast, have you ever amused yourself with the thought, on or about April 15th each year, that the filing of income tax returns is a bit more complicated? I'll confess that I have.

Turning our attention again to the timeless truths of the gospel, none are more vital than those associated with temple worship. They compose another link between ancient and modern Israel. The Bible Dictionary states that "whenever the Lord has had a people on the earth who will obey his word, they have been commanded to build temples in which the ordinances of the gospel and other spiritual manifestations that pertain to exaltation and eternal life may be administered" (Bible Dictionary, "Temple," 781).

The best-known temple of ancient Israel was Solomon's temple. Its baptismal font (see 2 Chronicles 4:15) and dedicatory prayer (see 2 Chronicles 6:12–42) provide patterns that are employed for temples today (see D&C 109:1–80). Old Testament scriptures refer to special clothing (see Exodus 28:4; 29:5; Leviticus 8:7–9; 1 Samuel 18:3–4) and ordinances (see Exodus 19:10, 14; 2 Samuel 12:20; Ezekiel 16:9) that are associated with temples (see D&C 124:37–40). How thankful we are that the Lord chose to restore the highest blessings of the priesthood to His faithful sons and daughters! He said: "For I deign to reveal unto my church things which have been kept hid from before the foundation of the world, things that pertain to the dispensation of the fulness of times" (D&C 124:41).

Revealed truth that we know as the Word of Wisdom came to the Prophet Joseph Smith in 1833. Every Latter-day Saint is familiar with it as one of the visible hallmarks of our faith. The final verse of that revelation forges another link back to ancient Israel: "And I, the Lord, give unto them a promise, that the destroying angel shall pass by them, as the children of Israel, and not slay them" (D&C 89:21).

This reference to the Passover shows that the Lord wanted obedient Saints of modern Israel to receive physical and spiritual protection just as He had provided for His faithful followers centuries before.

Summary

Ancient Israel and modern Israel are linked arm in arm. In our day, many Old Testament prophecies are being fulfilled. Isaiah foretold: "And it shall come to pass in the last days, that the mountain of the Lord's house shall be established in the top of the mountains, and shall be exalted above the hills; and all nations shall flow unto it" (Isaiah 2:2; see also 2 Nephi 12:2; JST, Isaiah 2:2).

During the past year, visitors from more than one hundred nations have come to visit world headquarters of The Church of Jesus Christ of Latter-day Saints.[33]

Ancient and modern Israel subscribe to an ageless message of the Old Testament: "Know therefore that the Lord thy God . . . keepeth covenant and mercy with them that love him and keep his commandments to a thousand generations" (Deuteronomy 7:9).[34]

All faithful members of the Church will receive their just reward: "All things are theirs, whether life or death, or things present, or things to come, all are theirs and they are Christ's, and Christ is God's" (D&C 76:59).

I would like to bear my testimony as one with you, my beloved brothers and sisters. We love our Heavenly Father. We love the Lord Jesus Christ. We are His people. We have taken His holy name upon us. We are His remnants now being gathered and gleaned into His eternal garners (see Alma 26:5). We are fulfilling "the covenant which the Father hath made unto his people" (3 Nephi 20:12). We are being brought to the knowledge of our Lord who has redeemed us (see 3 Nephi 20:12–13). We are "children of the covenant" (3 Nephi 20:26; see also Acts 3:25; 3 Nephi 20:25) destined to be as was ancient Israel—"a kingdom of priests, and an holy nation" (Exodus 19:6; see also D&C 76:56–57). We know that Joseph Smith is the great prophet of the Restoration and that President Gordon B. Hinckley is the prophet of the Lord today.

My testimony, my love, and my blessing, I leave with you, in the name of Jesus Christ, amen.

NOTES

1. Ten million members of the Church compose 0.0017 percent of a world population of 5.8 billion.
2. The term *saints* appears in sixty-two verses of the New Testament.
3. Joseph died at the age of 110 years (see Genesis 50:26).
4. Sixteen of fifty chapters equals 32 percent.
5. See J. Reuben Clark Jr., *On the Way to Immortality and Eternal Life* (Salt Lake City: Deseret Book, 1949), 133; Ezra Taft Benson, in Conference Report, April 1954, 58.
6. About 25 percent of the original manuscript is in the historical archives of the Church. The printer's manuscript is owned by the Community of Christ (formerly the Reorganized LDS Church) and was on loan to The Church of Jesus Christ of Latter-day Saints. It is reported to be complete except for two lines of the title page.
7. See Sydney B. Sperry, "The 'Isaiah Problem' in the Book of Mormon," *Improvement Era*, October 1939, 594.
8. Monte S. Nyman, in *Encyclopedia of Mormonism*, ed. Daniel H. Ludlow (New York: Macmillan, 1992), 2:702. Another is mentioned in Joseph Smith—History 1:40.
9. See 3 Nephi 24:1; D&C 110:14; 128:17; 133:64; 138:46; Joseph Smith—History 1:36.
10. See 3 Nephi 25:5; D&C 2:1; 27:9; 35:4; 110:13, 14; 128:17; 133:55; 138:46, 47; Joseph Smith—History 1:38.
11. Moses is mentioned in 1,300 verses of scripture, 515 (40 percent) of which are in modern revelation.

12. Personal communication from Elder Jeffrey R. Holland, June 1997.

13. Abraham is mentioned in 506 verses of scripture, 289 of which are in modern revelation.

14. The covenant may also be received by adoption (see Matthew 3:9; Luke 3:8; Galatians 3:27–29; 4:5).

15. Compare with Paul's prophecy of the Restoration in Ephesians 1:10.

16. Joseph Smith, quoted in Wilford Woodruff, *The Discourses of Wilford Woodruff*, sel. G. Homer Durham (Salt Lake City: Bookcraft, 1946), 39.

17. *Gather* is used to translate the Hebrew verb *qabats,* which means "to gather, assemble."

18. Spellings in James Strong, *The Exhaustive Concordance of the Bible* (1890; reprint, New York: Abingdon, 1965), "Hebrew and Chaldee Dictionary," 50, 15.

19. Joseph was "added" to Rachel's family because her handmaid, Bilhah, had given birth to Dan and Naphtali previously (see Genesis 30:5–8). See also Deuteronomy 33:16–17, which refers to the people of Joseph being pushed together "to the ends of the earth: and they are the ten thousands of Ephraim, and they are the thousands of Manasseh." JST, Genesis 50:34 also affirms that Joseph's seed would be preserved forever.

20. See Erastus Snow, in *Journal of Discourses* (London: Latter-day Saints' Book Depot, 1854–86), 23:183–84.

21. The pioneers were forced out of Missouri under threat of an order signed by Missouri's governor directing that the "Mormons must be treated as enemies and must be exterminated or driven from the state" (Joseph Smith, *History of The Church of Jesus Christ of Latter-day Saints,* ed. B. H. Roberts, 2nd ed. rev. [Salt Lake City: The Church of Jesus Christ of Latter-day Saints, 1980], 3:175). In 1887, the Congress of the United States of America took the unprecedented step of eliminating the Church's legal existence by revoking its corporate charter and authorizing federal receivers to assume ownership of virtually all of the Church's property and other assets, including its most sacred houses of worship—temples in Logan, Manti, St. George, and Salt Lake City (see *The Late Corporation of The Church of Jesus Christ of Latter-Day Saints v. United States,* 136 U.S. 1 [1890]). Yet the Saints knew that they were Abraham's seed and heirs to promises and protection from the Lord (see D&C 103:17–20).

22. See Smith, *History of the Church,* 2:6–12, 185; Leonard J. Arrington, *Brigham Young: American Moses* (New York: Knopf, 1985), 58.

23. See Smith, *History of the Church,* 2:529; 3:252, 261; Preston Nibley, *The Presidents of the Church* (Salt Lake City: Deseret Book, 1974), 41.

24. See Orson Pratt, in *Journal of Discourses,* 21:275–77.

25. Ordinances and covenants of ancient Israel are referenced in 1 Corinthians 10:1–3; for modern Israel, see D&C 84:26–27.

26. One hundred and eleven days.

27. For the people of ancient Israel, see Exodus 3:8, 17; 13:5; 33:3; Leviticus 20:24; Numbers 13:27; 14:8; 16:13, 14; Deuteronomy 6:3; 11:9; 26:9, 15; 27:3; 31:20;

Joshua 5:6; Jeremiah 11:5; 32:22; Ezekiel 20:6, 15; JST Exodus 33:1. For the pioneers, see D&C 38:18–19.

28. See Joseph Smith, *Teachings of the Prophet Joseph Smith,* sel. Joseph Fielding Smith (Salt Lake City: Deseret Book, 1938), 252.

29. President Spencer W. Kimball wrote of Brigham Young's role in that exodus: "Since Adam there have been many exoduses and promised lands: Abraham, Jared, Moses, Lehi, and others led groups. How easy it is to accept those distant in time as directed by the Lord, yet the ones near at hand as human calculations and decisions. Let us consider for a moment the great trek of the Mormon refugees from Illinois to Salt Lake Valley. Few, if any, great movements equal it. We frequently hear that Brigham Young led the people to make new tracks in a desert and to climb over mountains seldom scaled and to ford and wade unbridged rivers and to traverse a hostile Indian country; and while Brigham Young was the instrument of the Lord, it was not he but the Lord of heaven who led modern Israel across the plains to their promised land" (*Faith Precedes the Miracle* [Salt Lake City: Deseret Book, 1972], 28).

30. See Numbers 12:1–11 (Aaron and Miriam); for latter-day examples, see Smith, *History of the Church,* 1:104–5 (Oliver Cowdery); and 1:226 (William E. McLellin).

31. Other miracles were shared, such as food provided by the "miracle of the quails." (For ancient Israel, see Exodus 16:13; Psalm 105:40; for the pioneers, see Stanley B. Kimball, "Nauvoo West: The Mormons of the Iowa Shore," *BYU Studies* 18 [Winter 1978]: 142). Protection was provided for ancient Israel by the Lord, who "went before them by day in a pillar of a cloud, to lead them the way; and by night in a pillar of fire" (Exodus 13:21; see also v. 22; Numbers 14:14; Deuteronomy 1:33; Nehemiah 9:19). Similar care has been noted for the pioneers (see Smith, *History of the Church,* 3:34; Thomas S. Monson, in Conference Report, April 1967, 56).

32. See D&C 20:40, 75–79; 59:9; see also Matthew 26:26–28; Mark 14:22–24; Luke 22:19–20; Acts 20:7; 1 Corinthians 16:2; Revelation 1:10.

33. Estimate provided by the Temple Square Mission.

34. See also Deuteronomy 11:1, 27; 19:9; 30:16; Joshua 22:5; 1 John 5:2–3; Mosiah 2:4. Other Old Testament scriptures refer to rewards for those obedient to God's commandments through a "thousand generations" (see 1 Corinthians 16:15; Psalm 105:8).

Elder D. Todd Christofferson is a member of the Quorum of the Twelve Apostles. Address at a Brigham Young University–Idaho devotional assembly on January 27, 2009, published in *Religious Educator* 11, no. 2 (2010): 1–9.

13   "ALWAYS REMEMBER HIM"

THE SACRAMENTAL PRAYERS CONFIRM THAT one of the central purposes of that ordinance instituted by the Lord Jesus Christ is that we might "always remember him" (D&C 20:77, 79). Remembering the Savior obviously includes remembering His Atonement, which is symbolically represented by the bread and water, emblems of His suffering and death. We must never forget what He did for us, for without His Atonement and Resurrection life would have no meaning, whereas, given the reality of both the Atonement and the Resurrection, our lives have eternal, divine possibilities.

I would like today to elaborate with you what it means to "always remember him." I will mention three aspects of remembering Him: first, seeking to know and follow His will; second, recognizing and accepting our obligation to answer to Christ for every thought, word, and action; and third, living with faith and confidence in the realization that we can always look to the Savior for the help we need.

SEEK TO KNOW AND FOLLOW THE WILL OF CHRIST JUST AS HE SOUGHT THE WILL OF THE FATHER

First, remembering the Lord certainly means doing His will. The sacramental blessing on the bread commits us to be willing to take upon us the name of the Son "and always remember him and keep his commandments which he has given [us]" (D&C 20:77). It would also be appropriate to read this covenant as "always remember him *to* keep his commandments." This is how He always remembered the Father. As He said, "I can of mine own self do nothing: as I hear, I judge: and my judgment is just; because I seek not mine own will, but the will of the Father which hath sent me" (John 5:30).

Jesus achieved perfect unity with the Father by submitting Himself, both body and spirit, to the will of the Father. Referring to His Father, Jesus said, "I do always those things that please him" (John 8:29). Because it was the Father's will, Jesus submitted even to death, "the will of the Son being swallowed up in the will of the Father" (Mosiah 15:7). His focus on the Father is one of the principal reasons Jesus' ministry had such clarity and power. There was no distracting double-mindedness in Him.

In the same way, you can put Christ at the center of your life and become one with Him as He is one with the Father (see John 17:20–23). You could begin by stripping everything out of your life and then putting it back together in priority order with the Savior at the center. You would first put in place the things that make it possible always to remember Him—frequent prayer, studying and pondering the scriptures, thoughtful study of apostolic teachings, weekly preparation to partake of the sacrament worthily, Sunday worship, recording and remembering what the Spirit and experience teach you about discipleship. There may be other things that will come to your mind particularly suited to you at this point in your life. Once adequate time and means for centering your life in Christ have been put in place, you can begin to add other responsibilities and things you value insofar as time and resources will permit, such as education and family responsibilities. In this way the essential will not be crowded out by the merely good, and things of lesser value will take a lower priority or fall away altogether.

I recognize that aligning our will to that of Jesus Christ as He aligned His will to the Father's is something not easily achieved. President Brigham Young spoke understandingly of our challenge when he said:

> After all that has been said and done, after he has led this people so long, do you not perceive that there is a lack of

confidence in our God? Can you perceive it in yourselves? You may ask, "[Brother] Brigham, do you perceive it in yourself?" I do, I can see that I yet lack confidence, to some extent, in him whom I trust.—Why? Because I have not the power, in consequence of that which the fall has brought upon me. . . .

Something rises up within me, at times[,] that . . . draws a dividing line between my interest and the interest of my Father in heaven; something that makes my interest and the interest of my Father in heaven not precisely one. . . .

We should feel and understand, as far as possible, as far as fallen nature will let us, as far as we can get faith and knowledge to understand ourselves, that the interest of that God whom we serve is our interest, and that we have no other, neither in time nor in eternity.[1]

Though it may not be easy, you can consistently press forward with faith in the Lord. I can attest that over time one's desire and capacity to always remember and follow the Savior will grow. You should patiently work toward that end and pray always for the discernment and divine help you need. Nephi counseled, "But behold, I say unto you that ye must pray always, and not faint; that ye must not perform any thing unto the Lord save in the first place ye shall pray unto the Father in the name of Christ, that he will consecrate thy performance unto thee, that thy performance may be for the welfare of thy soul" (2 Nephi 32:9).

I witnessed a simple example of this kind of prayer a few weeks ago when Elder Dallin H. Oaks and I were assigned to conduct a videoconference interview of a couple in another country. Because we are conducting more and more business via videoconferences, we have a studio for that purpose set up on the fifth floor of the Church Administration Building, where our offices are located. Shortly before going up to the studio, I reviewed once again the information we had collected about the couple and felt I was prepared for the interview. As I came to the small elevator lobby on the fifth floor a few minutes before the appointed time, I saw Elder Oaks sitting alone there with head bowed. In a moment he raised his head and explained, "I was just finishing my prayer in preparation for this interview. We will need the gift of discernment." He had not neglected the most important preparation, a prayer to "consecrate our performance" for our good and the Lord's glory.

WE ANSWER TO CHRIST FOR EVERY THOUGHT, WORD, AND ACTION

A second aspect of always remembering the Redeemer is to live conscious of the responsibility we have to answer to Him for our lives. The scriptures make it clear that there will be a great day of judgment when the Lord shall stand to judge the nations (see 3 Nephi 27:16) and when every knee shall bow and every tongue confess that He is the Christ (see Romans 14:11; Mosiah 27:31; D&C 76:110). The individual nature and extent of that judgment are best described by Amulek and Alma in the Book of Mormon:

> And Amulek hath spoken plainly concerning death, and being raised from this mortality to a state of immortality, and being brought before the bar of God, to be judged according to our works.
>
> Then if our hearts have been hardened, yea, if we have hardened our hearts against the word, insomuch that it has not been found in us, then will our state be awful, for then we shall be condemned.
>
> For our words will condemn us, yea, all our works will condemn us; we shall not be found spotless; and our thoughts will also condemn us; and in this awful state we shall not dare to look up to our God; and we would fain be glad if we could command the rocks and the mountains to fall upon us to hide us from his presence.
>
> But this cannot be; we must come forth and stand before him in his glory, and in his power, and in his might, majesty, and dominion, and acknowledge to our everlasting shame that all his judgments are just; that he is just in all his works, and that he is merciful unto the children of men, and that he has all power to save every man that believeth on his name and bringeth forth fruit meet for repentance. (Alma 12:12–15)

When the Savior defined His gospel, this judgment was central to it. He said:

> Behold I have given unto you my gospel, and this is the gospel which I have given unto you—that I came into the world to do the will of my Father, because my Father sent me.
>
> And my Father sent me that I might be lifted up upon the cross; and after that I had been lifted up upon the cross, that I might draw all men unto me, that as I have been lifted up by men even so should men be lifted up by the Father, to stand before me, to be judged of their works, whether they be good or whether they be evil—
>
> And for this cause have I been lifted up; therefore, according to the power of the Father I will draw all men unto me, that they may be judged according to their works. (3 Nephi 27:13–15)

Being "lifted up upon the cross" is, of course, a symbolic or shorthand way of referring to the Atonement of Jesus Christ, by which He satisfied the demands that justice may have upon each of us. In other words, all that justice could demand of us for our sins, He has paid by His suffering and death in Gethsemane and on Golgotha. He therefore stands in the place of justice. He is now the personification of justice. Just as God is love, God is also justice. Our debts and obligations now run to Jesus Christ. He, therefore, has the right to judge us.

That judgment, He states, is based on our works. The especially "good news" of His gospel is that He offers the gift of forgiveness conditioned on our repentance. Therefore, if our works include the works of repentance, He forgives our sins and errors. If we reject the gift of pardon, refusing to repent, then the penalties of justice which He now represents are imposed. Remember He said, "For behold, I, God, have suffered these things for all, that they might not suffer if they would repent; but if they would not repent they must suffer even as I" (D&C 19:16–17).

Always remembering Him, therefore, means that we always remember that nothing is hidden from Him. There is no part of our lives, whether act, word, or even thought, that can be kept from the knowledge of the Father and the Son. No cheating on a test, no instance of shoplifting, no lustful fantasy or indulgence, no lie is missed, overlooked, hidden, or forgotten. Whatever one "gets away with" in life or manages to hide from other people must still be faced when the inevitable day comes that he or she is lifted up before Jesus Christ, the God of pure and perfect justice.

Speaking personally, this reality has helped impel me at different times either to repent or to avoid sin altogether. On one occasion in connection with the sale of a home, there was an error in the documentation, and I found myself in a position where I was legally entitled to get more money from the buyer. My real estate agent asked if I wanted to keep the money, a significant amount, since it was my right to do so. I thought about facing the Lord, the personification of justice, and trying to explain that I had a legal right to take advantage of the buyer and his mistake. I couldn't see myself being very convincing, especially since I would probably be asking for mercy for myself at the same time. And I knew I could not live with myself if I were so dishonorable as to keep the money. I replied to the agent that we would stick with the bargain as we all understood it originally. It is worth a great deal more to me than any sum of money to know that I have nothing to answer for in that transaction when I appear before the Great Judge.

Let me give you another example. In my youth I once was negligent in a way that later caused an injury to one of my brothers. It was not major, but it required some stitches in his hand. I was embarrassed about it and did not own up to my stupidity at the time, and no one ever knew about my role in the matter. Many years later, I was praying that God would reveal to me anything in my life that needed correction so that I might be found more acceptable before Him, and this incident came to my mind. Frankly, I had forgotten all about it. The Spirit whispered to me that this was an unresolved transgression that I needed to confess. I called my brother and apologized and asked for his forgiveness, which he promptly and generously gave. On reflection I realized that my embarrassment and regret would have been less if I had apologized when the accident happened. Of course, it would have been even better if I had followed the prompting of the Spirit at the time and avoided the injury to my brother altogether.

It was significant to me that the Lord had not forgotten about that event of the distant past even though I had. It was a comparatively small thing, but it still needed to be handled, or I would be answering for it at the judgment bar when the opportunity for repentance had passed. I realized once again that things do not get "swept under the rug" in the eternal economy of things. Sins do not take care of themselves or simply fade away with time. They must be dealt with, and the wonderful thing is that because of His atoning grace they can be dealt with in a much happier and less painful manner than directly satisfying offended justice ourselves.

We should also take heart when thinking of a judgment in which nothing is overlooked, because this also means that no act of obedience, no kindness, no good deed however small is ever forgotten, and no corresponding blessing is ever withheld.

We Need Not Fear Since We Can Look to the Savior for Help We Need

My third and final observation regarding what it means always to remember Him is that we can always look to the Savior for help. In the infant days of the Church, really before the actual reestablishment of the Church as an institution, Jesus counseled and comforted the two young men who were working to translate the Book of Mormon and who would soon have the priesthood conferred upon them, Joseph Smith and Oliver Cowdery. Joseph was twenty-three years old at the time, and Oliver twenty-two. Persecution and other obstacles were frequent if not constant. In these conditions, in April 1829, the Lord spoke these words to them:

> Fear not to do good, my sons, . . . let earth and hell combine against you, for if ye are built upon my rock, they cannot prevail.
>
> Behold, I do not condemn you; go your ways and sin no more; perform with soberness the work which I have commanded you.
>
> Look unto me in every thought; doubt not, fear not.

Behold the wounds which pierced my side, and also the prints of the nails in my hands and feet; be faithful, keep my commandments, and ye shall inherit the kingdom of heaven. Amen. (D&C 6:33–37)

Looking unto the Savior "in every thought" is, of course, another way of saying "always remember him." As we do, we need not doubt or fear. He reminded Joseph and Oliver, as He reminds us, that through His Atonement He has been given all power in heaven and earth (see Matthew 28:18) and has both the capacity and the will to protect us and minister to our needs—"Behold the wounds which pierced my side, and also the prints of the nails in my hands and feet." We need only be faithful and we can rely implicitly on Him and His grace.

Isaiah states it this way, "Hearken unto me, ye that know righteousness, the people in whose heart is my law; fear ye not the reproach of men, neither be ye afraid of their revilings. For the moth shall eat them up like a garment, and the worm shall eat them like wool: but my righteousness shall be for ever, and my salvation from generation to generation" (Isaiah 51:7–8; see also verses 12–16).

Preceding the comforting revelation to Joseph and Oliver that I have cited, the Prophet endured a poignant, painful experience, familiar to all of us, that taught him to look to the Savior and not fear the opinions, pressures, and threats of men. I quote from the account in our priesthood and Relief Society manual, *Teachings of Presidents of the Church: Joseph Smith*:

On June 14, 1828, Martin Harris left Harmony, Pennsylvania, taking the first 116 manuscript pages translated from the gold plates to show to some of his family members in Palmyra, New York. The very next day, Joseph and Emma's first child was born, a son they named Alvin. The baby died that same day, and Emma's health declined until she was near death herself. The Prophet's mother later wrote: "For some time, [Emma] seemed to tremble upon the verge of the silent home of her infant. So uncertain seemed her fate for a season that in the space of two weeks her husband never slept one hour in undisturbed quiet. At the end of this time, his anxiety became so great about the manuscript that he determined, as his wife was now some better, that as soon as she had gained a little more strength he would make a trip to New York and see after the same."

In July, at Emma's suggestion, the Prophet left Emma in her mother's care and traveled by stagecoach to his parents' home in Manchester Township, New York. The Prophet's trip covered about 125 miles and took two or three days to complete. Distraught about the loss of his firstborn son, worried about his wife, and gravely concerned about the manuscript, Joseph neither ate nor slept during the entire trip. A fellow traveler, the only other passenger on the stagecoach, observed the Prophet's weakened state and insisted on accompanying him for the 20-mile walk from the stagecoach station to the Smith home. For the last four miles of the walk, recalled the Prophet's mother, "the stranger was under the necessity of leading Joseph by his arm, for nature was too much exhausted to support him any longer and he would fall asleep as he stood upon his feet." Immediately upon reaching his parents' home, the Prophet sent for Martin Harris.

Martin arrived at the Smith home in the early afternoon, downcast and forlorn. He did not have the manuscript, he said, and did not know where it was. Hearing this, Joseph exclaimed, "Oh! My God, my God. . . . All is lost, is lost. What shall I do? I have sinned. It is I that tempted the wrath of God by asking him for that which I had no right to ask. . . . How shall I appear before the Lord? Of what rebuke am I not worthy from the angel of the Most High?"

As the day wore on, the Prophet paced back and forth in his parents' home in great distress, "weeping and grieving." The next day he left to return to Harmony, where, he said, "I commenced humbling myself in mighty prayer before the Lord . . . that if possible I might obtain mercy at his hands and be forgiven of all that I had done which was contrary to his will."

The Lord severely chastised the Prophet for fearing man more than God, but assured him he could be forgiven. "Thou art Joseph," the Lord said, "and thou wast chosen to do the work of the Lord, but because of transgression, if thou art not aware thou wilt fall. But remember, God is merciful; therefore, repent of that which thou hast done which is contrary to the commandment which I gave you, and thou art still chosen, and art again called to the work" (D&C 3:9–10).

For a time, the Lord took the Urim and Thummim and the plates from Joseph. But these things were soon restored to him. "The angel was rejoiced when he gave me back the Urim and Thummim," the Prophet recalled, "and said that God was pleased with my faithfulness and humility, and loved me for my penitence and diligence in prayer, in the which I had performed my duty so well as to . . . be able to enter upon the work of translation again." As Joseph moved forward in the great work before him, he was now fortified by the sweet feelings of receiving the Lord's forgiveness and a renewed determination to do His will.[2]

As you know, the Prophet's determination to rely upon God and not fear what men could do became fixed after this experience. His life thereafter was a shining example of what it means to remember Christ by relying upon His power and mercy. Joseph expressed this understanding during his very difficult and trying incarceration at Liberty, Missouri, in these words: "You know, brethren, that a very large ship is benefited very much by a very small helm in the time of a storm, by being kept workways with the wind and the waves. Therefore, dearly beloved brethren, let us cheerfully do all things that lie in our power; and then may we stand still, with the utmost assurance, to see the salvation of God, and for his arm to be revealed" (D&C 123:16–17).

In short, to "always remember him" means that we do not live our lives in fear. We know that challenges, disappointments, and sorrows will come to each of us in different ways, but we also know that in the end, because of our divine Advocate, all things can be made to work together for our good (see D&C 90:24 and 98:3). It is the faith expressed so simply by President Gordon B. Hinckley when he would say, "Things will work out." Because we always remember the Savior, we can "cheerfully do all things that lie in our power," confident that His power and love for us will see us through.

Now I bless you that you will be able to always remember our incomparable and divine Redeemer—that you will feel the need and be able to discern and follow His will in all aspects of your life, so that increasingly you will be one with Him as He is one with the Father; that you will always retain an awareness of your accountability to the Lord to sustain you in your fight against temptation or, where needed, in your repentance of any sin or misdeed; and finally, that you will always have with you the quiet assurance of His love and grace that will enable you to withstand the assaults of the adversary and his supporters and to feel the comfort and reality of your Lord's protecting care. I bless you that the promise to those who always remember Him—"that they may always have his spirit to be with them" (D&C 20:77)—will be fully realized in your life. I bear my witness of the power of the Atonement of Jesus Christ. I bear witness of the reality of the living, resurrected Lord. I bear witness of the infinite and personal love of the Father and the Son for each of you and pray that you will live in constant remembrance of that love in all its expressions.

Notes

1. Brigham Young, discourse in *Deseret News*, September 10, 1856, 212.
2. *Teachings of Presidents of the Church: Joseph Smith* (Salt Lake City: The Church of Jesus Christ of Latter-day Saints, 2007), 69–71.

President James E. Faust (1920–2007) was a member of the First Presidency. Address at the Sidney B. Sperry Symposium at Brigham Young University on October 20, 1990, published in *Sperry Symposium Classics: The New Testament* (Provo, UT: Religious Studies Center, Brigham Young University, 2006), 1–7.

14

"A Surety of a Better Testament"

MY CALLING PLACES UPON ME a responsibility to witness concerning the reality of the Savior and His mission. I hope that my assignment with the BYU Jerusalem Center and the Holy Land will be a helpful background against which to discuss some phase of the life and ministry of the Lord Jesus Christ.

I take my text from the Apostle Paul's Epistle to the Hebrews: "By so much was Jesus made a surety of a better testament" (Hebrews 7:22). What is a "surety"? We find in turning to the dictionary that surety is "the state of being sure"; it is an undertaking or a pledge. It also refers to "one who has become legally liable for the debt, default, or failure in duty of another."[1] Do not the Savior and His mission have claim upon all these meanings?

What is a testament? The primary meaning of "testament" is a "covenant with God." It is also holy scripture, a will, a witness, a tangible proof, an expression of conviction.[2] So the Savior as a surety is a guarantor of a better covenant with God.

We all know that moving from the Old Testament to the New Testament is moving from the rigid formality of the letter of the law to the spirit of the law. It is a better testament because the intent of a person alone becomes part of the rightness or wrongness of human action. So our intent to do evil or our desire to do good will be a free-standing element of consideration of our actions. We are told we will be judged in part by the intent of our hearts (see D&C 88:109). An example of being convicted by free-standing intent is found in Matthew: "Ye have heard that it was said by them of old time, Thou shalt not commit adultery: But I say unto you, That whosoever looketh on a woman to lust after her hath committed adultery with her already in his heart" (Matthew 5:27–28).

This New Testament is harder doctrine. In the old English common law, a formality and rigidity developed in the administration of the law to the point where, for justice to be obtained, the law of equity developed. One of my favorite maxims about equity is "Equity does what

Carl Heinrich Bloch, *Sermon on the Mount.*

ought to be done." The New Testament goes further. In a large measure we will be judged not only by what we have done but by what we should have done in a given situation.

Much of the spirit of the New Testament is found in the Sermon on the Mount. The New Testament requires a reconciliation of differences. "Therefore if thou bring thy gift to the altar, and there rememberest that thy brother hath ought against thee; leave there thy gift before the altar, and go thy way; first be reconciled to thy brother, and then come and offer thy gift" (Matthew 5:23–24).

In the New Testament, swearing becomes completely prohibited:

> Again, ye have heard that it hath been said by them of old time, Thou shalt not forswear thyself, but shalt perform unto the Lord thine oaths:
>
> But I say unto you, Swear not at all; neither by heaven; for it is God's throne:
>
> Nor by the earth; for it is his footstool: neither by Jerusalem; for it is the city of the great King.
>
> Neither shalt thou swear by thy head, because thou canst not make one hair white or black.
>
> But let your communication be, Yea, yea; Nay, nay: for whatsoever is more than these cometh of evil. (Matthew 5:33–37)

Then follows more of the difficult doctrine of the New Testament:

> But I say unto you, That ye resist not evil: but whosoever shall smite thee on thy right cheek, turn to him the other also.
>
> And if any man will sue thee at the law, and take away thy coat, let him have thy cloke also.
>
> And whosoever shall compel thee to go a mile, go with him twain.
>
> Give to him that asketh thee, and from him that would borrow of thee turn not thou away.
>
> Ye have heard that it hath been said, Thou shalt love thy neighbour, and hate thine enemy.

But I say unto you, Love your enemies, bless them that curse you, do good to them that hate you, and pray for them which despitefully use you, and persecute you. (Matthew 5:39–44)

The New Testament suggests a new form and content of prayer. It is profoundly simple and uncomplicated:

And when thou prayest, thou shalt not be as the hypocrites are: for they love to pray standing in the synagogues and in the corners of the streets, that they may be seen of men. Verily I say unto you, They have their reward.

But thou, when thou prayest, enter into thy closet, and when thou hast shut the door, pray to thy Father which is in secret; and thy Father which seeth in secret shall reward thee openly.

But when ye pray, use not vain repetitions, as the heathen do: for they think that they shall be heard for their much speaking.

Be not ye therefore like unto them: for your Father knoweth what things ye have need of, before ye ask him.

After this manner therefore pray ye: Our Father which art in heaven, Hallowed be thy name.

Thy kingdom come. Thy will be done in earth, as it is in heaven.

Give us this day our daily bread.

And forgive us our debts, as we forgive our debtors.

And lead us not into temptation, but deliver us from evil: For thine is the kingdom, and the power, and the glory, for ever. Amen. (Matthew 6:5–13)

The New Testament suggests that the doing of our good works ought to be in secret: "But when thou doest alms, let not thy left hand know what thy right hand doeth: That thine alms may be in secret: and thy Father which seeth in secret himself shall reward thee openly" (Matthew 6:3–4).

But the greatest challenge, the hardest doctrine, is also found in the Sermon on the Mount: "Be ye therefore perfect, even as your Father which is in heaven is perfect" (Matthew 5:48).

The Savior as "the mediator of the new testament" (Hebrews 9:15) introduced a higher law of marriage:

> And the Pharisees came to him, and asked him, Is it lawful for a man to put away his wife? tempting him.
>
> And he answered and said unto them, What did Moses command you?
>
> And they said, Moses suffered to write a bill of divorcement, and to put her away.
>
> And Jesus answered and said unto them, For the hardness of your heart he wrote you this precept.
>
> But from the beginning of the creation God made them male and female.
>
> For this cause shall a man leave his father and mother, and cleave to his wife;
>
> And they twain shall be one flesh: so then they are no more twain, but one flesh.
>
> What therefore God hath joined together, let not man put asunder. (Mark 10:2–9)

The challenge of Jesus was to replace the rigid technical "thou shalt not" of the law of Moses that the spiritually immature children of Israel needed with the spirit of the "better testament." How was that to be done? Time was short. He had only three years. How should He begin? Obviously He must begin with the Apostles and the small group of disciples around Him who would have the responsibility to carry on the work after His death. President J. Reuben Clark Jr., a counselor in the First Presidency, describes this challenge as follows: "This task involved the overturning, the virtual outlawing, of the centuries-old Mosaic law of the Jews, and the substitution therefore of the Gospel of Christ."[3]

It was not easy for even the Apostles to understand, of whom doubting Thomas is a good example. Thomas had been with the Savior when the Savior, on several occasions, foretold of His death and Resurrection. Yet when Thomas was told that the resurrected Christ lived, he said, "Except I shall see in his hands the print of the nails, and put my finger into the print of the nails, and thrust my hand into his side, I will not believe" (John 20:25). Perhaps Thomas can be forgiven because so great an event had never happened before.

What about Peter's conversion to the great principle that the gospel of Jesus Christ is for everyone? He had been an eyewitness, as he stated, that "we have not followed cunningly devised fables, when we make known unto you the power and coming of our Lord Jesus Christ, but were eyewitnesses of his majesty" (2 Peter 1:16). To what had Peter been an eyewitness? He had been an eyewitness to everything in the Savior's ministry. He had seen the Savior welcome the Samaritans, who were loathed by the Jews, following the encounter with the Samaritan at the well of Jacob (see John 4). Peter had seen a vision and heard the voice of the Lord, saying, "What God hath cleansed, that call not thou common" (Acts 10:15). Finally, fully converted and receiving a spiritual confirmation, Peter opened his mouth and said, "Of a truth I perceive that God is no respecter of persons: but in every nation he that feareth him, and worketh righteousness, is accepted with him" (Acts 10:34–35).

It is strengthening to review the testimonies of the Apostles that Jesus is, in fact, the Christ. These testimonies are also a surety of a better testament. The first recorded testimony of the divinity of the Savior is the occasion of Jesus walking on the water, which is most fully recorded in Matthew 14:24–33:

> But the ship was now in the midst of the sea, tossed with waves: for the wind was contrary.
>
> And in the fourth watch of the night Jesus went unto them, walking on the sea.
>
> And when the disciples saw him walking on the sea, they were troubled, saying, It is a spirit; and they cried out for fear.
>
> But straightway Jesus spake unto them, saying, Be of good cheer; it is I; be not afraid.
>
> And Peter answered him and said, Lord, if it be thou, bid me come unto thee on the water.
>
> And he said, Come. And when Peter was come down out of the ship, he walked on the water, to go to Jesus.

But when he saw the wind boisterous, he was afraid; and beginning to sink, he cried, saying, Lord, save me.

And immediately Jesus stretched forth his hand, and caught him, and said unto him, O thou of little faith, wherefore didst thou doubt?

And when they were come into the ship, the wind ceased.

Then they that were in the ship came and worshipped him, saying, Of a truth thou art the Son of God.

The second is that of Peter. The fullest account appears in Matthew, with which we are all familiar:

When Jesus came into the coasts of Cæsarea Philippi, he asked his disciples, saying, Whom do men say that I the Son of man am?

And they said, Some say that thou art John the Baptist: some, Elias; and others, Jeremias, or one of the prophets.

He saith unto them, But whom say ye that I am?

And Simon Peter answered and said, Thou art the Christ, the Son of the living God.

And Jesus answered and said unto him, Blessed art thou, Simon Bar-jona: for flesh and blood hath not revealed it unto thee, but my Father which is in heaven.

And I say also unto thee, That thou art Peter, and upon this rock I will build my church; and the gates of hell shall not prevail against it. (Matthew 16:13–18)

The third instance again involves Peter. After the great sermon on the bread of life, in which the Savior made clear to those who had been fed by the loaves and the fishes that He and His doctrine were the Bread of Life, John records: "From that time many of his disciples went back, and walked no more with him. Then said Jesus unto the twelve, Will ye also go away? Then Simon Peter answered him, Lord, to whom shall we go? thou hast the words of eternal life. And we believe and are sure that thou art that Christ, the Son of the living God" (John 6:66–69).

The testimony of the divinity of the Savior given by God the Father and heard by Peter, James, and John is recorded in connection with the happenings on the Mount of the Transfiguration. The accounts of Matthew, Mark, and Luke all tell of the appearance of Moses and Elias talking to the Savior. Matthew records:

> Then answered Peter, and said unto Jesus, Lord, it is good for us to be here: if thou wilt, let us make here three tabernacles; one for thee, and one for Moses, and one for Elias.
>
> While he yet spake, behold, a bright cloud overshadowed them: and behold a voice out of the cloud, which said, This is my beloved Son, in whom I am well pleased; hear ye him.
>
> And when the disciples heard it, they fell on their face, and were sore afraid.
>
> And Jesus came and touched them, and said, Arise, and be not afraid.
>
> And when they had lifted up their eyes, they saw no man, save Jesus only.
>
> And as they came down from the mountain, Jesus charged them, saying, Tell the vision to no man, until the Son of man be risen again from the dead.
>
> And his disciples asked him, saying, Why then say the scribes that Elias must first come?
>
> And Jesus answered and said unto them, Elias truly shall first come, and restore all things.
>
> But I say unto you, That Elias is come already, and they knew him not, but have done unto him whatsoever they listed. Likewise shall also the Son of man suffer of them.
>
> Then the disciples understood that he spake unto them of John the Baptist. (Matthew 17:4–13)

We are grateful for these profound statements of the "eyewitnesses of his majesty" (2 Peter 1:16). They form part of the footings of our faith. But the miracles performed by the Savior and the testimonies of those who saw and heard were far from convincing to everyone, perhaps because a testimony is such a personal, spiritual conviction.

The New Testament is a surety of better testament because so much is left to the intent of the heart and of the mind. The refinement of the soul is part of the reinforcing steel of a personal testimony. If there is no witness in the heart and in the mind, there can be no testimony. The Sermon on the Mount produces deep, spiritual reinforcing that moves us to higher spiritual attainment.

I leave with you my blessing. May the Lord watch over you and strengthen you. I invoke a blessing upon the institutions sponsoring the Sperry Symposium to be powerful in instructing faith and witness and testimony. And I witness to you in the authority of the holy apostleship of the divinity of the calling and mission of the Savior and of the Restoration of the gospel by Joseph Smith. To this I bear witness and testimony in the name of the Lord Jesus Christ, amen.

Notes

1. *Merriam-Webster's New Collegiate Dictionary*, 11th ed., s.v. "surety."
2. *Merriam-Webster's New Collegiate Dictionary*, s.v. "testament."
3. J. Reuben Clark Jr., *Why the King James Version* (Salt Lake City: Deseret Book, 1979), 51.

Elder Neal A. Maxwell (1926–2004) was a member of the Quorum of the Twelve Apostles. Address at the Book of Mormon Symposium at Brigham Young University on October 10, 1986, published in *A Book of Mormon Treasury: Gospel Insights from General Authorities and Religious Educators* (Provo, UT: Religious Studies Center, Brigham Young University, 2003), 1–18.

15 THE BOOK OF MORMON: A GREAT ANSWER TO "THE GREAT QUESTION"

T HE BOOK OF MORMON PROVIDES resounding and great answers to what Amulek designated as "the great question"—namely, is there really a redeeming Christ? (Alma 34:5–6). The Book of Mormon with clarity and with evidence says, "Yes! Yes! Yes!" Moreover, in its recurring theme, the book even declares that "all things which have been given of God from the beginning of the world, unto man, are the typifying of [Christ]" (2 Nephi 11:4). How striking its answers are, considering all that God might have chosen to tell us! He, before whom all things—past, present, and future—are continually (see D&C 130:7), has chosen to tell us about the "gospel" (3 Nephi 27:13–14, 21; D&C 33:12; D&C 39:6; 76:40–41)—the transcending "good news," the resplendent answers to "the great question."

Astoundingly, too, God, who has created "worlds without number" (Moses 1:33, 37–38; see Isaiah 45:18), has chosen to reassure us on this tiny "speck of sand" that he "doeth not anything save it be for the benefit of [this] world; for he loveth [this] world" (2 Nephi 26:24); and "for behold, this is my work and my glory—to bring to pass the immortality and eternal life of man" (Moses 1:39).

It should not surprise us that this glorious gospel message is more perfect than any of its messengers, save Jesus only. Nor should it surprise us that the gospel message is more comprehensive than the comprehension of any of its bearers or hearers, save Jesus only.

Apparently translated by Joseph Smith at an average rate of eight or more of its printed pages a day, the Book of Mormon's full significance could not have been immediately and fully savored by the Prophet Joseph. Given this average, according to Professor Jack Welch, only one and a half days, for instance, would have been spent translating all of the first five chapters of Mosiah, a remarkable sermon about which books will be written.

Coming forth as the Book of Mormon did in Bible Belt and revival conditions early in this dispensation, we of the Church have been slow to appreciate its special relevance to the erosive conditions in our time, the latter part of this dispensation. Questioning and doubting has grown rapidly on the part of some scholars and even some clerics about the historicity of Jesus. Such, however, was not the America of 1830. Demographically speaking, therefore, the majority of the "ministry" of the Book of Mormon is occurring in a time of deep uncertainty and unrest concerning "the great question"—the very question which the Book of Mormon was created to answer!

Another strong impression is how the Book of Mormon foretells the latter-day emergence of "other books" of scripture (1 Nephi 13:39), of which it is one, "proving to the world that the holy scriptures are true, and that God does inspire men and call them to his holy work in this age and generation, as well as in generations of old" (D&C 20:11).

With regard to omissions from the precious Holy Bible, in just one chapter of 1 Nephi, chapter 13, four phrases appear: *taken away,* four times; *taken out,* once; *kept back,* twice; and *taken away out of,* once. Eight indications of omissions because of transmission deficiencies appear in one chapter! Moreover, as Nephi indicated, it was the "precious things" which had been lost. You will recall that Joseph Smith's translation of Luke 11:52 shows Jesus criticizing those, then, who had "taken away the key of knowledge, the fulness of the scriptures" (Joseph Smith Translation, Luke 11:52).

While we do not know precisely what was "kept back" or "taken away" (see 1 Nephi 13:40), logically there would be a heavy representation of such plain and precious truths in the Restoration. Therefore, the "other books" provide precisely that which God is most anxious to have "had again" among the children of men, so that we might know the truth of things, in Jacob's felicitous phrase, of "things as they really are" (Jacob 4:13).

The convergence of these "other books" of scripture with the precious Bible is part of the rhythm of the Restoration. The rhythm would have been impossible except for devoted and heroic individuals, including the Jewish prophets and the Jewish people of antiquity who, in the words of the Book of Mormon, had "travails," "labors," and "pains" to preserve the Bible for us. Lamentably, as foreseen, for that contribution the Jews have been unthanked, as a people, and instead have been "cursed," "hated," and made "game" of (see 2 Nephi 29:4–5; 3 Nephi 29:4, 8). A much later expression of the rhythm of the Restoration is symbolically reflected, too, in the graves of some Church members of the 1830s buried in Ohio and Indiana. Recently discovered, there is a trail of testifying tombstones which display, in stone, replicas of both the Bible *and* the Book of Mormon. These members felt doubly blessed and wanted the world to know it.

The existing scriptures advise of more than twenty other books to come forth[1] (see 1 Nephi 19:10–16). One day, in fact, "all things shall be revealed unto the children of men which ever have been . . . and which ever will be" (2 Nephi 27:11). Hence, the ninth article of faith is such an impressive statement! My personal opinion, however, is that we will not get additional scriptures until we learn to appreciate fully those we already have.

The "other books," particularly the Book of Mormon, fulfill—if constitutional lawyers will forgive me—Nephi's "establishment clause": "These last records . . . shall *establish* the truth of the first, which are of the twelve apostles of the Lamb" (1 Nephi 13:40). What the latter-day seer, Joseph Smith, brought forth will actually aid some people in accepting God's word which had already gone forth, namely the Bible (see 2 Nephi 3:11), by convincing them "that the records of the prophets and of the twelve apostles of the Lamb are true" (1 Nephi 13:39). There is high drama ahead!

Meanwhile, even as the criticism of the Book of Mormon continues to intensify, the book continues to testify and to diversify its displays of interior consistency, conceptual richness, and its connections with antiquity.

The plentitude of the Restoration followed as foreseen by Amos: "a famine in the land, not a famine of bread, nor a thirst for water, but of hearing the words of the Lord" (Amos 8:11). The end of that famine was marked by the coming of the Book of Mormon and the "other books."

Such books have been and are the Lord's means of preserving the spiritual memory of centuries past. Without moral memory, spiritual tragedy soon follows: "Now . . . there were many of the rising generation that . . . did not believe what had been said concerning the resurrection of the dead, neither did they believe concerning the coming of Christ" (Mosiah 26:1–2).

And on another occasion: "And at the time that Mosiah discovered them . . . they had brought no records with them; and they denied the being of their Creator" (Omni 1:17).

Belief in Deity and the Resurrection are usually the first to go. Ironically, though we gratefully accept the Bible as the word of God, the very process of its emergence has, alas, caused an unnecessary slackening of the Christian faith on the part of some. Because available Bible sources are not original but represent dated derivations and translations, "other books" of scripture, which have come to us directly from ancient records and modern revelations, are even more prized.

Paul, for instance, wrote his first epistle to the Corinthians about AD 56. We do not, of course, have that original parchment. Instead, the earliest document involving the first epistle to the Corinthians was discovered in the 1930s and is dated to about AD 200. By comparison, King Benjamin's sermon was given in about 124 BC by a prophet. In the late fourth century AD it was selected by another prophet— Mormon— to be a part of the Book of Mormon. Benjamin's sermon was translated into English in AD 1829 by Joseph Smith, another prophet. There was, therefore, an unbroken chain of a prophet-originator, a prophet-editor, and a prophet-translator collaborating in a remarkable process.

Even so, some discount the Book of Mormon because they cannot see the plates from which it was translated. Furthermore, they say that we do not know enough about the process of translation. But Moroni's promise to serious readers, to be discussed shortly, involves reading and praying over the book's substance, not over the process of its production. We are "looking beyond the mark" (Jacob 4:14), therefore, when, figuratively speaking, we are more interested in the physical dimensions of the cross than what was achieved thereon by Jesus. Or when we neglect Alma's words on faith because we are too fascinated by the light-shielding hat reportedly used by Joseph Smith during some of the translating of the Book of Mormon.[2]

Most of all, I have been especially struck in rereading and pondering the Book of Mormon with how, for the serious reader, it provides a very, very significant response to what might be called modern man's architectonic needs—that is, our deep needs to discern some design, purpose, pattern, or plan regarding human existence.

No less than fifteen times, the Book of Mormon uses the word *plan* in connection with the plan of salvation or its components. The very use of the word *plan* is itself striking. In bringing back this particular "plain and precious" truth—namely, God not only lives but does have a plan for mankind—the Book of Mormon is unusually relevant for our age and time. Phrases about God's planning from the "foundation of the world" appear not at all in the Old Testament but ten times in the New Testament and three times as often in the other books.[3] *Foundation*, of course, thus denotes a creation overseen by a loving and planning God.

The Book of Mormon lays further and heavy emphasis on how the gospel, in fact, has been with mankind from Adam on down. Only six pages into the book, we read of the testifying words of all the prophets "since the world began" (1 Nephi 3:20); five pages later, a recitation notes the words of the "holy prophets, from the beginning" (1 Nephi 5:13). This one verse represents many: "For behold, did not Moses prophesy unto them concerning the coming of the Messiah, and that God should redeem his people? Yea, and even all the prophets who have prophesied ever since the world began—have they not spoken more or less concerning these things?" (Mosiah 13:33; see also 2 Nephi 25:19).

It seems probable that there will be some additional discoveries of ancient records pertaining to the Old and New Testaments, further shrinking the time between the origination of those scriptures and the earliest available documentation. However, this *shrinking* will not automatically lead to an *enlarging* of the faith—at least of some. Future discoveries of ancient documents that may "throw greater views upon [His] gospel" (D&C 10:45) may also focus on portions of Jesus' gospel which existed *before* Jesus' mortal ministry. Unfortunately, a few may unjustifiably use such discoveries to diminish the divinity of the Redeemer, inferring that Jesus is therefore not the originator, as previously thought. However, the restored gospel, including the Book of Mormon, gives us such a clear reading of the spiritual history of mankind, showing God's "tender mercies" (see 1 Nephi 1:20; Ether 6:12) from Adam on down. There is thus no need for us to be anxious about finding a reliable portion of Christ's gospel before Christ's mortal ministry. The gospel was preached and known from the beginning (see Moses 5:58–59).

The detailed, interior correlation of the Book of Mormon—indeed of all true scripture—is marvelous to behold. Centuries before Christ's birth, King Benjamin prophesied: "And he shall be called Jesus Christ, the Son of God, the Father of heaven and earth, the Creator of all things from the beginning" (Mosiah 3:8).

The resurrected Jesus introduced Himself to the Nephites with strikingly similar words centuries later: "Behold, I am Jesus Christ the Son of God. I created the heavens and the earth, and all things that in them are. I was with the Father from the beginning" (3 Nephi 9:15).

But back to God's enfolding plan: Alma, after a discussion of the Fall, declared it was "expedient that man should know concerning the things whereof [God] had appointed unto them; therefore [God] sent angels to converse with them . . . and [make] known unto them the plan of redemption, which had been prepared from the foundation of the world" (Alma 12:28–30). This is the very process which was followed, of course, in North America in the first half of the nineteenth century through angelic visitations to Joseph Smith.

At the center of this architectonic responsiveness, with its related dispensational emphasis, is the Book of Mormon's steady, Christian core. Jacob wrote, "We knew of Christ . . . many hundred years before his coming; . . . also all the holy prophets which were before us. Behold, they believed in Christ and worshipped the Father in his name, . . . [keeping]

the law of Moses, it pointing our souls to him" (Jacob 4:4–5). Jacob was emphatic: "None of the prophets have written . . . save they have spoken concerning this Christ" (Jacob 7:11).

God witnesses to us in so many ways: "Yea, and all things denote there is a God; yea, even the earth, and all things that are upon the face of it, yea, and its motion, yea, and also all the planets which move in their regular form do witness that there is a Supreme Creator" (Alma 30:44; see also Moses 6:63).

A believing British scientist has observed that our planet is especially situated: "Just a bit nearer to the sun, and Planet Earth's seas would soon be boiling; just a little farther out, and the whole world would become a frozen wilderness." This scientist noted: "If our orbit happened to be the wrong shape, . . . then we should alternately freeze like Mars and fry like Venus once a year. Fortunately for us, our planet's orbit is very nearly a circle."[4]

"The 21 percent of oxygen is another critical figure. Animals would have difficulty breathing if the oxygen content fell very far below that value. But an oxygen level much higher than this would also be disastrous, since the extra oxygen would act as a fire-raising material. Forests and grasslands would flare up every time lightning struck during a dry spell, and life on earth would become extremely hazardous."[5]

When, therefore, we know the affirmative answers to "the great question," we can, in Amulek's phrase, "live in thanksgiving daily" (Alma 34:38) with gratitude for the many special conditions which make daily life on this earth possible.

God's encompassing purposes are set forth to the very end of the Book of Mormon. Moroni urged a precise method of study and verification which, if followed, will show among other things how merciful the Lord has been unto mankind "from the creation of Adam" (Moroni 10:3). Foretelling can be convincing too, along with remembering, in showing the sweep of God's love. "Telling them of things which must shortly come, that they might know and remember at the time of their coming that they had been made known unto them beforehand, to the intent that they might believe" (Helaman 16:5; see also Mormon 8:34–35).

Every age needs this architectonic message, but none more desperately than our age, which is preoccupied with skepticism and hedonism: "For how knoweth a man the master whom he has not served, and who is a stranger unto him, and is far from the thoughts and intents of his heart?" (Mosiah 5:13).

If, however, one gets too caught up in the warfare in the Book of Mormon, or if he is too preoccupied with the process of the book's emergence, such transcendent truths as the foregoing can easily be overlooked.

Even the title page[6] declares, among other things, that the Book of Mormon was to advise posterity "what great things the Lord hath done for their fathers." The very lack of such a spiritual memory once led to a decline of ancient Israel: "There arose another generation after them, which knew not the Lord, nor yet the works which he had done for Israel" (Judges 2:10).

Why was it so difficult for a whole people—or for Laman and Lemuel—to maintain faith? Because they were uninformed and unbelieving as to "the dealings of that God who had created them" (1 Nephi 2:12; 2 Nephi 1:10). Many efforts were made: "I, Nephi, did teach my brethren these things; . . . I did read many things to them, which were engraven upon the plates of brass, that they might know concerning the doings of the Lord in other lands, among people of old" (1 Nephi 19:22).

The prophetic emphasis on the Book of Mormon, therefore, is so pertinent!

Even the criticisms of the book will end up having their usefulness in God's further plans. Granted, the great answers in the book will not now be accepted by disbelievers. Such people would not believe the Lord's words—whether coming through Paul or Joseph Smith—even if they had an original Pauline parchment or direct access to the gold plates. The Lord once comforted Joseph Smith by saying such individuals "will not believe my words . . . if [shown] all these things" (D&C 5:7).

Thus, some decry the Book of Mormon. However, for those who have ears to hear, it represents an informing but haunting "cry from the dust" (2 Nephi 3:20). It is the voice of a fallen people sent to lift us. Described as a "whisper out of the dust" (2 Nephi 26:16) from "those who have slumbered" (2 Nephi 27:9), this sound from the dust is the choral cry of many anguished voices with but a single, simple message. Their spiritual struggles span a few centuries but concern the message of the ages—the gospel of Jesus Christ! The peoples of the Book of Mormon were not on the center stage of secular history. Instead, theirs was a comparatively little theater. Yet it featured history's largest message.

Not pleasing to those who crave other kinds of history, the Book of Mormon is pleasing to those who genuinely seek answers to "the great question" (Alma 34:5). Contrary to the sad conclusion now reached by many, the Book of Mormon declares to us again and again that the universe is not comprised of what has been called "godless geometric space."[7]

Granted, too, usually the "learned shall not read [these things], for they have rejected them" (2 Nephi 27:20). This is not solely a reference to Professor Anthon, since the plural pronoun *they* is used. The reference suggests a mind-set of most of the learned of the world, who, by and large, do not take the Book of Mormon seriously. Even when they read it, they do not *really* read it, except with a mind-set which excludes miracles, including the miracle of the book's coming forth by the "gift and power of God." Their flawed approach diverts them from scrutinizing the substance. Sometimes, as has been said, certain mortals are so afraid of being "taken in," they cannot be "taken out" of their mindsets.[8]

How dependent mankind is, therefore, upon emancipating revelation: "Behold, great and marvelous are the works of the Lord. How unsearchable are the depths of the mysteries of him; and it is impossible that man should find out all his ways. And no man knoweth of his ways save it be revealed unto him; wherefore, brethren, despise not the revelations of God" (Jacob 4:8).

Now to Moroni's promise, which is a promise that rests on a premise, a promise with several parts. The reader is (1) to read and ponder, (2) while remembering God's mercies to mankind from Adam until now, and (3) to pray in the name of Christ and ask God with real intent if the book is true, (4) while having faith in Christ, then (5) God will manifest the truth of the book. The reverse approach, scanning while doubting, is the flip side of Moroni's methodology and produces flippant conclusions. Moroni's process of verification is surely not followed by many readers or reviewers of this book. This leads to misapprehension—like mistakenly labeling rumor with her thousand tongues as the gift of tongues!

Therefore, we should not be deluded into thinking that these "other books" will be welcomed, especially by those whose sense of sufficiency is expressed thus: "There cannot be any more" such books and "we need no more" such books (2 Nephi 29:3, 6).

Another strong impression from my rereading is how the Book of Mormon peoples, though Christians, were tied, until Jesus came, much more strictly to the preexilic law of Moses than we in the Church have fully appreciated. "And, notwithstanding we believe in Christ, we keep the law of Moses, and look forward with steadfastness unto Christ, until the law shall be fulfilled" (2 Nephi 25:24).

People back then were thus to "look forward unto the Messiah, and believe in him to come as though he already was" (Jarom 1:11). Moses indeed prophesied of the Messiah, but not all of his words are in the treasured Old Testament. Recall the walk of the resurrected Jesus with two disciples on the road to Emmaus? Their walk probably covered about twelve kilometers and provided ample time for Jesus' recitation of not merely three or four, but many prophecies by Moses and others concerning Christ's mortal ministry (Luke 24:27).

Scriptures attesting to Jesus' divinity are vital in any age. Otherwise, as the Book of Mormon prophesies, He will be considered a mere man (Mosiah 3:9) or a person of "naught" (1 Nephi 19:9). Over the decades, what has been called the "dilution of Christianity from within"[9] has resulted in a number of theologians not only diminishing their regard for Christ but likewise regarding the Resurrection as merely "a symbolic expression for the renewal of life for the disciple."[10] Once again we see the supernal importance of the "other books" of scripture: they reinforce the reality of the Resurrection, especially the Book of Mormon's additional gospel with its report of the visitation of and instruction by the resurrected Jesus. The resurrection of many others occurred and, by Jesus' pointed instruction, was made record of (see 3 Nephi 23:6–13).

Thus the Book of Mormon resoundingly, richly, and grandly answers the "great question." Granted, in our day, the post-Christian era, many who are preoccupied are not even asking that great question anymore, regarding Christianity "not as untrue or even as unthinkable, but simply irrelevant,"[11] just like some in Benjamin and Mosiah's times (see Mosiah 28:1–2; Omni 1:17).

If the answer to the "great question" were "no," there would quickly come a wrenching surge of what Professor Hugh Nibley has called the "terrible questions."

Even the historical, political, and geographical setting of the emergence of the Book of Mormon was special. President Brigham Young boldly declared: "Could that book have been brought forth and published to the world under any other government but the Government of the United States? No. [God] has governed and controlled the settling of this continent. He led our fathers from Europe to this land . . . and inspired the guaranteed freedom in our Government, though that guarantee is too often disregarded."[12]

In the midst of this continually unfolding drama, a few members of the Church, alas, desert the cause; they are like one who abandons an oasis to search for water in the desert. Some of these few will doubtless become critics, and they will be welcomed into the "great and spacious building." Henceforth, however, so far as their theological accommodations are concerned, they are in a spacious but third-rate hotel. All dressed up, as the Book of Mormon says, "exceedingly fine" (1 Nephi 8:27), they have no place to go except—one day, hopefully, home.

The great answers to the "great question" repeatedly focus us, therefore, on the reality of the "great and last sacrifice." "This is the whole meaning of the law, every whit pointing to that great and last sacrifice; and that great and last sacrifice will be the Son of God, yea, infinite and eternal" (Alma 34:14). These great answers reaffirm that mortal melancholy need not be, however frequently and poignantly expressed.

Furthermore, what we receive in the Book of Mormon is not a mere assemblage of aphorisms, nor is it merely a few individuals offering their philosophical opinions. Instead, we receive the cumulative witness of prophetic individuals, especially those who were eyewitnesses of Jesus, including Lehi, Nephi, Jacob, Alma, the brother of Jared, Mormon, and Moroni. The biblical account of the five hundred brothers and sisters witnessing the resurrected Jesus (1 Corinthians 15:6) is joined by the witnessing throng of twenty-five hundred in the land of Bountiful (3 Nephi 17:25). All of these are thus added to the burgeoning cloud of witnesses about whom the Apostle Paul wrote (Hebrews 12:1).

The Book of Mormon might have been another kind of book, of course. It could have been chiefly concerned with the ebb and flow of governmental history; that is, "Princes come and princes go, an hour of pomp, an hour of show." Such would not have offset, however, the many despairing books and the literature of lamentation so much of which we have already, each reminiscent in one way or another of the hopelessness of these lines from Shelley:

> . . . *Two vast and trunkless legs of stone*
> *Stand in the desert. Near them, on the sand,*
> *Half sunk, a shattered visage lies, . . .*
> *And on the pedestal, these words appear:*
> *"My name is Ozymandias, king of kings:*
> *Look on my works, ye Might, and despair!"*
> *Nothing beside remains. Round the decay*
> *Of that colossal wreck, boundless and bare*
> *The long and level sands stretch far away.*[13]

Because the editing of the Book of Mormon, with its gospel of hope, occurred under divine direction, it has a focus which is essentially spiritual. Yet some still criticize the Book of Mormon for not being what it was never intended to be, as if one could justifiably criticize the phone directory for lack of a plot!

Some verses in the Book of Mormon are of tremendous salvational significance, others less so. The book of Ether has a verse about lineage history: "And Jared had four sons" (and names them) (Ether 6:14). However, Ether also contains another verse of tremendous salvational significance:

"And if men come unto me I will show unto them their weakness. I give unto men weakness that they may be humble; and my grace is sufficient for all men that humble themselves before me; for if they humble themselves before me, and have faith in me, then will I make weak things become strong unto them" (Ether 12:27).

We read of a battle "when . . . they slept upon their swords . . . were drunken with anger, even as a man who is drunken with wine. . . . And when the night came there were thirty and two of the people of Shiz, and twenty and seven of the people of Coriantumr" (Ether 15:20–26). Such, however, is of a much lower spiritual significance for the development of our discipleship than are these next lines. In all of scripture, these constitute the most complete delineation of Jesus' requirement that we become as little children (see Matthew 18:3): ". . . and becometh as a child, submissive, meek, humble, patient, full of love, willing to submit to all things which the Lord seeth fit to inflict upon him, even as a child doth submit to his father" (Mosiah 3:19).

One reason to "search the scriptures" is to discover these sudden luxuriant meadows of meaning, these green pastures to nourish us in our individual times of need. The Book of Mormon surely has its share and more of these. Immediately after words about economic conditions in the now vanished city of Helam, we encounter an enduring and bracing truth: "Nevertheless the Lord seeth fit to chasten his people; yea, he trieth their patience and their faith" (Mosiah 23:20–21; see also D&C 98:12; Abraham 3:25).

Similarly, the Book of Mormon provides us with insights we may not yet be ready to manage fully. Astonishingly, Alma includes our pains, sicknesses, and infirmities, along with our sins, as being among that which Jesus would also "take upon him" (Alma 7:11–12). It was part of the perfecting of Christ's mercy by His experiencing "according to the flesh." Nephi in exclaiming "O how great the plan of our God" (2 Nephi 9:13) also declared how Jesus would suffer "the pains of all . . . men, women, and children, who belong to the family of Adam" (2 Nephi 9:21). The soul trembles at those implications. One comes away weeping from such verses, deepened in his adoration of our Redeemer.

Given such richness, it is unsurprising that the prophets urge us to read the Book of Mormon. In closing his writings to those who do not respect (1) the words of the Jews (the Bible), (2) his words (as found in the Book of Mormon), and (3) also the words from Jesus (from the future New Testament), Nephi said simply, "I bid you an everlasting farewell" (2 Nephi 33:14).

Mormon is equally emphatic regarding this interactiveness between the Bible and the Book of Mormon (see Mormon 7:8–9). The interactiveness and cross-supportiveness of holy scripture was attested to by Jesus: "For had ye believed Moses, ye would have believed me: for he wrote of me. But if ye believe not his writings, how shall ye believe my words?" (John 5:46–47).

Meanwhile, from those who say, "We have enough, from them shall be taken away even that which they have" (2 Nephi 28:30). Obviously, this refers not to the physical loss of the Bible, which may still be on the bookshelf or may be used as a bookend, but to a sad loss of conviction concerning it on the part of some.

When we "search the scriptures," the luminosity of various verses in the various books is focused, laserlike. This illumination arcs and then converges, even though we are dealing with different authors, people, places, and times: "Wherefore, I speak the same words unto one nation like unto another. And when the two nations shall run together the testimony of the two nations shall run together also" (2 Nephi 29:8).

Believing, however, is not a matter of accessing antiquity with all its evidence, though we welcome such evidence. Nor is it dependent upon accumulating welcomed historical evidence either. Rather, it is a matter of believing in Jesus' words. Real faith, like real humility, is developed "because of the word"—and not because of surrounding circumstances (Alma 32:13–14)!

How fitting it is that it should be so! The test is focused on the message, not on the messengers; on principles, not on process; on doctrines, not on plot. The emphasis is on belief, per se, "because of the word." As Jesus told Thomas on the Eastern Hemisphere, "Blessed are they that have not seen, and yet have believed" (John 20:29). He proclaimed to the Nephites: "More blessed are they who shall believe in your words because that ye shall testify that ye have seen me" (3 Nephi 12:2).

True faith therefore, is brought about by overwhelming and intimidating divine intervention. The Lord, the Book of Mormon tells us, is a shepherd with a mild and pleasant voice (see Helaman 5:30–31; 3 Nephi 11:3)—not a shouting and scolding sheepherder. Others may, if they choose, demand a "voiceprint" of the "voice of the Lord," but even if so supplied, they would not like His doctrines anyway (see John 6:66). The things of the Spirit are to be "sought by faith"; and they are not to be seen through slit-eyed skepticism.

Without real faith, individuals sooner or later find one thing or another to stumble over (Romans 9:32). After all, it is a very difficult thing to show the proud things which they "never had supposed," especially things they do not really want to know. When Jesus was speaking about Himself as the bread of life, a powerful doctrine laden with life-changing implications, there was murmuring. Jesus asked them, "Doth this offend you?" (John 6:61). "Blessed is he, whosoever shall not be offended in me" (Luke 7:23).

As if all this were not enough, the splendid Book of Mormon advises that a third scriptural witness is yet to come from the lost tribes (see 2 Nephi 29:12–14). Its coming is likely to be even more dramatic than the coming forth of the second testament. Those who doubt or disdain the second testament of Christ will not accept the third either. But believers will then possess a triumphant triad of truth (see 2 Nephi 29:12–13). Were it not for the Book of Mormon, we would not even know about the third set of records!

We do not know when and how this will occur, but we are safe in assuming that the third book will have the same fundamental focus as the Book of Mormon: "that . . . their seed [too] . . . may be brought to a knowledge of me, their Redeemer" (3 Nephi 16:4). If there is a title page in that third set of sacred records, it is not likely to differ in purpose from the title page in the Book of Mormon, except for its focus on still other peoples who likewise received a personal visit from the resurrected Jesus (see 3 Nephi 15:20–24; 16:1–4).

Thus in the dispensation of the fulness of times there is not only a "welding together" (D&C 128:18) of the keys of all the dispensations but there will also be a "welding together" of all the sacred books of scripture given by the Lord over the sweep of human history. Then, as prophesied, "my word also shall be gathered in one" (2 Nephi 29:14).

Then there will be one fold, one shepherd, and one stunning scriptural witness for the Christ!

Given all the foregoing, it is touching that a jailed Joseph Smith, during his last mortal night, 26 June 1844, bore "a powerful testimony to the guards of the divine authenticity of the Book of Mormon, the restoration of the Gospel, the administration of angels"[14] (see Alma 12:28–30). The guards apparently did not hearken then any more than most of the world hearkens now. Heeded or unheeded, however, the Book of Mormon has a further rendezvous to keep: "Wherefore, these things shall go from generation to generation as long as the earth shall stand; and they shall go according to the will and pleasure of God; and the nations who shall possess them shall be judged of them according to the words which are written" (2 Nephi 25:22).

For my part, I am glad the book will be with us "as long as the earth shall stand." I need and want additional time. For me, towers, courtyards, and wings await inspection. My tour of it has never been completed. Some rooms I have yet to enter, and there are more flaming fireplaces waiting to warm me. Even the rooms I have glimpsed contain further furnishings and rich detail yet to be savored. There are panels inlaid with incredible insights and design and decor dating from Eden. There are also sumptuous banquet tables painstakingly prepared by predecessors which await all of us. Yet, we as Church members sometimes behave like hurried tourists, scarcely venturing beyond the entry hall to the mansion.

May we come to feel as a whole people beckoned beyond the entry hall. May we go inside far enough to hear clearly the whispered truths from those who have "slumbered," which whisperings will awaken in us individually the life of discipleship as never before.

Notes

1. Wars of the Lord, Jasher, more from Samuel, the Acts of Solomon, the book of Nathan, Shemaiah, Ahijah, Iddo, Jehu, the Sayings of the Seers, at least two epistles of Paul, books of Enoch, Ezias, Adam's Book of Remembrance, and Gad the Seer. Thus we are dealing with over twenty missing books. We also have certain prophecies from Jacob, or Israel, and extensive prophecies by

Joseph in Egypt, only a portion of which we have (see 2 Nephi 3:1–25; 4:1–3; Joseph Smith Translation, Genesis 50:24–37; Alma 46:24–26).

2. Furthermore, too few people are inclined to follow the counsel of Moroni regarding the book's substance: "Condemn me not because of mine imperfection, neither my father, because of his imperfection, neither them who have written before him; but rather give thanks unto God that he hath made manifest unto you our imperfections, that ye may learn to be more wise than we have been" (Mormon 9:31).

3. Twenty-two times in the Book of Mormon, ten times in the Doctrine and Covenants, and three times in the Pearl of Great Price.

4. Alan Hayward, *God Is* (Nashville: Thomas Nelson, 1980), 62–63.

5. Hayward, *God Is*, 68.

6. *Teachings of the Prophet Joseph Smith*, comp. Joseph Fielding Smith (Salt Lake City: Deseret Book, 1976), 7.

7. Michael Harrington, *The Politics at God's Funeral: The Spiritual Crisis of Western Civilization* (New York: Holt, Rinehart, and Winston, 1983), 114.

8. C. S. Lewis, *The Last Battle* (New York: Collier, 1970), 148.

9. Harrington, *Politics*, 153.

10. Harrington, *Politics*, 164.

11. Penelope Fitzgerald, *The Knox Brothers* (New York: Coward, McCann & Geoghegen, 1977), 106–7.

12. Brigham Young, in *Journal of Discourses* (London: Latter-day Saints' Book Depot, 1854–86), 8:67.

13. Percy Bysshe Shelley, "Ozymandias," *Norton Anthology of English Literature* (New York: W. W. Norton & Company, 1986), 2:691.

14. *Teachings of the Prophet Joseph Smith*, 383.

Index

Page numbers in italics indicate images.